THE RADIUM GIRLS

YOUNG READERS' EDITION

The Scary but True Story of the POISON
that Made People GLOW in the Dark

KATE MOORE

sourcebooks
eXplore

Published by Sourcebooks eXplore, an imprint of Sourcebooks Kids
P.O. Box 4410, Naperville, Illinois 60567-4410
(630) 961-3900
sourcebookskids.com

Library of Congress Cataloging-in-Publication data is on file with the publisher.

This product conforms to all applicable CPSC and CPSIA standards.

Source of Production: Sheridan Books, Chelsea, Michigan, United States
Date of Production: July 2020
Run Number: 5018859

Printed and bound in the United States of America.
SB 10 9 8 7 6 5 4 3 2 1

For all the dial-painters
and those who loved them

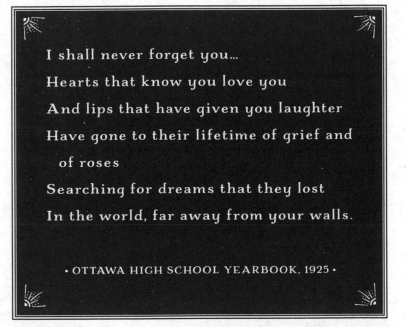

I shall never forget you...

Hearts that know you love you

And lips that have given you laughter

Have gone to their lifetime of grief and

   of roses

Searching for dreams that they lost

In the world, far away from your walls.

• OTTAWA HIGH SCHOOL YEARBOOK, 1925 •

CONTENTS

AUTHOR'S NOTE

Dear Reader,

The women you're about to meet in this book are incredibly special, for so many reasons. I feel very lucky that I'm the one who gets to introduce them to you. For these women are my heroes, and I hope by the time you've finished reading that they may be heroes to you too. Or, at the very least, good friends.

Their story is a true one, and it happened about a hundred years ago. It started with what they thought of as a piece of luck: when they were teenagers, they landed jobs that everybody wanted, paid really well, and were glamorous, artistic, and fun. They had no idea that, one day, you would be reading their story. You are doing so only because of how they faced what happened next. Because that piece of luck had a very dark flip side. Yet when the radium girls faced pain and heartache and injustice and tragedy, they did not suffer in silence.

They chose, as a sisterhood, to rise up and fight back—with everything they had.

As a result, America's shining girls now shine through history as an inspirational example of standing up for your rights. They stand as an example that no matter how small and powerless you may sometimes feel, *you can make a difference.* Because against all the odds, the radium girls made the world a better place. They made it better for every single person on this planet. These courageous women left us all an extraordinary legacy—in science, health-and-safety laws, and human rights—that their teenage selves would likely be astonished by.

But you never know what you may achieve when you grow up.

Their story may have started a hundred years ago, but please don't think that just because their story is old, it doesn't have any meaning today. If you look around, you may see echoes of it on the nightly news. You may see men and women fighting for justice just as the radium girls once did. And perhaps one day, like these young women, you too will lend your voice to a cause in order to fight for what *you* believe in. I hope you may take inspiration from them when that day comes.

The radium girls' story is a sad one. While I was writing their book, I cried many times. Yet I hope, when you finish it, that you're left with a feeling that's like sunshine after rain. Because for all the sadness in their tale, you can still take hope from it. You can take strength from their strength and courage from their courage. Even though they're not with us anymore, these amazing women live on—in the beating hearts of those whose lives they saved, in their enduring gift of knowledge, and in the minds of those who read their incredible story... which now includes you.

Thank you for being part of their legacy.

I hope you may use it, in your own way, to become a hero too.

Yours truly,

Kate Moore

— x —

LIST OF
KEY CHARACTERS

NEWARK AND ORANGE, NEW JERSEY

The Dial-Painters

The Carlough Sisters

- Marguerite Carlough
- Sarah Carlough Maillefer

The Maggia Sisters

- Albina Maggia Larice
- Amelia "Mollie" Maggia
- Quinta Maggia McDonald

Their Colleagues

- Edna Bolz Hussman
- Ella Eckert
- Grace Fryer
- Hazel Vincent Kuser
- Irene Rudolph, *Katherine Schaub's cousin*
- Katherine Schaub, *Irene Rudolph's cousin*

The United States Radium Corporation

- Arthur Roeder, *president (from 1921)*
- Edwin Leman, *chief chemist*
- Howard Barker, *chemist and vice president*
- Sabin von Sochocky, *founder and inventor of the paint*

Doctors

- Dr. Frederick Flinn, *company doctor*
- Dr. Harrison Martland, *Newark doctor*
- Dr. Joseph Knef, Dr. Walter Barry, Dr. James Davidson, *local dentists*
- Dr. Robert Humphries, *doctor at the Orange Orthopedic Hospital*
- Dr. Theodore Blum, *New York dentist*

Investigators

- Dr. Alice Hamilton, *Harvard School of Public Health, Katherine Wiley's ally and colleague of Cecil K. Drinker*
- Andrew McBride, *commissioner of the Department of Labor*
- Dr. Cecil K. Drinker, *professor of physiology at the Harvard School of Public Health*
- Ethelbert Stewart, *commissioner of the Bureau of Labor Statistics, Washington, DC*
- Dr. Frederick Hoffman, *investigating statistician*
- John Roach, *deputy commissioner of the Department of Labor*

- Katherine Wiley, *executive secretary of the Consumers League, New Jersey*

- Swen Kjaer, *national investigator from the Bureau of Labor Statistics, Washington, DC*

OTTAWA, ILLINOIS

The Dial-Painters

- Catherine Wolfe Donohue

- Charlotte Nevins Purcell

- Ella Cruse

- Inez Corcoran Vallat

- Margaret "Peg" Looney

- Marie Becker Rossiter

The Radium Dial Company

- Joseph Kelly, *president*

- Lottie Murray, *superintendent*

- Rufus Fordyce, *vice president*

- Rufus Reed, *assistant superintendent*

PROLOGUE
Paris, France
1901

T he scientist had forgotten all about the radium. It was tucked within his waistcoat pocket, enclosed in a slim glass tube in such a small quantity that he could not feel its weight. He had a lecture to give in London, England, and the vial of radium stayed within that shadowy pocket throughout his journey across the sea.

He was one of the few people in the world to possess it. Discovered by Marie and Pierre Curie in December 1898, radium was so difficult to extract from its source that there were only a few grams available anywhere in the world. He was lucky to have been given a tiny amount by the Curies to use in his lectures. They barely had enough themselves to continue their experiments.

Yet this did not affect the Curies' progress. Every day, they discovered something new about their element. It made ghostly white pictures on photographic plates. It destroyed the materials in which it was wrapped. Marie called it "my beautiful radium"—and it truly was. Deep in the dark pocket of the scientist, the radium broke through the gloom with an unending, eerie glow. "These gleamings," Marie wrote of its luminous effect, "stirred us with ever-new emotion and enchantment."

Enchantment... It implies a kind of sorcery, almost supernatural power. No wonder the U.S. surgeon general said of radium that "it reminds one of a mythological super-being." An English physician would call its enormous radioactivity "the unknown god."

Gods can be kind. Loving. Generous. Yet as the playwright George Bernard Shaw once wrote, "The gods of old are constantly demanding human sacrifices." Enchantment—in the tales of the past and present—can also mean a curse.

So although the scientist had forgotten about the radium, the radium had not forgotten him. As he traveled to England, the radium shot out its powerful rays toward his pale, soft skin. Days later, he would peer in confusion at the red mark blooming mysteriously on his stomach. It looked like a burn, but he had no memory of coming near any flame. Hour by hour, it grew more painful. It didn't get bigger, but it seemed, somehow, to get *deeper*, as though that unknown flame was burning him still. It blistered into an agonizing flesh burn. The pain made him suck in his breath sharply and rack his brains. What on earth could have inflicted such damage without him noticing? And it was then that he remembered the radium.

PART ONE

—

KNOWLEDGE

1.

FIRST DAY

Newark, New Jersey
1917

Katherine Schaub had a jaunty spring in her step as she walked the brief four blocks to work. It was February, but the cold didn't bother her. She had always loved the winter snows of her hometown. Yet the frosty weather wasn't the reason for her high spirits on that particular icy morning. Today, she was starting a brand-new job at the watch-dial factory of the Radium Luminous Materials Corporation.

To her excitement, Katherine had been hired to work in the company's glamorous-sounding studio. Her job was to paint watch dials with glow-in-the-dark radium paint. Katherine was just fourteen—her fifteenth birthday was in five weeks' time—but she was sure to fit in. Most of her fellow dial-painters were

Katherine Schaub.

teenagers too. Katherine was blond-haired and blue-eyed, and she loved to sing, play piano, and write—her dream was to become an author. Most of all, she was a go-getter. She'd gotten the job at the studio simply by asking the boss for one outright.

As Katherine walked into the studio on her first day, she saw the other dial-painters were already hard at work. Young girls sat in rows, painting dials at top speed. Yet it wasn't the dials that caught Katherine's eye. It was the material they were using to paint them. It was the radium.

Radium was a wonder element. Everyone knew that. Katherine had read all about it in magazines and newspapers, which were always full of advertisements for new radium products. At the turn of the century, scientists had discovered that radium could destroy human tissue. After that, it had quickly been used to treat cancerous tumors, with remarkable results. It saved lives. People therefore assumed it must be healthful. So all of Katherine's life, radium had been marketed as a magnificent cure-all. It wasn't just used to treat cancer but also hay fever and constipation...really, anything you could think of. People popped radioactive pills to treat their ailments, yet they also used radium products to ward off ill health and to give them energy. Radium water was drunk daily as a health tonic. The recommended dose was five to seven glasses a day.

The element was dubbed "liquid sunshine," and it was an entrepreneur's dream. Also on sale were radium butter, milk, and chocolate, radium toothpaste (guaranteeing a brighter smile with every brushing), and even a range of Radior cosmetics, which offered radium-laced face creams, soap, and makeup. But because radium was the most valuable substance on earth—selling for $120,000 for a single gram, which is $2.2 million in today's values—these products weren't aimed at poor working-class girls like Katherine. It was mainly the rich and famous who were lucky enough to get up close with radium.

Well, the rich and famous—*and the dial-painters*. They perhaps got closest to radium of all.

To her delight, Katherine could see that there was luminous radium dust scattered all over the studio. Even as she watched, little puffs of it seemed to hover in the air before settling on the shoulders or hair of a dial-painter at work. To her astonishment, it made the girls themselves gleam. Each girl mixed her own paint. She dabbed a little radium powder into a small white dish, then added water and some glue to make the greenish-white luminous paint. The company called this paint "Undark." The fine yellow powder contained only a tiny amount of radium. It was mixed with zinc sulfide, which reacted with the radium to give a brilliant glow. But tiny amount or not, the stunning, shining radium was even more beautiful than Katherine had imagined.

A tray of radium dials like the ones
Katherine would have worked on.

Her very first task that morning was to learn the technique that all new dial-painters were taught. Katherine carefully picked up the finely bristled, camel-hair paintbrush she was given. She saw that the smallest pocket watch the girls had to paint measured only three and a half centimeters across. The tiniest element to be painted on the watch was just a single millimeter in width. Yet the girls would be fired if they painted outside the lines. So even though their paintbrushes were thin, the girls had to make the brushes even finer.

There was only one way they knew of to do that. They put the brushes in their mouths.

It was a technique called lip-pointing. Katherine had to suck on the brush to make it taper to a point. Following the company's instructions, Katherine put the brush to her lips, dipped it in the radium, and painted the dials. It was a "lip, dip, paint routine." All the girls did it that way—they lipped and dipped and painted all day long.

The dial-painters did not adopt the technique without checking it was safe. "The first thing we asked [our bosses was] 'Does this stuff hurt you?'" remembered one of Katherine's colleagues. "And they said, 'No.' [They] said that it wasn't dangerous, that we didn't need to be afraid." After all, radium was the wonder element. The girls, if anything, should find that swallowing it did them good. They soon grew so used to the brushes in their mouths that they stopped even thinking about it.

But for Katherine, it felt peculiar, that first day, as she lip-pointed over and over. Yet she was constantly reminded why she wanted to be part of the glamorous workforce. The dust-covered dial-painters shone like otherworldly angels all around her. And they dressed like queens, in expensive silks and furs. The women were paid a flat rate for every watch they painted, which meant the most skilled workers could take home, in today's money, almost $40,000 a year. This ranked them in the top 5 percent of female wage earners nationally and gave them plenty of spare cash for shopping. So Katherine persevered. She and the well-dressed dial-painters soon became friends, sitting together to eat lunch, sharing sandwiches and gossip over the dusty tables. They had fun at company picnics too.

Yet in that spring of 1917, there was not much fun happening in the wider world. For the past two and a half years, a terrible war had been raging in Europe. Most Americans had been happy to stay out of the conflict. But in 1917, that neutral position became impossible. So on April 6, just a few short months after Katherine started work, Congress voted America into what would become known as "the war to end all wars."

In the dial-painting studio, the impact of America entering the First World War was immediate. Demand for the company's luminous paint rocketed. It was applied not only to watches but also to gunsights, ships' compasses, and aeronautical instruments, and it had many more military uses. The studio in Newark, New Jersey, where Katherine worked was far too small to produce the numbers required. So her bosses opened a purpose-built plant just down the road in Orange, New Jersey. This time, there wouldn't only be dial-painters on-site. The company was expanding, now doing its own radium extraction, which required laboratories and processing plants.

Katherine was among the first workers through the door

of the two-story brick building that housed the new studio. She and the other dial-painters were delighted by what they found. The second-floor studio was charming, with huge windows on all sides and skylights in the roof. The spring sunshine streamed in, giving excellent light for dial-painting.

An appeal for new workers to help the war effort was made. Just four days after war was declared, Grace Fryer answered the call. She had more reason than most to want to help, because two of her brothers were heading to France to fight. Lots of dial-painters were motivated by the idea of helping the troops. "The girls," wrote Katherine, "were but a few of the many who through their jobs were 'doing their bit.'"

Grace was a woman who really cared about her community. Her father was a representative of the carpenters' union, and Grace had picked up his political principles. Aged eighteen, she was an exceptionally bright and pretty girl with curly chestnut hair and hazel eyes. Many called her striking, but her looks weren't of much interest to Grace. Instead, she preferred to focus on her career. She soon excelled at dial-painting, regularly completing 250 dials a day.

Grace, Katherine, and the other women sat side by side at long wooden tables running the full width of the room. Wartime demand was so high that as many as 375 girls were soon recruited. Hazel Vincent was one. She had an oval

Grace Fryer (far left) on a makeshift bridge
behind the studio with two colleagues.

face with a button nose and fair hair. Other new joiners
included the music-loving Edna Bolz, who was nicknamed
the "Dresden Doll" because of her beautiful golden locks, and
Ella Eckert, who had a great sense of fun. Dial-painting was
such a desirable profession that the radium girls promoted
the vacancies to their loved ones. Katherine's orphaned cousin
Irene Rudolph was hired. It wasn't long before whole sets of
siblings were seated alongside each other too, merrily painting away. These included the Maggia sisters—Mollie, Quinta,
and Albina—and the Carlough girls, Sarah and Marguerite.

That summer, the plant was full of activity. "The place
was a madhouse!" one worker exclaimed. The girls did
overtime, working seven days a week, with the studio operating night and day. There was a lot of work to do. In 1918, an

11

The dial-painting studio in Orange, New Jersey, in the early 1920s.

estimated 95 percent of all the radium produced in America was used to make radium paint and applied to military dials. By the end of the year, one in six American soldiers would own a luminous watch.

Though the pace was demanding, the setup was still rather fun for the women. They reveled in the drama of long shifts painting dials for their country. Now and then, they even found time for a game. One favorite was to scratch their name and address into a watch, a message for the soldier who would wear it. Sometimes, he would respond with a note.

Despite the occasional games, the girls were under pressure. If a worker failed to keep up the breakneck pace, she was criticized. If she fell short repeatedly, she was fired. The company's biggest concern was any wasting of the expensive radium. The girls were covered in it—their "hands, arms, necks, the dresses, the underclothes, even the corsets of the dial-painters were luminous," wrote one observer. So when a shift was over, the women were ordered to brush the radium from their clothes. The sparkling particles were swept from the floor into a dustpan for use the next day.

But no amount of brushing could get all the dust off. Edna Bolz remembered that even after the brushing down, "When I would go home at night, my clothing would shine in the dark." Grace recalled that even her boogers became luminously green! The girls glowed like ghosts as they walked home through the streets of Orange.

The company was haunted by the waste. Soon, it banned the water dishes in which the women cleaned their radium-encrusted brushes. The bosses said that too much valuable material was lost in the water. Now the girls had no choice but to lip-point, as there was no other way to clean off the radium that hardened on the brush. As Edna Bolz observed, "Without so doing, it would have been impossible to have done much work."

So Edna and Grace, Katherine and Irene, and the Maggia and Carlough sisters did just as they were told. *Lip... Dip... Paint.*

———— ≋ ————

The dial-painters' boss was Sabin von Sochocky. He was an Austrian-born, thirty-four-year-old doctor who'd invented the radium paint back in 1913. In his first year in business, he'd sold two thousand glow-in-the-dark watches. Now, the company's output ranked in the millions. His company had made him a very rich man. *American* magazine called him "one of the greatest authorities in the world on the subject of radium."

Von Sochocky, like many others, was bewitched by the wonder element. He was known to play with it. He would hold tubes of glowing radium with his bare hands or immerse his arm up to the elbow in radium solutions. His careless attitude was striking because von Sochocky knew that radium was in fact very dangerous.

The doctor had studied under the very best radium experts on the planet: Marie and Pierre Curie. The Curies by that time were familiar with radium's hazards because they'd suffered many radiation burns themselves. Pierre had even gone on record in 1903 to say that radium could probably kill a man. It *was* true that radium could save your life if you had cancer by destroying your tumor. But it could devastate *healthy* tissue too.

Von Sochocky knew that only too well. Radium had badly damaged his left index finger, so he'd hacked the tip of it off. It now looked as though an animal had gnawed it. But the doctor's dangerous brush with radium still didn't stop him playing with it...

Although the company founder seemed to care little for himself, he did at least protect his laboratory workers in

Orange. The men who were extracting and refining radium in the labs were provided with safety equipment, such as lead-lined aprons and ivory-tipped forceps.

But in the sunny second-floor studio, the dial-painters were given nothing. The amount of radium in the paint was so small that their bosses didn't think safety equipment was necessary.

The girls themselves had no clue any precautions might be needed. To them—to most people—the effects of radium were *all* positive. That was what it said in the newspapers and magazines and on the product packaging. The dial-painters thought themselves lucky to be so close to it. Carefree, they laughed among themselves and bent their heads to their work.

Von Sochocky seldom spent time with them, preferring to work in his laboratory. So Grace Fryer remembered her boss passing through the studio—it happened just the once. She didn't pay his visit much attention at the time, but it would come to take on a great significance.

She was at her desk as usual that day, lipping and dipping her brush, as were all the other girls. As von Sochocky passed by, he suddenly stopped and looked straight at her—and at what she was doing, as though seeing her actions for the very first time.

Grace glanced up at him. He was a memorable-looking

man, with a big nose and ears that stuck out. Conscious of the pace of work around her, she bent again to her task and slipped the brush between her lips.

"Do not do that," von Sochocky said.

Grace looked up, perplexed. This was how you did the job. It was how all the girls did it.

"Do not do that," he said again. "You will get sick." And then he was on his way.

Grace was utterly confused. Never one to back down from something she thought needed further investigation, she went straight over to the forewoman. But Miss Rooney merely repeated what the girls had already been told. "She told me it was not harmful," Grace recalled.

So Grace went back to her work. *Lip... Dip... Paint.*

3.

ALL CHANGE

On November 11, 1918, the First World War came to an end. Peace reigned. Across the globe, around seventeen million people had died. Now, surely, it was time for living.

The end of the war brought change to the dial-painting studio. Many girls—Quinta Maggia was one—left to get married and start a family. Others, such as Mollie Maggia and Ella Eckert, who became great friends, continued to lip-point their brushes day in and day out. They liked being able to earn good money. Mollie became so independent that she left her family home and moved into an all-female boarding house. Her career gave her a sense of empowerment, a feeling that only increased in the summer of 1919 when Congress finally gave women the right to vote.

At the factory, too, change was afoot. The company began experimenting with the recipe of the luminous paint. The bosses now swapped radium for mesothorium. Mesothorium was an isotope—a different type—of radium, named radium-228. ("Normal" radium was called radium-226.) Mesothorium was also radioactive but had a half-life of 6.7 years, much shorter than radium-226's half-life, which was 1,600 years. (A half-life is the length of time that a radioactive substance is at full strength, before it diminishes into an ever-less-powerful version of itself.) Mesothorium was more abrasive than radium, and—most importantly—much cheaper.

Not that the company *needed* to cut corners. It was not struggling financially. With the war over, the company's glow-in-the-dark paint was used for all sorts of things. Radium paint was now applied to fun and frivolous items, such as dolls' eyes, theater seats, fish bait, and even slippers (so you'd never lose them in the night). In 1919, meanwhile, there was a new production high of 2.2 million luminous watches.

No wonder Katherine Schaub was feeling tired. That fall, she noticed her legs felt curiously stiff. Yet she could do nothing but knuckle down to work.

But the postwar changes weren't over yet. Next, the firm laid off most of its dial-painters. The company had devised a new strategy. It helped watch manufacturers set up their own studios and still made money by supplying them with paint. Soon, there were fewer than a hundred dial-painters left in Orange. Katherine Schaub took a job in an office, while clever Grace Fryer landed an impressive position at a high-end bank. She loved traveling daily to her office, her dark hair neatly set and

A group of Orange dial-painters, including Mollie Maggia (second from left), Ella Eckert (third from right, partially hidden), and Sarah Carlough Maillefer (first from right).

an elegant string of pearls around her neck, ready to jump into work that challenged her.

Mollie Maggia, however, kept working in the studio. Every morning, she went to work full of energy and enthusiasm, which was more than she could say for some of her colleagues. Marguerite Carlough, who could normally be relied on for a laugh, kept saying she felt tired all the time, while Hazel Vincent complained that her jaw ached something rotten. Hazel eventually left too. She asked the company doctor at her new office to examine her, but he was unable to diagnose her strange illness.

In October 1920, Hazel's former employer was featured

in the local news. The radium company sold its industrial waste—which looked like seaside sand—to schools and playgrounds to use in children's sandboxes. Recently, kids' shoes were reported to have turned white because of it. One little boy even complained to his mother of a burning sensation in his hands. Yet in comments that were reassuring for ill dial-painters such as Hazel, von Sochocky said the radioactive sand was "most hygienic" for children to play in.

Katherine Schaub certainly had no worries about returning to the radium firm in November 1920. She took a temporary position training the new radium girls at the watch-company studios. These were mostly based in Connecticut, including at the Waterbury Clock Company. Katherine taught dozens of girls the lip-pointing technique that she herself had learned.

The new girls were excited to be working with radium. The craze around the wonder element continued, brought to fever pitch by a visit of Marie Curie herself to the United States in 1921. In January of that same year, as part of radium's constant press coverage, von Sochocky wrote an article for *American* magazine. "Locked up in radium is the greatest force the world knows," he wrote. "Through a microscope, you can see whirling, powerful, invisible forces, the uses of which," he admitted, "we do not yet understand." He added, "What radium means to us today is a great romance in itself. But what it may mean to us tomorrow, no man can foretell."

In fact, no man can foretell much, von Sochocky included. And there was one change in particular that the doctor didn't see coming.

Sabin von Sochocky (center), the radium firm's founder, at a company picnic.

In summer 1921, he was fired from his own company after a corporate takeover. The newly named United States Radium Corporation (USRC) seemed destined for great things in the postwar world, but von Sochocky wouldn't be at the helm to guide it through whatever lay ahead.

Instead, it was the treasurer, Arthur Roeder, who slipped graciously into the vacant president's chair.

4.

THE MYSTERIOUS MALADIES OF MOLLIE MAGGIA

Mollie Maggia poked her tongue gingerly into the gap where her tooth had once been. *Ouch.* The dentist had removed it a few weeks ago after she'd gotten a toothache. But it was still incredibly sore. She gave herself a little shake and turned back to her dials. Anxiously, she smoothed down her bouffant brown hair, which was covered all over, as usual, with glowing dust.

The studio was very quiet. So many girls had gone. Of the original women, it was really only Mollie and the Carlough sisters left now. Saddest of all was that Ella Eckert had quit to go to Bamberger's, a department store. It sure wasn't the same place anymore, not since Roeder had taken over.

Mollie completed her tray of dials and stood to take it up

to Miss Rooney. Despite herself, she found her tongue flicking back to that hole. If it didn't get better soon, she thought, she would go to the dentist again, but a different one this time, someone who really knew what he was doing.

It didn't get better soon.

So in October 1921, she made an appointment with a dentist named Dr. Joseph Knef. He diagnosed pyorrhea, a common disease that affects the tissues around the teeth. But despite his treatment, Mollie still didn't get better. In fact, she got much, much worse. Knef pulled out more of her teeth, hoping to stop the infection. But he failed. Painful ulcers sprouted in the holes left behind, hurting Mollie even more than the teeth had.

Mollie struggled on, continuing to work at the studio, even though using her mouth on the brush was very uncomfortable. Marguerite Carlough, who was feeling completely well again, tried to engage her in chatter. But Mollie barely responded. It wasn't just the pain of her bloody gums, which seemed to take up all her concentration, but the bad breath that came with it. There was a nasty odor whenever she opened her mouth, and she was embarrassed by it.

In November 1921, Mollie's sister Albina married James Larice, a bricklayer. At the wedding, the family couldn't help but be concerned by Mollie's ill health. By then, it wasn't just her mouth that was sore. She'd started to have aches and pains

The Maggia family. Back row: Albina (far left),
Mollie (center), and Quinta (far right).

in completely unconnected places. "My sister," Quinta Maggia McDonald remembered, "began having trouble with her teeth and her jawbone and her hips and feet. We thought it rheumatism [a disease that makes your joints and muscles stiff and usually occurs in older people]." The doctor prescribed aspirin.

But both the doctor and Knef seemed powerless to save Mollie from her mysterious infection. It appeared to be attacking her from the inside. Soon, it became so aggressive that Knef no longer had to pull her teeth. They fell out on their own.

As 1922 began, Knef came up with a new diagnosis. He wondered if Mollie might be a victim of phosphorus poisoning. In recent years, this had hurt and killed many local women who'd worked in match factories. "Phossy jaw"—as the victims of the condition had grimly nicknamed it—had very similar symptoms to Mollie's. So at her next appointment, Knef asked Mollie what her job was.

"Painting numbers on watches so that they will shine at night," she responded. She winced as her tongue formed the words and touched the ulcers in her mouth.

With that, Knef's suspicions increased. He visited the radium plant for answers. But the company would not cooperate beyond assuring him there was no phosphorus in the paint. No phosphorus at all: only radium.

None of this helped Mollie. She was in agony. Her mouth had become a mass of sores. She could barely speak, let alone eat. Mollie's entire lower jaw, the roof of her mouth, and even the bones of her ears were like one huge abscess. She couldn't work in such a condition. She quit her job at the studio, where she had spent so many happy hours painting dials, and stayed at home. Surely, one day soon, the doctors would find out what was wrong and cure her. Then she could get on with her life again.

But no cure came. In May 1922, Mollie limped into Knef's office once more. The rheumatism in her hips and feet was now so bad she was almost lame. But it was her mouth that took up all her thoughts, all her time, and consumed *her*. There was no escaping the pain.

She hobbled into Knef's dental chair and leaned back.

Gingerly, she opened her mouth for him. He bent over her and prepared to probe inside.

There were barely any teeth left now, he saw. Raw, red ulcers peppered the inside of her mouth instead. Mollie tried to indicate that her jaw was hurting especially. Knef prodded delicately at the bone in her mouth.

To his horror and shock, even though his touch had been gentle, her jawbone broke against his fingers. He then removed it, "not by an operation, but merely by putting his fingers in her mouth and lifting it out."

A week or so later, her entire lower jaw was removed in the same way.

Mollie couldn't bear it, but there was no relief. All the doctors could offer were painkillers that barely helped. Her whole face beneath her bouffant brown hair was just pain, pain, *pain*. She soon became anemic, meaning she didn't have enough red blood cells. This made her weaker still.

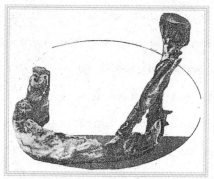

Mollie Maggia's lower jawbone, riddled with holes and crumpled from the radium.

Everyone was confused by her condition. After all, she should be full of health. Not only was she young, in her twenties, but she had worked with radium for years. Only that February, the local paper had declared, "Radium may be eaten... In years to come we shall be able to buy radium tablets—and add years to our lives!"

But, for Mollie, it seemed time was running out. After her jaw was gone, an important discovery was made. Knef had always hoped that by removing a tooth or a piece of infected bone, the progress of the mysterious disease would be stopped. But it became obvious the opposite was true. Removing teeth and bone actually sped up Mollie's illness. Over the summer, her condition got even worse. Her jaw, at times, would spontaneously bleed.

Then, in September 1922, the peculiar infection that had plagued Mollie Maggia for less than a year spread to the tissues of her throat. The disease "slowly ate its way through her jugular vein." On September 12, her mouth flooded suddenly with blood. She bled so fast from her throat that her nurse could not stop it. Her mouth, empty of teeth, empty of jawbone, empty of words, filled with red, hot blood instead. It spilled over her lips and down her stricken, shaken face. She died, her sister Quinta said, a "painful and terrible death."

She was just twenty-four years old.

Her family buried her on September 14, 1922, in a wooden coffin with a silver nameplate. They hoped that now, at last, she would find peace.

T wo days after Mollie's funeral and eight hundred miles away from Orange, a small advertisement appeared in the local paper of a little town called Ottawa, in Illinois. "Girls Wanted," it declared. And then continued, "Several girls, 18 years or over, for fine brushwork. This is a studio proposition, the work is clean and healthful, surroundings pleasant. Apply to Miss Murray, old high school building, 1022 Columbus Street."

It sounded *wonderful*.

Ottawa was a tiny town—population 10,816—located eighty-five miles southwest of Chicago. It was a community where folks were happy simply to get on with life: raise their families, do good work, live decent lives. It seemed the perfect place for this new dial-painting opportunity.

It wasn't the United States Radium Corporation hiring, although they knew their competitor well. The employer was the Radium Dial Company. Its president was Joseph A. Kelly, but he was based at the

The "Girls Wanted" advertisement that ran in the Ottawa Daily Times on September 16, 1922.

head office in Chicago. So it was to Miss Murray, the studio's superintendent, the Ottawa girls applied.

One of the very first successful applicants was nineteen-year-old Catherine Wolfe. She was Ottawa born and bred, a devoted parishioner of St. Columba Church, which was located across the street from the studio. Despite her young age, Catherine had already had some hard knocks in life. When she was only six, her mother had died. Then, just four years later, her father passed too. As a result, ten-year-old Catherine had been sent to live with her elderly aunt and uncle at 520 East Superior Street, where she still resided in 1922.

Catherine was a shy, quiet person. She had short, thick, jet-black hair and very pale skin. The job at the studio would be her first, painting the dials of timepieces and aeronautical

Charlotte Nevins.

instruments. "It was fascinating work, and the pay was good," she enthused, "but every line had to be just so."

And there was only one known way to get the necessary point on their brushes. "Miss Lottie Murray taught us how to point camel-hair brushes with our tongues," Catherine remembered. "We would first dip the brush into water, then into the powder, and then point the ends of the bristles between our teeth."

It was the "lip, dip, paint routine" all over again, but with an entirely new cast.

Joining Catherine at the studio was sixteen-year-old Charlotte Nevins. The ad had said "18 years or over," but she wasn't going to let a little thing like that stop her. All her friends were there, and she wanted to join them. Charlotte wasn't the only one to tweak the truth about her age. Records show that some dial-painters were as young as eleven. In truth, the nimble fingers of young girls suited the delicate work of dial-painting. So all were welcomed.

Charlotte remembered, "When I was working in the plant painting dials they always told me the radium would never hurt me. They even encouraged us to paint rings on our fingers and paint our dress buttons and buckles." The girls did exactly as instructed. Lots of them took paint home to practice painting. One woman even painted her walls with it: interior decoration with a difference.

Radium Dial didn't seem to be as concerned as USRC had been about wasting material. Former employees report that the radium was handled carelessly. And in contrast to the brushing down in Orange, "washing was a voluntary procedure and not many of the workers made use of the washing facilities."

Why would they when they could go home glowing like angels? "The girls were the envy of others in the little Illinois town when they stepped out with...their dresses and hats and some-times even their hands and faces aglow with the phosphorescence of the luminous paint,"

An advertisement for clocks with radium dials.

a newspaper reported. The women were "humorously termed the ghost girls."

They worked six days a week, using a similar greenish-white paint to that used in Orange. The girls declared, "We were extremely happy in our work." Radium Dial was equally content. It followed the attitude of its main client, Westclox. Their *Manual for Employees* read, "We expect you to work hard, and the pay is accordingly large... If you do not expect to work hard and carefully, you are in the wrong place."

But for Catherine, Charlotte, and all the other girls, this place felt very, very right indeed.

Miss Irene Rudolph?"

Irene got tentatively to her feet as she heard her name being called by Dr. Barry. She shuffled awkwardly into his office. Her trouble had first started in her feet, though they were currently the least of her worries. She could just about get by if she took things slow. Her family, including her cousin Katherine Schaub, helped out a lot. It was now her mouth that was the real problem.

She'd been coming to this dental practice since August, though she'd been having tooth trouble since the spring of 1922. Despite the attentions of various dentists, her condition had worsened, so much so that in May, she'd had to give up her job in a corset factory. Without a job yet with increasing medical

Irene Rudolph.

bills, Irene soon found herself poverty-stricken. She'd been sensible when she'd worked as a dial-painter, squirreling away her high wages rather than splurging on silks and furs like some of the other girls. But her mysterious condition had used up all her hard-earned savings.

With every expensive appointment, she hoped for improvement. As she lowered herself into Dr. Barry's chair, she opened her mouth wide and prayed that this time he would have good news to offer.

Walter Barry, an experienced, forty-two-year-old dentist, examined Irene's mouth with deepening confusion. He and his partner, Dr. James Davidson, had been operating on Irene since the summer. Yet every course of treatment they tried, such as cutting out the diseased bone in her mouth and removing teeth, seemed only to increase her suffering. As Barry examined Irene's butchered mouth at this latest appointment, on November 8, 1922, he could see that there was only more infection, inflaming her empty gums with an unhealthy yellow sheen.

James Davidson had experience in treating phossy jaw. He and Barry became convinced this was Irene's trouble.

Unknowingly, the dentists were following in the footsteps of Dr. Knef, who had treated Mollie Maggia. But the two investigations didn't cross. Nor did Knef have opportunity to share his own discovery of how Mollie's jaw was destroyed faster and faster the more of her he removed. That same accelerated infection was affecting Irene.

Barry told his patient it was his opinion she was suffering from "some occupational trouble." In other words, he thought her dial-painting job had caused it. But as Katherine Schaub later said, "The word radium was never brought into it." With everyone believing that radium was safe and healthful, people didn't even suspect it as a possible cause of the dial-painters' problems. Barry thought the luminous paint was poisonous, but he suspected that phosphorus, not radium, was at fault.

In December, Irene was admitted to the hospital. She was shockingly pale and found to be anemic. And it was in the hospital that she decided she was not going to lie down and suffer quietly.

Although Irene's dentists may not have crossed paths with Knef, the dial-painters' friendships were a stronger network. Through those friendships, they were gaining knowledge that the dentists didn't have. By that time, Irene had heard about Mollie Maggia's death. She knew, too, that Hazel Vincent was very sick. Hazel's mouth and nose were now constantly oozing with a garlic-scented, black discharge, and her doctor suspected phossy jaw too. Irene bravely told her own doctor about the other girls. She thought their cases were just too similar to be mere coincidence.

Her doctor agreed. On December 26, 1922, he reported Irene Rudolph as a case of phosphorus poisoning to the Industrial Hygiene Division and asked them to investigate.

The authorities launched straight into action. Within days, an inspector was at the Orange studio, looking into the claims the girls' work had made them sick.

The inspector observed with shock that all the girls were lip-pointing. He asked the executive accompanying him about the technique. The company man replied promptly that he had warned the girls repeatedly about this "dangerous practice" but could not get them to stop it.

Had the dial-painters overheard this conversation, they would probably have been stunned. Other than Sabin von Sochocky's one-off warning to Grace Fryer that lip-pointing would make her ill, not a single other dial-painter ever reported such advice being issued. They were certainly never told that lip-pointing was a "dangerous practice." On the contrary, they'd received countless assurances of the exact opposite.

The inspection concluded with the official taking a sample of the luminous paint. He sent it to John Roach, the deputy commissioner of the New Jersey Department of Labor, who arranged for it to be examined by Dr. Szamatolski, a chemist. Szamatolski thought it extremely unlikely any phosphorous would be in the paint, as it had never been listed as an ingredient. Without having run a single test, he wrote to Roach on January 30, 1923, that he believed Irene's jaw condition had been "caused by the influence of radium."

This was a seemingly unconventional idea, given radium's reputation as a cure-all. Yet Szamatolski's suggestion did have some science to back it up. In a collection of radium studies that USRC itself had published just four months before, there was an article called "Radium Dangers—Injurious Effects." In fact, the collection contained articles from as far back as 1906 on the damage radium could cause. USRC later admitted in an internal memo that there were a considerable number of articles about the hazards from the early twentieth century. A woman had even died in Germany in 1912 after being treated with radium. Her doctor had said the element was undoubtedly the cause.

Yet the flip side of the coin was all the *positive* literature about radium, which seemed to contest these scare stories. This literature acknowledged that radium could deposit in bones and cause changes in the blood, but all these changes were interpreted as a good thing.

If you looked a little closer at all the positive publications, however, there was a common factor: nearly all the researchers worked for radium firms. Those making money from radium were the very same people who were publishing the positive literature. As radium was such a rare and costly element, the companies selling it could control its image and most of the knowledge about it. So effective was their marketing campaign that Szamatolski's opinion seemed radical.

But that didn't mean it was wrong. By April 1923, Szamatolski had completed his tests. As he had suspected, there was not a single trace of phosphorus in the luminous paint.

"I feel quite sure," he therefore wrote on April 6, 1923, "that the opinion expressed in my former letter is correct. Such trouble as may have been caused is due to the radium."

The radium, the girls in Ottawa thought, was one of the best things about their new job. Most women who worked in the town at that time were shopgirls, secretaries, or factory workers. This was something a little different. The dial-painters were even listed as artists in their town directory in a nod to the glamour of their work. No wonder it was the most popular gig in town.

Radium Dial had initially advertised that it was hiring fifty girls, but it would eventually employ as many as two hundred. More workers were needed to keep up with demand. In 1923, Westclox, Radium Dial's main client, had a 60 percent share of the U.S. alarm-clock market, worth $5.97 million ($83 million in today's money). Ottawa's high-school students were among

Margaret "Peg" Looney.

the new employees. They worked during the school holidays, earning pocket money to buy candy. The dial-painters would keep the sweets on their desks, snacking between painting dials without washing their hands.

So many girls wanted to become dial-painters that the company could afford to be choosy. "The practice," a former employee recalled, "was to hire about ten girls at a time and try them out. Out of the ten, they would usually keep about five."

One who made the cut was seventeen-year-old Margaret Looney. Her family called her Peg. She and her nine siblings lived in a cramped house right on the railroad tracks, sleeping three or four kids to a bed. Given her dirt-poor background, Peg was thrilled to land a job as a well-paid dial-painter. She earned $17.50 ($242) a week and gave her mom most of it, though occasionally she kept a little back to treat her younger sisters. A slender, freckled redhead who was known for her giggling fits, Peg was very intelligent. She dreamed of becoming a schoolteacher, but she couldn't turn down the high wages of a dial-painter. She was still young, she reasoned, and there was plenty of time to teach later in life.

Anyway, she had a good time at work. The old high school was a lovely Victorian building with huge arched windows and high ceilings. Peg enjoyed painting there with her friends, such as her old parish schoolmate Catherine Wolfe and girls like Ella Cruse and Marie Becker.

Like Peg, Marie came from a poor background. When she was only thirteen, her stepfather sent her out to work. She'd done all sorts of jobs since then: the bakery, factory work, and sales at the dime store. Her stepfather's instruction had been something Marie took in her stride, as she did all things in life. "Her attitude was wonderful," a close relative said. "I don't ever remember her being in a bad mood... She laughed a lot. She laughed loud. Her laugh would make you laugh."

She was an instant hit in the dial-painting studio. Marie—a skinny girl with striking dark eyes and long brown hair—was a real character, full of opinions and wisecracks. Her feistiness was a sign of the times.

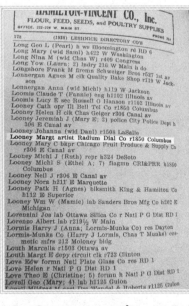

An Ottawa town directory, listing Margaret Looney as an artist at Radium Dial.

Marie Becker.

It was the Roaring Twenties, after all, and even in a tiny town like Ottawa, the breeze of female independence was stirring the sidewalks, blowing the winds of change. What a time to be alive! The Charleston dance craze took America by storm in 1923, and the Radium Dial girls swiveled their knees as they partied to the new jazz tunes. The glow of the radium on their hair and clothes made those dances even more special. "Many of the girls," Catherine Wolfe recalled, "used to wear their good dresses to the plant so that they would become luminous when they went out to parties later."

Nor was it just after work that the good times roared. In the studio, too, the girls had a blast. In their lunch hour, the dial-painters would sneak into the darkroom with the leftover radium paint. They'd had a swell idea for a new game.

"We used to paint our eyebrows, our lips, and our eyelashes," recalled Marie. She'd even give herself an elaborate mustache with the glowing paint. Then the girls would make faces at one another. They all thought it was hilarious.

Charlotte Nevins remembered that they would "turn the lights off and then [we] could look in the mirror and laugh a lot. [We] glowed in the dark!"

Yet for all the laughter, it was a strangely spooky vision. In the darkroom, no daylight shone. There was no light at all, except for the glowing element the girls had painted on their bare skin. They themselves were completely invisible. All you could see was the radium. But as Marie herself said, it was "just for fun."

They were such happy days, and a little later in the 1920s, Radium Dial took a company photograph to commemorate them. It stands now as a snapshot in time. All the girls, including Catherine, Peg, and Marie, filed outside to have their picture taken. Some sat on benches while others stood on the grand steps of the old high school. Many of the women had their hair bobbed short in the latest flapper style. They wore fabulous drop-waisted dresses, accessorized with strings of pearls.

Catherine sat in the front row in the center of the picture, just to the right of the assistant superintendent, Mr. Reed. He was a tall, bald, deaf New Yorker who was a company man to his bones. Catherine's position in the picture was perhaps a sign of her seniority. Already, she was one of the studio's longest-serving employees. Some of the other early starters

A section of the Radium Dial company photograph, including Catherine Wolfe (second row, second from left in black dress), Peg Looney (third row, first from left), and Marie Becker (third row, eighth from left).

who'd joined with Catherine when the studio first opened had already left. Charlotte Nevins, for example, quit to become a seamstress after just thirteen months.

But now all the girls remaining—the jokers and the quiet ones, the conscientious and the unconcerned—sat still for the photographer. Some hugged each other or interlinked their arms. They sat close together, staring at the camera. As the shutter closed, it captured them all together, frozen in time for just one moment. The girls of Radium Dial, outside their studio: forever young and happy and well.

On the photographic film at least.

8.

STRANGE SYMPTOMS

Orange, New Jersey
June 1923

I t was the Roaring Twenties in Orange, too, but Grace Fryer wasn't in the mood for dancing. It was odd: she had this slight pain in her back and feet. It was nothing major but enough to make it uncomfortable to walk. Dancing definitely wasn't on her agenda.

She tried to put it to the back of her mind. She'd had a few aches the year before, too, but they had come and gone. Hopefully, these latest pains would soon go for good. She was just run-down, she reasoned, and did nothing about it. Grace had far more important things to think about. She'd been promoted at the bank and was now head of her department.

It wasn't just an achy foot troubling her, however. Back in January, Grace had gone to the dentist for a routine checkup.

He'd removed two teeth. Now, six months on, a hole had appeared at the site of the extraction and was leaking pus. It was painful and smelly and tasted *disgusting*. Grace had health insurance and was prepared to pay to get it sorted out. The doctors, she was sure, would be able to fix her trouble.

But had she known what was happening just a few miles away in Newark, she might have had reason to doubt her faith in physicians. Grace's former colleague Irene Rudolph was still paying doctor after doctor to treat her but without relief. She had by now undergone both operations and blood transfusions, all to no avail. The decay in Irene's jaw was eating her alive, bit by bit.

She could feel herself weakening. Her pulse would pound in her ears as her heart beat quicker. But although her heart was drumming faster and faster, it felt to her as if her life was slowing down.

On July 15, 1923, the drumbeat suddenly stopped.

Irene died at twelve noon in Newark General Hospital. She was twenty-one. Her death was attributed to her work, but the cause was given as phosphorus poisoning. The doctors admitted it was a diagnosis that was "not decisive."

Katherine Schaub, who had watched her cousin suffer through every stage of what she called her "terrible and mysterious illness," was angry and confused as well as grief-stricken. She knew Irene had spoken to her doctor about her fears that her sickness had been caused by her job, but since then, the family had heard nothing. They didn't know the names John Roach or Dr. Szamatolski. They knew nothing of the chemist's verdict following his tests. In fact, after reviewing Szamatolski's report, the Department of Labor took no action. No action whatsoever. Even though, by that time, Mollie and Irene were not the only former dial-painters to have passed away.

Katherine was an intelligent, determined young woman. If the authorities weren't going to do anything, well then, *she* would. On July 18, the Schaubs buried Irene, who had lived such a short, sad life. The very next day, fueled by sorrow and the senseless waste, Katherine went to the Department of Health. She had a report she wished to make, she told the official there. And she told him all about Irene and her tragic death, how Mollie Maggia had died of the same sort of poisoning a year before, and how all the dial-painters had to lip-point. They'd all worked, she made sure to say, at the United States Radium Corporation.

Report filed, Katherine left. She hoped and assumed that something would be done.

A memo *was* filed about her visit. At the end, it said simply, "A foreman [at the plant] said [her] claims were not true."

And that was that.

———————≈———————

While the authorities did nothing, more and more girls got sick. That year, Quinta McDonald's back and bones began to ache. Marguerite Carlough, who was still working in the studio, developed a severe toothache that made her face swell up. And Hazel Vincent had more and more teeth extracted until her own mouth felt like a stranger's.

Then, in November, another young woman fell ill.

"I began to have trouble with my teeth," wrote Katherine Schaub.

Katherine had seen firsthand what her cousin Irene went through. When her mouth started to throb, it must have shot a bolt of terror right through her. She was brave. She didn't ignore it. Instead, she went to the same dentist who had treated Irene. Dr. Barry removed two of her teeth, noting they were "flinty" and broke easily. Katherine was told to come back soon.

And she did, again and again. Following the tooth extraction, her gum did not heal. So she returned very frequently to Dr. Barry's office. She went five times within that same month, at a charge of $2 ($27) each visit. The extraction had cost $8 ($111). Katherine wasn't stupid. "I kept thinking about Irene," she said anxiously, "and about the trouble she had had with her jaw... There was some relationship between Irene's case and mine."

Katherine's always vivid imagination, fueled by the knowledge of what she'd seen Irene endure, soon became a constant, flickering movie in her mind. Silently, it played out the fate that must lie before her. Katherine became mentally unwell. And her condition did not improve when, on December 16, 1923, another former coworker passed away. Another ghost girl began to haunt her thoughts...

As Christmas approached, Grace Fryer was conscious that although her jaw seemed better, the pain in her back and foot was worse. "My foot was stiff; I couldn't bend it," she remembered. "[When] I walked I had to walk with my foot real flat." Yet she'd soldiered on throughout the fall and still didn't ask for help. "I said nothing about [my condition] to anyone."

But she couldn't pull the wool over her parents' eyes. Daniel and Grace Fryer watched their eldest daughter as she went about her life—commuting to the bank, helping out at home, playing with her young nieces and nephews—and saw that she was limping. They insisted Grace see a doctor. Dutifully, she made an appointment at the Orthopedic Hospital in Orange for January 5, 1924.

Before that was Christmas. By Christmas Eve 1923, Marguerite Carlough felt at her wits' end. All fall, she'd battled on, continuing her work at the studio in spite of increasing ill health—and in spite of a new painting technique. To the girls' surprise, lip-pointing was banned by USRC in late 1923. The peculiar explanation was that acid in the dial-painters' mouths spoiled the paint.

No mention was made of any danger.

Marguerite had followed the new orders, but her mind wasn't on the job. She was tired, pale, and weak. Her tooth-ache, which had started in October, was agonizing. Unable to eat, weight dropped off her at an alarming rate.

When she left work that December 24, she didn't know

Marguerite Carlough.

it, but it would be for the very last time. Because that same evening, she visited her dentist. There were two teeth that were especially hurting her, and her dentist advised that both should be removed that same day.

When her dentist pulled the teeth, a piece of decayed jawbone came out too.

She wasn't going back to the studio after that. She went home instead to her sister, Sarah, and her mom and dad, and she tried to tell them what had happened. Christmas Day was a solemn occasion after her gruesome experience. But at least they were all together.

Given the absences in other New Jersey homes that winter, that was something to be grateful for.

"SOMETHING GOING ON"

Dr. Barry had never had such a busy January. Patient after patient came through his door with pale hands clutched to thin cheeks. Discomfort was obvious in the women's questioning eyes as they asked him what was wrong.

Perhaps worst of all was Marguerite Carlough, who came to him on January 2. She had recently had a tooth extraction, which had begun the process of the jaw decay he was now seeing in so many girls. Katherine Schaub was back again, as was the newly married Hazel Vincent Kuser. The sheer number of cases seemed to prove the dentist's previous theory that the problem must stem from the dial-painters' jobs. Dr. Barry and his partner, Dr. Davidson, truly believed that phosphorus in the paint was to blame because the girls' symptoms were so like those of phossy jaw. That spring, their suspicions came to a head when they confronted one of the firm's executives.

"You ought to close down the plant," Davidson told the vice president

Hazel Vincent Kuser.

angrily. "You've made $5 million. Why go on killing people for more money?"

Yet the vice president had no answer.

"If I could have my way," Davidson told him bitterly, "I would close your plant."

Yet the plant was making far too much money for that to be an option. Undark was now considered the standard radium paint for government use. Arthur Roeder's company had contracts with the U.S. Navy and Army Air Corps as well as many hospitals and doctors. Naturally, the firm wanted nothing to get in the way of all these business opportunities. So when the company learned of the dentists' accusations that the radium girls had been harmed by their work, the firm took action. They wrote to their insurance company in January 1924 to reassure them. "We do not recognize that there is any such hazard in the occupation," the company said.

But by this time, their former dial-painters disagreed. On January 19, 1924, there was a meeting held in Dr. Barry's office with at least Katherine Schaub and Marguerite Carlough present. The girls talked over their identical conditions with their increasingly concerned dentist. "We discussed employment at the radium plant," Katherine remembered. "There [was] some talk of industrial disease." The girls agreed "there was something going on about this thing."

Yet what could they do about it? Katherine had already complained to the authorities, and nothing had come of it. The evidence pointed to some problem at the plant, but no one really knew the cause. Even though in December 1923, the U.S. Public Health Service had issued an official recommendation that safety precautions should be used by all those handling radium, no one put the pieces of the puzzle together.

Much more pressing for the women than the cause, anyway, was searching for a cure or at least some relief. But there was nothing the doctors could do. Barry point-blank refused to operate on the women. He was scared that if he did, they would all be killed by the aggressive infection that had murdered Irene and others.

Just down the road at the Orange Orthopedic Hospital, Grace Fryer wasn't having much more luck. Just as she'd promised her parents, she'd kept her appointment with Dr. Robert Humphries. Humphries was the head doctor at the hospital. He listened carefully to Grace's complaints and diagnosed muscle-bound feet and chronic arthritis. He strapped her up, wrapping her feet tightly in bandages that stayed on for several weeks, but there was little improvement.

Grace's mouth was still infected, too, so she had an operation to cut out some of her jawbone. Sadly, as her former colleagues had discovered before her and as Dr. Barry had feared, once an operation had been carried out, another was soon needed and then another after that. "I have been compelled to go to the hospital so often," Grace later said, "that it seems like a second home."

Dr. Humphries was treating another young woman that spring by the name of Jennie Stocker. He didn't connect her with Grace Fryer, who worked in a bank, but Jennie had been a dial-painter until 1922. She and Grace had worked together during the war. Jennie had a strange knee complaint, which had been mystifying Humphries ever since he'd taken her case.

So many doctors across New Jersey were confused in that first month of 1924. But they didn't share notes, so each case was viewed in isolation. As January drew to a close, Hazel Kuser and her husband, Theo, decided they would look elsewhere for treatment. New Jersey was just a short distance from New York City, where some of the best doctors and dentists in the world had their practices. On January 25, Hazel made the journey into the Big Apple for treatment with Dr. Theodore Blum, one of America's first oral surgeons. His fees were very high, but Theo insisted that they visit him anyway. He could borrow money to pay the bills, he reasoned. If it eased Hazel's pain, and if Dr. Blum could stop this endless decay in her mouth, then it would all be worth it.

Blum was a balding man with a neatly trimmed mustache, spectacles, and a high forehead. As he introduced

himself to Hazel and began his examination, he quickly realized that he had never seen a condition quite like hers before. Her face was swollen with "pus bags," but it was the condition of her jawbone that was most perplexing. It seemed almost moth-eaten. It literally had holes in it.

Dr. Theodore Blum.

56

But what, Dr. Blum pondered, could have caused it?

Blum was worth his money. He made a correct if unspecific diagnosis. Hazel was suffering from poisoning by a radioactive substance. He admitted her to the hospital to operate on her jaw. It would be the first but not the last of such procedures Hazel had to endure.

Yet although Blum offered a diagnosis and swift and specialist treatment, he didn't offer the one thing that Theo had been yearning for. Hope. That was all he really wanted. To know that there was light at the end of the tunnel. To know that he and his childhood sweetheart could get through this and come out the other side into a shining day—and another day, and another one after that.

Instead, Blum told him "there is little chance of recovery."

All the money in the world couldn't save his wife now.

———≈———

The radium girls' agony hadn't gone unnoticed in the community. That same month, a concerned resident wrote to the Department of Labor about the Orange plant. This time, it was John Roach's boss, Commissioner Andrew McBride, who stepped in. He questioned the health officers about Katherine Schaub's complaint from the previous summer. They apologized for seeming negligent and finally interviewed the affected girls. Afterward, the officers recommended that the Public Health Service be called in.

Yet McBride felt there was not enough evidence for that. This may have been a political decision, because the Department of Labor was pro-business. In addition, under state law, it had no power to stop an industrial process even if it was harmful. So the department gave USRC a clean bill of health and stopped looking into the dial-painters' illnesses. They made this decision even though more and more women were getting sick with the same symptoms.

It was a stalemate. No diagnosis. No clue as to the cause. No one lifting a finger to find out what was really going on in that radium studio in Orange.

But then the stalemate was ended by an unexpected source: USRC itself.

As more and more girls fell ill, the company found that it was very difficult to recruit staff. A number of the girls had quit, and no one wanted to replace them. Production was being held up.

There was also another worrying development around the same time that really made the firm sit up and take note of what was happening to their former workers. For more than three years, Grace Vincent, Hazel's mother, had been watching her daughter suffer. Hazel was in constant agony. No mother could bear it. Dr. Blum had said there was no hope now, and Mrs. Vincent had nothing to lose. So she went down to the studio in Orange and left a letter there. In it, she told the firm that she was going to make a legal claim against them for compensation.

That got their attention.

At once, these developments were reported to the company's New York headquarters. Not long after, USRC executives decided to launch an investigation to find out if there was anything dangerous in dial-painting. For too long, there had been rumor and suspicion. It couldn't continue. After all, now it was bad for business.

10.

INVESTIGATIONS UNDERWAY

ompany president Arthur Roeder took charge of the investigation. It was a sign of how seriously the company was taking the holdup in its operations. In March 1924, Roeder approached Dr. Cecil K. Drinker, professor of physiology at the Harvard School of Public Health, to ask if he would conduct a study at the Orange plant. Drinker was a qualified medical doctor as well as a recognized authority in diseases caused by people's jobs. Roeder was taking no chances and bringing in the very best. Drinker arranged to visit the studio in April 1924, bringing with him his equally brilliant wife, Dr. Katherine Drinker.

Their study started not a moment too soon. On April 15, 1924, another young woman lost her life. Former dial-painter

Jennie Stocker—whom Dr. Humphries had been trying to treat for her peculiar knee condition—had died suddenly at the age of twenty.

The day after she passed, Roeder met the Drinkers. He showed them around the studio, and they spoke to several dial-

Dr. Cecil K. Drinker.

painters, including Marguerite Carlough. It is surprising she was in the studio, and not simply because she no longer worked there. Since Christmas Eve 1923, she had been confined to her home, except for her visits to Dr. Barry. The company may have asked her to come in specially to meet the Drinkers, being determined to lay to rest the rumors that Marguerite's work had made her sick.

Marguerite was accompanied by her sister, Sarah Carlough Maillefer, who now walked with a limp. Sarah was still working at USRC as a dial-painter. The Carlough family was poor, and with Marguerite no longer able to work and the medical bills mounting, they needed every cent they could get. Nobody thought that Sarah's lame leg was in any way connected to the awful disease plaguing Marguerite's mouth. After all, it appeared to be a completely different problem...

At the end of their visit, Katherine Drinker informed Roeder that a one-day tour was not long enough for an in-depth investigation. So over two more days, from May 7 to 8, 1924, the Drinkers returned to make a comprehensive study of the plant.

During this time, they met USRC's chief chemist, Dr. Edwin Leman. They couldn't help but notice that he had dreadful lesions on his hands. Yet when they mentioned them, he scoffed at the idea that the lesions could hurt him long-term.

The Drinkers soon realized that this unconcerned attitude was shared by all those who ran the company. "There seemed to be," Cecil Drinker later wrote, "an utter lack of realization of the dangers inherent in the material which was being manufactured." Roeder even told him that radium-induced lesions could never develop into malignant tumors, a statement the Drinkers knew was untrue.

Up in the studio, the doctors carried out thorough medical examinations of the workers. Twenty-five employees were selected as a representative number. One by one, the chosen dial-painters knocked nervously on the door of the restroom, where the women's tests were held. Sarah Maillefer was one. As the doctors requested, she opened her mouth wide so they could prod at her teeth, kept still as they probed firmly around her nose and throat, and offered the vulnerable inside of her arm so they could take a vial of blood. The exam then transferred to the darkroom. Here, Katherine Drinker closely examined the women to see for herself how they shone in the dark.

Oh, that luminosity. That *glow*. Katherine Drinker was stunned by it. As the women undressed, she witnessed the dust lingering on their bodies. It scattered everywhere, leaving its traces on the women's limbs, across their cheeks, down the backs of their necks, and around their waists. Every inch of them was marked by it. It was spectacular—and stubborn, once it had gotten beneath the women's clothing. The Drinkers noted that it "persisted in the skin" even after the women had tried to scrub themselves clean.

The Drinkers didn't limit their study to the plant. They also visited Dr. Barry and met some of the other suffering dial-painters, including Grace Fryer.

And it turned out that they were not alone in investigating the women's illnesses. That same spring, a woman named Katherine Wiley began her own independent research. Wiley was the executive secretary of the New Jersey branch of the National Consumers League, an organization that fought for better working conditions for women. A smart, driven lady in her early thirties, Wiley was shocked by what she found. The

Katherine Wiley.

level of sheer suffering was difficult to witness. She later wrote, "After seeing one of the victims, I can never rest until I have seen something done whereby I am assured it will not happen again." She resolved "to stick to this thing until there is some action somewhere."

And stick to it she did. Hearing of Hazel's mother's desire to claim compensation, she spoke to a local judge to get his advice on how the families could take legal action. But the judge told her bluntly that the women could not be helped under the New Jersey laws.

In fact, the state had pioneered legislation when it came to workers' rights. A new law had come in only that January that allowed injured employees to claim compensation for diseases caused by their jobs. But—and it was a big *but*—only nine diseases were on the permitted list; radium poisoning—if indeed that was what the girls were suffering from—was not on the list. In addition, the law had a five-month statute of limitations, which meant any legal claim had to be filed within five months of the person being hurt. Most of the dial-painters had not worked at USRC for years, let alone five months.

And there was even more bad news. The judge told

Wiley that even if a new law was passed to help the women, it would not be retroactive. In other words, it would only apply to women who were hurt *after the law was passed* and not those who had gotten sick beforehand. The judge told Wiley frankly, "As far as these girls [are] concerned, nothing [can] be done."

The families had hit the same legal brick wall. Broke and desperate, Marguerite Carlough was also now considering legal action in order to get some money to pay for her treatment. But neither she nor Hazel Kuser's family had been able to find a lawyer who would take the case without getting cash up front. And as Wiley noted grimly, "They have none."

On May 19, 1924, Wiley delivered the results of her independent investigation to the Department of Labor. She took them straight to the top: to Commissioner Andrew McBride. But he was furious to find that the Consumers League had stuck its nose into the matter. Wiley wasn't daunted one bit by McBride's anger, however. She continued to argue with him that action was required. McBride, frustrated with this nagging woman, asked her what she wanted to happen.

"An investigation by the U.S. Public Health Service," she said immediately.

"Put it in writing," he replied wearily.

She did—at once. But still no investigation began.

Even as Wiley was championing the women's cause,

developments were afoot at the center of all the trouble: USRC. The Drinkers had been busy assessing the results of all their tests. On June 3, 1924, they delivered their full and final report to the firm.

Fifteen days later, on June 18, USRC wrote to John Roach at the Department of Labor to share the doctors' verdict. The firm didn't send the full report, which was lengthy. They simply shared a table of the medical-test results of the workers. This showed the employees' blood to be "practically normal."

The company was in the clear. Arthur Roeder wasted no time in spreading the news. "He tells everyone," an observer commented, "he is absolutely safe because he has a report exonerating him from any possible responsibility in the illness of the girls." Immediately, just as Roeder had hoped, the situation improved at the plant. "Rumors quieted consider-ably," noted an internal memo with satisfaction as the produc-tion line resumed.

However, it was at this moment that Dr. Blum begged the company to help his patient Hazel Kuser. Since she'd first visited Blum in January, her condition had gone rapidly downhill despite many operations, two blood transfusions, and multiple hospital stays. The medical bills were coming in faster than Theo Kuser could pay them, even though he was mortgaging everything he owned. His father loaned him his entire life savings, but it still wasn't enough. Her family simply could not afford the care that Hazel needed. So Blum appealed directly to the company for help.

The response from USRC was swift. Full of the confidence given them by the Drinkers' report, the company refused to assist in any way whatsoever.

They were guiltless, and they said they had a report that proved it.

11.

WARNING SHOTS

Katherine Schaub couldn't wait for her summer holiday. It had been a horrible twelve months: her cousin Irene dying last July, almost a year ago now, and then Katherine's own trouble with her teeth starting in November. She knew she was now called a "nervous case" by her doctors too. But as much as she tried not to think about her situation, it was very hard not to. She had recently taken work in an office with the idea that it would help take her mind off things.

But it did not.

That summer, Katherine planned to take a much-needed rest. She was only twenty-two, and she needed to remember what it was to feel young. All this worry was dragging her down.

Yet when July 1924 arrived, Katherine noted, "I could not go away. The condition in my jaw was causing me considerable anxiety and I decided to consult a skilled dental surgeon in New York City; I had to use my vacation money for a new set of X-rays."

She chose to consult Dr. Blum, who was also treating Hazel Kuser. Katherine was at his office again and again that summer, finding herself in agony. "The pain [I have] suffered," she later said, "could only be compared with the pain caused by a dentist drilling on a live nerve hour after hour, day after day, month after month." But no matter what Blum did for her, no cure came. "I had stopped at nothing in an effort to regain my lost health, but so far I had failed," Katherine wrote dejectedly. "No one was able to help me."

On one of her visits to Blum, she ran into Hazel. Her former colleague was unrecognizable. This mysterious new disease, in some patients, led to grotesque facial swellings: football-sized balls of pus sprouting from their jaws. It seems Hazel may have suffered in this way. "Why should I be so afflicted?" Katherine would later ask, and she could have been speaking for all the radium girls. "What have I done to be so punished?"

Nor were Hazel and Katherine the only ones in pain. In Orange, Quinta McDonald was hobbling about now with more than just a noticeable limp. It was more like a lurch as she stumbled from one foot to the next. It was the strangest thing, but, she said, "It seemed to me that one leg was shorter than the other."

She must be imagining it. All the twenty-four years of her life, her limbs had measured up straight. Why would that suddenly change?

Nevertheless, she made an appointment with Dr. Humphries at the Orange Orthopedic Hospital. In August 1924, Humphries took an X-ray of her hip and stared grimly at it. *Ah, there it was. But* what *was it?*

On the X-ray, there was a "white shadow," as Humphries called it. It was peculiar, showing a white mottling through-out the bone. He had never seen anything quite like it. As John Roach later wrote of the bewildering maladies, "The whole situation is baffling and perplexing... This strange and destructive [force] is an unknown quantity to medical and surgical science."

In fact, there was one person who had realized exactly what the problem was. In September 1924, Dr. Blum made an address to the American Dental Association about jaw necro-sis. (*Necrosis* meant decay or death of living tissue. It was the technical term that dentists used to describe the aggressive destruction of the dial-painters' jawbones.) Blum referenced only Hazel Kuser's case and merely in a brief footnote. But it was he who made the first-ever mention in medical literature of what he now termed "radium jaw."

One might have thought that the dentist's groundbreaking diagnosis would have captured the imagination of the medical community. But in fact, it went entirely unnoticed by everyone. By other dentists. By the dial-painters, who did not read medical publications. And by physicians, like Dr. Humphries in Orange.

Standing before Quinta McDonald's X-ray in that summer of 1924, Humphries was completely at a loss. Nevertheless, he had to offer a diagnosis to his patient. So he told her she had arthritis. But standard treatments failed to help. Consequently, that summer, Quinta McDonald was encased in plaster, from her diaphragm down to her knees, in the hope that it would mend her troubles.

At least Quinta had hope. Later that year, there was none left for her former colleague Hazel Kuser. On December 9, 1924, she passed away at the age of twenty-five, with her husband and mother by her side. By the time she died, her body was in such a distressing condition that the family would not allow her friends to see it at the funeral. And the family was financially ruined. Their bills—for hospitals, X-rays, ambulances, physicians, house calls, medicine, and transport to New York—ran to almost $9,000 ($125,000). They had tried everything to save her, but it had all been for nothing.

Katherine Wiley of the Consumers League found the situation unbearably unjust. Frustrated that nothing had been done by the authorities, she now pursued two leads.

First, she wrote to Dr. Alice Hamilton, a brilliant scientist who was the first-ever female faculty member of Harvard University. The head of Hamilton's department happened to be Cecil Drinker. Yet Hamilton at that time knew nothing of the Drinkers' report on the Orange plant. Company president Roeder may have been using it to calm the fears of his employees and to justify the company's refusal to help the sick dial-painters, but Drinker had not yet published it. Hamilton therefore didn't know that an expert had already looked into the link between the girls' jobs and their mysterious illnesses. She enthusiastically agreed to help Wiley.

Wiley's second line of attack was to reach out to Dr. Frederick Hoffman, a fifty-nine-year-old statistician who specialized in work-related diseases. After reading Wiley's letter, Hoffman began making inquiries. His first port of call, at Wiley's urging, was to visit Marguerite Carlough.

It had been almost a year since Marguerite had made that fateful Christmas Eve trip to the dentist. By the time Hoffman visited her in December 1924, he found her "lingering between

Dr. Alice Hamilton.   Dr. Frederick Hoffman.

life and death, with apparently no hopeful outlook for the future." He couldn't help but be moved.

Before the year was out, Hoffman had sent a strongly worded letter to Roeder at USRC. He told him that if Marguerite's disease ever met the legal rules that would allow her to claim financial compensation, "I seriously doubt...your company would escape liability." In other words, he believed the company would lose any legal case she brought. Then Hoffman added, somewhat threateningly, that if any more dial-painters got sick, he thought it highly likely their conditions *would* eventually be made legally compensable.

A warning shot had been fired. And the New Jersey dial-painters were determined that this would be only the start of it. Marguerite in particular could not stop thinking that she had given her all to that company—and this was how they repaid her. Out in the cold, not a cent to spare to ease her suffering. And not just her but her friends too.

Though it had been a long time since she had felt like herself, Marguerite could dimly remember how she used to be. Once upon a time, a dynamic young woman in sleekly fitted tailored clothes and fabulous hats had smiled back at her when she looked in the mirror. That winter, as the calendar pages turned and the New Year began, she tried to be that dynamic girl again. She gathered all her courage and what little strength she had left. She asked her family for help, being too weak now to do what she needed. But this was important. This she would do, even if it was her last act on earth.

Against all the odds, Marguerite Carlough found a lawyer to take her case. And on February 5, 1925, she filed suit against USRC for $75,000 ($1 million).

The dial-painters' fight back had begun.

12.

LIP... DIP... PAINT

Ottawa, Illinois
1925

Marguerite's legal case made the local news in Newark. It's unlikely that the Radium Dial girls in Ottawa heard about it, but their employers certainly did. The radium industry was a small pond, and Radium Dial was one of the biggest fishes of them all.

By 1925, the studio in Ottawa had become the largest dial-painting plant in the country, supplying forty-three hundred dials a day. Business was booming, and Radium Dial wanted to take no chances of having a holdup in their operations as USRC had suffered when the rumors first started in New Jersey.

Radium Dial now conceived a master plan to avoid the same problem. They opened a second dial-painting studio in Streator, sixteen miles south of Ottawa, where even less was

Ottawa dial-painters in 1924.

known about radium. Both plants ran simultaneously for nine months. But once it was clear the Ottawa workers hadn't heard the rumors from the east and weren't going to quit, the firm shut down the second studio.

The company also decided, just as USRC had done before them, to have their workers medically tested later in the year. The exams were conducted by a company doctor in Mr. Reed's home on Post Street. Not all the women were tested; Catherine Wolfe was not among them. That was a shame, because just lately, she had not been feeling well. After two years of working at Radium Dial, she said, "I began to feel pains in my left ankle, which spread up to my hip." She'd started to limp just a little.

Red-haired Peg Looney, however, *was* summoned by Mr.

Reed to his home for a test. Yet when her colleagues asked her how it had gone, she had to tell them she hadn't a clue. The medical-exam results were only given to the corporation, and Peg and her coworkers weren't told what they said. Peg settled back at her desk in the studio without worry, however. She picked up her brush and licked her lips in preparation for painting. She wasn't at all concerned. The company, she was sure, would tell her if anything was wrong.

All the girls in Ottawa still lip-pointed, little knowing that eight hundred miles away, the practice had been banned. Yet behind the scenes at Radium Dial's headquarters, its executives—mindful of the New Jersey lawsuit—now started putting some half-hearted effort into finding an alternative method of applying the paint. Eventually, they tasked Mr. Reed with this job. He began tinkering with the idea of a glass pen like the ones Swiss dial-painters used. In the meantime, the Ottawa girls kept on. *Lip... Dip... Paint.*

Their fun times kept right on too, as the young women started courting. Back in high school, Peg Looney's favorite song had been the independent-minded "I Ain't Nobody's Darling," but she had changed her tune. She was stepping out with a bright young man named Chuck Hackensmith. Anyone with half a brain could see that any one of these days, he was going to propose.

Peg Looney and Chuck
Hackensmith, with two
of her little sisters.

Chuck grew up living just around the block from Peg and her large family. Although he was now away at college, he came home on weekends, and that was when the young couple really let their hair down. Chuck had a shack at his house where he would throw parties, serving home-brewed root beer and playing records on his beat-up old gramophone, to which the dial-painters danced. Everybody would go down to the shack. Marie Becker would be there with her new boyfriend, Patrick Rossiter. Catherine Wolfe would also attend as a good friend of Peg; she was single at that time. And all the Looneys would be there as well. "The whole family!" exclaimed Peg's sister Jean. "And there were ten of us!"

There was so much happening in Ottawa in that spring of 1925 that the visit from the government inspector to the studio barely registered with the women. But that was just what Radium Dial wanted.

The inspector came from the Bureau of Labor Statistics, a government organization. The bureau was based in the capital, Washington, DC, and run by a white-haired man named Ethelbert Stewart. Recently, the bureau had launched a national investigation into workplace poisons. Stewart sent his inspector, Swen Kjaer, out into the field. He was to investigate dial-painting studios across America.

Kjaer began his study in April 1925. He went first to the Chicago office of Radium Dial, where he interviewed the company's vice president, Rufus Fordyce, and some laboratory workers. Kjaer noticed the latter had lesions on their fingers. The lab workers openly acknowledged that radium was dangerous to handle without protection. And the company acknowledged the danger too, because the men in Radium Dial's labs were provided with safety equipment. Kjaer noted that the operators were shielded by lead screens and also given vacations from work to limit their exposure.

When Kjaer met with Fordyce, the vice president had a special request for him. Fordyce knew that Kjaer was about to inspect the Ottawa studio, and Fordyce asked him to be discreet while there, "so as not to cause an alarm among the workers."

Maybe as a result of that request, only three Ottawa dial-painters would be questioned.

On April 20, Kjaer arrived in the little town of Ottawa for the studio inspection. His first port of call was to speak with Miss Murray, the superintendent.

"Why," she told him, "[I] never heard of any illness which might in the slightest manner be caused by the work." In fact, she thought the opposite had occurred, believing some workers had shown "physical improvement" after working in the studio.

Kjaer asked her about lip-pointing. She told him that the girls had been warned "not to tip the brushes in the mouths without washing them carefully first in the water provided." But she conceded, "Tipping in the mouth is constantly practiced."

Kjaer could see that for himself as he toured the studio the same day. Every single girl there was lip-pointing. Yet they were all, he noted, "healthy and vigorous." On the day he toured the plant, he observed that the girls did have water on their desks, in which they were cleaning their brushes. But later, when Fordyce supplied him with a photograph of the studio taken at a different time, Kjaer noticed that water was not in evidence on the tables.

As part of his inspection, Kjaer also interviewed Ottawa's dentists. He wanted to find out if they'd come across any unusual conditions in their patients. In New Jersey, it had been Drs. Barry and Davidson who'd first raised the alarm. So should there be a problem in Ottawa too, it seemed logical that its dentists might be the first to know of it. Consequently, Kjaer called on three different dentists on that April afternoon, including one who had the largest dental practice in town. Yet they all told Kjaer there had been no problems. They promised to notify the bureau promptly if anything should turn up.

Kjaer spent only three weeks on his national study. That was an incredibly short time, given the size of the country and the potential seriousness of the situation. But he had no say in the matter. After those three weeks were up, the study was suddenly stopped. Kjaer's boss, Ethelbert Stewart, later said of the decision, "Radium paints came to our attention in connection with our campaign against white phosphorus; phosphorus then was our chief interest and we found that it was not used in the elements which go into luminous paint." The dial-painting investigation had simply been an offshoot of a wider study into industrial poison.

Yet there was another reason too, as Stewart later confessed. He didn't stop the inquiry because he was sure there was no danger in dial-painting but because "the expense of follow-up made it impossible for the Bureau to continue." Safety had a price tag, or so it seemed.

In those three short weeks, however, Kjaer had reached a conclusion. Radium, he determined, *was* dangerous.

It was just that nobody told the girls...

Arthur Roeder was having a very bad day. Ever since the Carlough girl had brought her lawsuit, every day seemed to be a bad day. The publicity had been horrendous, with his company's name dragged through the mud as this little upstart charged that the firm had hurt her. To his frustration, the coverage was affecting business. There were now only a few dial-painters left.

Roeder was fighting the case with the help of expensive lawyers. They'd immediately asked that Marguerite's claim be presented before the Workmen's Compensation Bureau. It would instantly fail there, as she wasn't suffering from one of the nine diseases covered by the law. So far, however, the legal maneuvering wasn't working. The judge had directed that a jury should decide the case.

Arther Roeder.

The situation, from Roeder's perspective, grew worse by the day. The family of Hazel Kuser joined the lawsuit, with a claim of $15,000 ($203,000). It was just as well, Roeder thought, that Miss Carlough's sister, Sarah Maillefer, quit her job in the dial-painting studio when Marguerite filed suit. There was no way she could have continued in their employ. He mused on Mrs. Maillefer for a moment. His executives had told him what a sickly woman she was—lame for three years now, walking with a cane. Well, in Roeder's opinion, apples didn't fall far from trees, and if one sister was sickly, the chances were it ran in the family.

He blamed the women's clubs for all this bother, such as the Consumers League. Their New Jersey executive secretary, Katherine Wiley, had been writing to him since the start of the year. She had an unusual interest in the matter, he thought disapprovingly. He'd done his best to put her off but had not succeeded.

Then there was the statistician, Dr. Hoffman. His investigation was really troubling Roeder. Hoffman planned to publish his report, probably before the influential American Medical Association. Why, Roeder thought in frustration, he hadn't even visited the factory! Though, to be fair, that was perhaps because Roeder had offered no assistance. Nevertheless, Hoffman's study had continued. Roeder couldn't understand his determination.

Unbeknownst to the company president, it was perhaps partly driven by the fact that even the paint's inventor now acknowledged the girls' trouble was due to their work. In February 1925, Sabin von Sochocky had written to Hoffman to say that "the disease in question is, without doubt, an occupational disease."

Roeder sighed and turned back to his desk to read his correspondence. Yet his heart sank further when he saw what was before him. Another letter from Miss Wiley.

"My dear Mr. Roeder," she wrote. "I [have] learned that Dr. Drinker made an investigation [last spring]. I have heard nothing of the result, but have been looking with great interest to the time when it would be published."

A troubled look crossed Arthur Roeder's affluently rounded face. The Drinker investigation... That was another thorn in his side. He'd so looked forward to the delivery of the doctors' report last June. Here, finally, would be the scientific proof of what he knew to be the truth: that these grim illnesses and deaths had absolutely nothing to do with his firm.

He had been stunned when he read the letter Cecil K. Drinker had enclosed with the report.

"We believe that the trouble which has occurred is due to radium," Drinker had written, almost a year ago now, on June 3, 1924.

Well, that was...unexpected. The Drinkers *had* delivered an early opinion on April 29, following their one-day visit and some initial academic research, that "it would seem that radium is the probable cause of the trouble." But that was before they'd even returned to the plant, and Roeder had been certain that further study would prove them wrong.

Yet the final report hadn't made for better reading. "In our opinion, so great an incidence among these employees of this unusual disease...cannot be a coincidence."

The Drinkers had carefully examined the paint's ingredients. They dismissed each ingredient in turn as nontoxic—except for radium. At radium, they declared there was ample evidence of the dangers.

They even supplied a theory of what they thought was happening inside the women. Radium, they noted, was chemically similar to calcium, and the human body is programmed to deliver calcium straight to the bones. The Drinkers thought that radium would act in the same way, as a bone seeker. Essentially, radium had masked itself as calcium. Fooled, the girls' bodies had deposited it inside their bones. Radium was like a silent stalker, hiding behind that mask, using its disguise to burrow deep into the women's jaws and teeth.

And once there, it began to kill them.

Since the beginning of the century, radium had been proven to cause serious flesh wounds. That was why workers exposed to large amounts of radium wore heavy lead aprons. It was why Dr. von Sochocky didn't have the tip of his left index finger anymore and why Dr. Leman, the chief chemist at USRC, had lesions all over his hands. The impact radium had externally could easily kill a man, as Pierre Curie had noted back in 1903.

That was the effect it had on the outside. Now imagine the impact of it once it had craftily concealed its way inside your bones.

"Radium, once deposited in bone," wrote Dr. Drinker in his report, "would be in a position to produce peculiarly effective damage, many thousand times greater than the same amount outside."

It was radium, lurking in Mollie Maggia's bones, that had caused her jaw to splinter. It was radium, making itself at home in Hazel Kuser, that had eaten away at her skull until her jawbones had holes riddled right through them. It was radium, shooting out its constant rays, that was battering Marguerite Carlough's mouth, even at this moment.

It was radium that had killed Irene and Mollie and so many more...

It was radium, the Drinkers said, that was the problem.

The doctors enclosed the results of the tests they'd run on the workers. "No blood [from the USRC employees]," they wrote, "was entirely normal." While some employees registered significant changes in their blood, other results were noted to be "practically normal." But not one worker had completely normal blood, not even a woman who had been with the firm for only two weeks.

Roeder had been aghast at the Drinkers' report by the time he'd finished reading. Surely, it couldn't be true. He'd taken a few days to collect his thoughts. Then, over the course of several weeks in June 1924, he'd exchanged further letters with Dr. Drinker. Seeming to forget the doctor's undoubted brilliance—the very thing that had driven Roeder to recruit him in the first place—Roeder now said he was "mystified" by Drinker's conclusions. On June 18, 1924—the same day that the company wrote to the Department of Labor to share its sleight-of-hand summary of the Drinker report—Roeder told

Drinker that he didn't accept his conclusions. He rejected the evidence. He felt strongly that the question of whether the girls' jobs had hurt them was still open to discussion. He had decided to ignore the report.

It then all went quiet. In time, Drinker asked for Roeder's permission to make his report public. Since Roeder was the person who'd commissioned the study, Drinker felt it was not right to publish it without Roeder's say-so. But with USRC having deliberately manipulated the Drinkers' true results with the Department of Labor, the company did not *want* the report made public. Permission was not given. So the real report stayed secret. The lies worked well. For the past year, to his satisfaction, Arthur Roeder had been able to get on with business as usual.

Until now.

Until Katherine Wiley had stuck her nose in where it wasn't wanted.

Unknown to Roeder, Wiley was making great strides in her independent investigations. She was working closely with Dr. Alice Hamilton, who worked in the same department as Drinker. By this time, the women had learned of the Drinkers' unpublished report and become determined to bring it into the light. Katherine Wiley's letter to ask Roeder about it was just part of this plan. In another line of attack, the women asked John Roach at the Department of Labor to *request* the Drinkers' report from Roeder. They didn't know that USRC had already given Roach their deceitful version of the study.

Naturally, Roach told Wiley that he'd *already* seen the Drinkers' report—and that it put the company in the clear. Shocked, the women informed the Drinkers that the firm had lied to the authorities about their conclusions. The scientists were outraged. Katherine Drinker called Roeder "a real villain," while her husband wrote to Roeder to urge him to make the full study public at last.

Wheels set in motion, Hamilton wrote to Wiley that she believed the situation resolved. Surely, she said, Arthur Roeder would not be "stupid enough [as] to refuse to let Dr. Drinker publish the report."

But she had underestimated the nerve of the company president.

14.

HOFFMAN HELPS

A rthur Roeder had not become the head of USRC without being a clever businessman. He was an expert negotiator, skilled in manipulating situations to his advantage. It was always wise, he thought, to keep your friends close. But one should always keep one's enemies closer.

On April 2, 1925, Roeder invited Frederick Hoffman to the Orange plant.

The statistician, in fact, visited two or three times, noting in particular the lack of warning signs about lip-pointing. It's possible Roeder observed his notes. On Hoffman's final visit, Roeder called his attention to brand-new notices in the studio, which commanded employees not to put the brushes in their mouths. Hoffman approved. "They had impressed me," he later said, "with improved conditions."

Roeder knew what he was doing. Now that the two men were friendly, Roeder asked Hoffman to delay publishing his report.

But Roeder was too late. The paper had already been submitted to the American Medical Association. Not only that, Hoffman had agreed to supply the Bureau of Labor Statistics—the government agency led by Ethelbert Stewart—with a copy of it too.

One can only imagine Roeder's reaction to that news. However, he had recently tried to calm the concerns of the bureau as well. When the inspector, Swen Kjaer, had interviewed Roeder that spring about Marguerite Carlough, Roeder told him frankly that he thought she was trying to "palm off" her illness on the firm. In other words, that she was lying about her job having hurt her and in so doing trying to cheat the company.

At least the Carlough girl gave him an excuse to put off John Roach. As a result of Katherine Wiley's meddling, Roach had been in touch. Now that the Department of Labor knew the report supplied by USRC in June 1924 was a whitewash, they were demanding a copy of the full study. But Roeder had replied that he could not help because of the Carlough lawsuit. He said the same in response to Drinker's plea for him to publish it: "We are not issuing any reports now except on advice of [our lawyers]."

Roeder did not seem troubled by any of these new developments. And with good reason. He had an ace up his sleeve. Drinker, he thought, wasn't the only expert in town.

Enter Dr. Frederick Flinn.

Dr. Flinn specialized in industrial health, just like Drinker. He was the assistant professor of physiology at the Institute of Public Health at Columbia University. Within a day or so of being asked to undertake research into the supposed harmful effects of radioactive paint, he had met with Roeder, who agreed to give him money for his study.

A serious man in his late forties with thinning hair and wire-framed glasses, Flinn began work the very next morning with a tour of the Orange plant. But he didn't stop there. Through the contacts of USRC, Flinn soon met the dial-painters of other firms, too, giving them physical checkups.

One such company was the Luminite Corporation in Newark, where he now encountered Edna Bolz Hussman, the "Dresden Doll" dial-painter who'd worked at the Orange plant during the war. At that time, Edna had slight knee pains. But she was paying them no attention. She'd probably heard the rumors about the Carlough lawsuit, however. So it must have come as a huge relief when Flinn gave his verdict following the tests. "[He] told me," she later said, "that my health was perfect."

If only her former colleagues were as fortunate.

Dr. Frederick Flinn.

Katherine Schaub was having a dreadful time. It had been, she later wrote, "a very depressing winter." Her stomach was now troubling her, so much so that she could not retain solid food and had endured an operation. She felt as if she was being passed from dentist to doctor, yet still no one offered any answers. "Since [my] first visit [to a doctor], it had been nothing but doctors, Doctors, DOCTORS," she wrote in frustration. "To be under the care of a skilled physician and yet not show any sign of improvement was most discouraging." She was so ill, she'd been forced to stop work.

Grace Fryer, however, was still managing to carry on with her job at the bank. But although the infection in her jaw seemed to have cleared up, her back still plagued her.

No one was suffering as much as Marguerite Carlough. With the lawsuit dragging on, her family was forced to spend money they didn't have on her care. By May 1925, the medical bills ran to $1,312 (almost $18,000 today). Sarah Maillefer was distraught over her little sister's condition. She tried to keep talking to her—soothing words or jokes to lift her spirits— but Marguerite's hearing was greatly impaired in both ears because of her infected facial bones. Though her sister tried to cheer her up, Marguerite really struggled to hear what Sarah said. And the pain was *awful*. By this time, Marguerite's lower jaw was fractured on the right side of her face and most of her teeth were missing. Her head, essentially, was "extremely rotten." But she was alive. Her whole head was rotting, but she was still alive.

```
X ray photographs.............$15
Dr. Lane's bills to date.....500.
Hospital,4 weeks.............. 84.
Trips to hospital(2persons)  92.80
medicine to date.............511.00
Blood tests(5 at $5).......... 25.00
Blood transfusion............. 60.00
3 trips to see Dr. Ivy(2person84.80
                             ‾‾‾‾‾‾‾‾‾
                             $1312.60
Dr. Ivy  has not yet rendered a bill.
```

A tally of Marguerite Carlough's medical bills. By May 1925, they totaled $1,312.60, almost $18,000 in today's dollars.

Appalled at her rapid decline, the doctors caring for her sought aid from an unlikely source—USRC founder Sabin von Sochocky.

Von Sochocky was no longer part of his company. He had no ties to the corporation anymore. If anything, he may even have felt bitter about the way he had been treated by them. Perhaps, too, he felt some responsibility. When Marguerite's doctors asked him for help, he willingly gave it. Working together with Dr. Hoffman, von Sochocky admitted Marguerite to St. Mary's Hospital in Orange. She was anemic and weighed ninety pounds. Her pulse was "small, rapid, and irregular."

She was hanging on, but barely.

A week or so after she was admitted, which was partly thanks to Hoffman, the statistician did the dial-painters his biggest service yet. He read his paper on their problems before the American Medical Association. His was the first major study to connect the women's illnesses to their work—the first, that is, to be made public. And his opinion was this: "The women were slowly poisoned as a result of introducing into the system minute quantities of radioactive substance."

That *minute* was important, for the company—*all* the radium companies—believed dial-painting to be safe because there was such a tiny amount of radium in the paint. But

Hoffman had realized that it wasn't the amount that was the problem. It was the cumulative effect of the women taking the paint into their bodies day in and day out, dial after dial. The amount of radium in the paint may have been small, but by the time you had been swallowing it every single day for three or four or five years in a row, there was enough there to cause you damage, particularly when, as the Drinkers had already realized, radium was even more powerful internally and headed straight for your bones.

As early as 1914, specialists knew that radium could deposit in bone and cause changes in the blood. The radium companies researching these effects interpreted them in a positive way. They thought that the radium stimulated the bone marrow to produce extra red blood cells, which was a good thing for the body. In a way, they were right—that was exactly what happened. Ironically, the radium did, at first, boost the health of those it had poisoned. There were more red blood cells, something that gave an illusion of excellent health.

But it was an illusion only. That stimulation of the bone marrow, by which the red blood cells were produced, soon became *over*stimulation. The body couldn't keep up. In the end, Hoffman said, "The cumulative effect was disastrous, destroying the red blood cells, causing anemia and other ailments, including necrosis." He concluded emphatically, "We are dealing with an entirely new occupational affection demanding the utmost attention." And then—perhaps thinking of Marguerite's lawsuit, which was dragging sluggishly through the legal system—he added that the disease should be brought under the workmen's compensation laws.

Katherine Wiley was, in fact, attempting to do just that through her work with the Consumers League. She was valiantly campaigning to have radium necrosis added to the list of compensable diseases. In the meantime, Marguerite's only hope for justice was the federal court. But her case was unlikely to be heard before the fall. As Alice Hamilton noted with dismay, "Miss Carlough may not live till then."

Hoffman continued to present his discoveries. He noted that although he had looked for cases of radium poisoning in other studios across the United States, he found none. Unwittingly, Hoffman *had* stumbled on the reason for that, but didn't realize it. He wrote that radium poisoning was a very sinister disease because several years might pass before its victims experienced any symptoms.

Several years. The Radium Dial studio in Ottawa had been running for less than three.

Both Hoffman and von Sochocky, whom he'd consulted for his paper, were struck by the lack of other cases. For

USRC, the fact that no other dial-painters were sick was clear evidence that the girls' illnesses could not have been caused by their jobs. But Hoffman and von Sochocky were both convinced that dial-painting *was* the source of the girls' sickness. So they did what any scientists would do. They looked for a scientific reason to explain it. And when von Sochocky gave Hoffman the top-secret paint formula, Hoffman believed he had found it. Von Sochocky explained that while other companies still used standard radium (radium-226) in their paint, USRC had long ago switched to using mesothorium (radium-228) instead.

That *had* to be the answer. Hoffman thought that radium was *not* at fault. It must be *mesothorium* that was the real problem. So Hoffman, building on Dr. Blum's work, commented in his paper, "It has seemed to me more appropriate to use the term 'radium (mesothorium) necrosis.'"

But while Hoffman's paper attracted some publicity, it didn't *prove* the connection between the girls' poisoning and their careers completely. And who was Frederick Hoffman, anyway, to come up with all these theories? He was not a medical doctor who might *really* know about these things.

What the women needed was a champion. A medical mastermind—someone who could not only command authority but also, perhaps, find a way of definitively diagnosing their disease. Most importantly of all, they needed a doctor who wasn't in the pocket of the company.

Sometimes, the Lord works in mysterious ways. On May 21, 1925, a Newark trolley car was traveling along its tracks on Market Street when there was a commotion on board. The commuters, making their way home in the evening rush hour, made room for the passenger who had collapsed to the floor. They called out to give him some air, for the trolley car to stop. A kindly passerby no doubt bent to mop his brow.

It was all in vain. Only a few minutes after the man first collapsed, he died.

His name was George L. Warren. In life, he had been the county physician for Essex County, a senior medical figure with responsibility for all residents within the county borders. And within those borders lay Newark and Orange, the locations where former dial-painters were now dying unstoppably.

With Warren's passing, his position became vacant. The role of county physician—what would become the powerfully titled chief medical examiner—was now open.

Whoever filled it would make or break the case.

15.

MAKING HISTORY

It was a unanimous appointment. The board congratulated the new county physician with firm handshakes and much approving nodding of heads.

Dr. Harrison Martland, please step up.

Martland was a man of extraordinary talents. He ran his own laboratory at Newark City Hospital, where he was chief pathologist. Forty-one years old, he had graying brown hair, circular glasses, and wobbly jowls. A colorful personality who drove open-top cars and exercised to bagpipes every morning, he was an extremely hard-working man. As chance would have it, he was also a Sherlock Holmes enthusiast.

The Case of the Radium Girls was a mystery to challenge even the greatest of medical detectives.

Martland was already aware of the dial-painters' illnesses, having briefly met some of Dr. Barry's patients a year or so before. But by his own admission, he had then lost interest in the case. Now, he took his new responsibilities seriously.

Dr. Harrison Martland.

As he himself said, "One of the main functions of a medical examiner is to prevent wastage of human life in industry."

The cynical would say, however, that these noble words had absolutely nothing to do with why he took an interest in the radium cases at that moment. The cynical would say there was only one reason a high-profile specialist finally took up the cause.

On June 7, 1925, the first male employee of USRC died.

"The first case that was called to my attention," Martland later remarked, "was a Dr. Leman."

The chief chemist of USRC, who had scoffed at the Drinkers when they'd expressed concern about the blackened lesions on his hands the year before, was dead. He died at the age of thirty-six of pernicious anemia after an illness of only a few weeks. His death had occurred much too quickly for a normal case of anemia. So Martland was called in to conduct an autopsy.

He suspected radium poisoning. But the chemical analyses he carried out on Leman's body failed to show any sign of the element. Specialist testing would clearly be required. Martland turned to Sabin von Sochocky, an authority on radium, for assistance. And he asked someone else for help too. Where could he possibly find the best-qualified radium expert in town? Surely, USRC knew a little bit about it?

Together, Martland, von Sochocky, and USRC's Howard Barker tested Leman's tissues and bones in the radium-factory laboratory. In exchange for its help, USRC asked Martland to keep his conclusions secret.

The tests were a success. The doctors reduced Leman's bones to ashes, then tested the ash with an instrument called an electrometer. In so doing, they made medical history in measuring radioactivity in a human body for the first time. They determined that Leman had died from radium poisoning. His remains were all radioactive.

As Martland and von Sochocky worked together, von Sochocky asked the new medical examiner to help the dial-painters. So only a day or two after Leman had died, Martland found himself in St. Mary's Hospital, meeting a brave young woman named Marguerite Carlough.

She lay weakly in her hospital bed, her shockingly pale face surrounded by limp, dark hair. At that point, the roof of her mouth was so decayed that there was no bone left between her mouth and nose at all.

Also visiting Marguerite that day was her sister, Sarah. Sarah still had her limp, but a new ailment was more worrying. In the past week, large black-and-blue spots had broken out all over her body. Sarah had come to see Marguerite anyway, not wanting to miss the visit. With difficulty, she limped up the stairs with her walking cane. Her teeth were aching, too, but you had to put things into perspective. Look at her sister; she was far worse off. Even when her gums started to bleed, Sarah thought only of her sister, who was so close to death.

As Martland met the Carlough girls, he observed that although Marguerite was more ill than Sarah, Sarah was also not well. When he asked her, she confessed that the black-and-blue spots were causing her intense pain.

Martland ran tests and found Sarah to be very anemic. He told her the results and spoke with her about her mouth problems. And then Sarah, perhaps becoming anxious about what it might all mean, worsened rapidly and had to be admitted to the hospital. But at least she wasn't alone. She and Marguerite shared a hospital room. Two sisters together, facing whatever might lie ahead.

Martland wanted to test the two women to find out if radium was the cause of their illnesses. But the only tests he knew that could extract radium from a human body—those he had conducted with von Sochocky and Barker on Dr. Leman—required burning bone to ash. You couldn't very well do that with living patients.

It was von Sochocky who came up with the answer. If radium *was* in the women, it would make the girls themselves radioactive. Therefore, all they had to do was devise tests that could measure radioactivity in living humans. These tests, which would be developed and largely invented by Martland and von Sochocky, were created specifically to test the dial-painters' bodies. No physician had ever attempted to test living patients in this way before.

The pair devised two methods. First, the gamma-ray test, which involved sitting the patient before an electroscope to read the gamma radiation coming from their skeleton. Second, the expired-air method, in which the patient blew through a series of bottles into an electroscope so that the amount of radon could be measured. This latter test was based on a simple idea. Martland knew that as radium decayed, it turned into radon gas. If radium was present in the girls' jawbones, he thought that radon might be exhaled when they breathed out.

The doctors took their equipment to the hospital to try

on Marguerite. But when they got there, it was Sarah Maillefer they decided to test first.

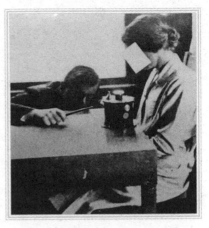

A dial-painter being tested for radioactivity, ca. 1920s.

Being in the hospital had not helped her. Despite being given a blood transfusion on June 14, Sarah had become so ill that she'd had to be removed from the room she shared with her sister. When Marguerite asked where she was, the nurses told her Sarah had been "removed to receive special treatments."

That was true, in a way. The tests Sarah was about to have *were* special, for she was the first dial-painter ever to be tested for the presence of radium. The first who would prove whether all the guesswork was correct.

This was the moment of truth.

In a hospital room in St. Mary's, Martland and von Sochocky set up the equipment. They first tested Sarah's body. As she lay weakly on the bed, Martland held the electrometer eighteen inches above her chest to test her bones. A "normal leak" would be ten subdivisions in sixty minutes. Sarah's body was leaking fourteen subdivisions in that time. *Radium.*

Next, they tested her breath. The normal result they were looking for was five subdivisions in thirty minutes. This test wasn't as easy as simply holding the measuring device over Sarah's prone body. This test, she had to help with.

It was very hard for her to do, because she was so unwell she found it difficult to breathe. Yet Sarah was a fighter. So when Martland asked her to breathe into his machine, she tried very, very hard for him. *In...out... In...out.* She kept it going, even as her pulse raced and her gums bled and her leg ached and ached. *In...out... In...out.* Sarah Maillefer breathed. She lay back on the pillows, exhausted, and the doctors checked the results.

The subdivisions were 15.4. With every breath she gave, the radium was there: carried on the very air, slipping out through her painful mouth, passing by her aching teeth, moving like a whisper across her tongue. *Radium.*

Sarah Maillefer was a fighter. But there are some fights that you cannot win. The doctors left her in the hospital that day, on June 16, 1925. They didn't see as the poison set in more strongly, as new bruises bloomed on her body, blood vessels bursting under her skin. Her mouth would not stop bleeding. Pus oozed from her gums. Her bad leg was a constant source of pain. *Everything* was a constant source of pain. She couldn't take it anymore. She became delirious and lost her mind.

But it didn't take too long, not after that. In the early

hours of June 18, only a week after she'd been admitted to the hospital, Sarah Maillefer died.

The same day, Martland conducted an autopsy. The results would take some weeks to come back. Yet he spoke to the media on the day Sarah died. "I have nothing more than my suspicions now," he told them. "[But] this poisoning, if my suspicions are correct, is so insidious, and sometimes takes so long to manifest itself, that I think it possible it has been going on for some time throughout the country without being discovered." That time was now at an end, although Martland wasn't rushing into anything. "We have nothing more definite than a theory at present," he said. "I will not make the statement that commercial 'radium poisoning' exists until we can prove it." But *once he could...*

The press was all over it. Sarah's death even made the front page of the *New York Times*. Yet while the whole world knew of her passing, there was someone who didn't.

Her little sister, Marguerite. She hadn't seen Sarah since June 15, the night she'd been taken from their shared room. She'd inquired several times as to how her sister was. Even though Marguerite had seen Sarah decline, she must have had hope. Sarah had always been the strong one once Marguerite had sickened, and she had only been seriously ill for a few days.

The nurses put her off when she asked after her big sister. But on June 18, when the papers were filled with the news of Sarah's death, Marguerite had innocently asked to see a newspaper.

"No," the nurses said, wanting to spare her.

"Why?" asked Marguerite. Of course Marguerite Carlough would ask why.

So the nurses told her of her sister's death. She was said to have borne the news with courage and expressed regret that she could not attend the funeral. She was far too ill to go.

It was Sarah's father who told the authorities of her death and arranged her memorial service. It was he who watched her coffin being lowered into the ground at Laurel Grove Cemetery, shortly after 2:00 p.m. on Saturday, June 20.

Sarah may have been thirty-five, but it was his little girl who'd gone.

16.

HOPE

Sarah wasn't even in her grave before her former company was denying that it was to blame.

"Nothing was found in our plant not found among average industrial employees," protested USRC's vice president. Despite the Department of Labor now knowing the truth about the Drinker report, the firm was still manipulating its results, and USRC now chose to ignore the recent conclusions of Dr. Hoffman too. The firm said it was absurd to connect the deaths of Dr. Leman and Sarah Maillefer. They reasoned "the latter could not have handled in one hundred years of her work half the amount of radium Dr. Leman handled in one year. The amounts handled by [Sarah] were so infinitesimal that in the opinion of company officials the work could not be considered as hazardous."

Yet those tiny amounts still left a trace—something that Martland was discovering. Sarah's autopsy was conducted nine hours after her death. She was the first-ever dial-painter to be autopsied. The first radium girl to have an expert examine every inch of her body for clues as to what could have caused her mysterious downfall.

The medical detective made notes as he moved down her silent corpse, working from head to toe. He stretched her mouth wide, looked inside. It was filled with old, dark, clotted blood. He inspected her left leg, the one she'd been limping on for three years. It was, the doctor noted, four centimeters shorter than her right.

He weighed and measured her internal organs, stripped out her bones to run his tests. He looked inside those bones, into the bone marrow where the blood-producing centers lay. In a healthy adult, the bone marrow is usually yellow and fatty. Sarah's was a dramatic dark red.

Martland was a medical man. He had seen for himself how radium was used to treat cancers in hospitals, and he knew how that worked. Radium had three types of radiation that it constantly emitted: alpha, beta, and gamma. The alpha particles could be cut off by a thin sheet of paper, while beta particles could be blocked by a sheet of aluminum. The gamma rays, however, could penetrate both those things, which is what made radium so good at treating cancer. The gamma rays could travel through the body and be specifically directed at a tumor.

Healthy lab workers protected themselves from the gamma and beta radiation by wearing lead aprons, because the gamma rays could be blocked by lead. But they didn't need to worry about the alpha particles, as they were unable to penetrate their skin. That was just as well, for the alpha particles, which formed 95 percent of the total radiation, were biologically the most dangerous.

In Sarah Maillefer's body, Martland now realized, the alpha particles had not been blocked by paper or by skin—they were not blocked by anything. The radium was in the very heart of her bones, right next to her bone marrow. No wonder it was red. It had been constantly bombarded by those powerful, destructive, radioactive rays.

Given the extreme danger of the alpha particles, Martland now realized that it didn't matter that the amount of radium Sarah had worked with was so small. From the tests, the doctor estimated that her body contained 180 micrograms of radium, a tiny amount. But it was enough. It was "a type of radiation never before known to have occurred in human beings."

He continued his tests. And now he discovered something that no one had ever appreciated before. For he didn't just test

Sarah's affected jaw and teeth for radioactivity—the site of all the dial-painters' necroses—he tested her organs, and he tested her bones.

They were all radioactive.

Her spleen was radioactive, her liver, her lame left leg. He found it all over her but chiefly in her bones, with her legs and jaw being considerably radioactive. They were the parts most affected, just as her symptoms had shown.

It was an extremely important discovery. Dr. Humphries in Orange had never connected the cases he had seen because the women all presented different complaints. Why would he have thought that Grace Fryer's aching back might be connected to Jennie Stocker's peculiar knee or to Quinta McDonald's arthritic hip? But it was the same thing affecting all the girls. It was radium, heading straight for their bones, yet on its way seeming to decide, almost on a whim, where to settle in the greatest degree. So some women felt the pain first in their feet. In others, it was in their jaw. In others still, it was their spine. It had totally fooled their doctors. But it was the same cause in all of them. In all of them, it was the radium.

There was one final test that Martland conducted. "I then took from Mrs. Maillefer," he remembered, "portions of the femur [thigh bone] and other bones and placed dental films over them...and left them in a dark room in a box." When he'd tried this experiment on normal bones, leaving the films in place for three or four months, he had not gotten the slightest photographic impression.

Within sixty hours, Sarah's bones caused exposure on the film: white fog-like patches against the ebony black. Just as the girls' glow had once done as they walked home through the streets of Orange, her bones had made a picture: an eerie, shining light against the dark.

And from that strange white fog, Martland now understood another critical concept. Sarah was dead, but her bones seemed very much alive, making impressions on photographic plates and carelessly emitting measurable radioactivity. It was all due, of course, to the radium. Sarah's own life may have been cut short, but the radium inside her had a half-life of sixteen hundred years. It would be shooting out its rays from Sarah's bones for centuries, long after she was gone. Even though it had killed her, it kept on bombarding her body, and would do every day of every week for month after month and year after year.

It is bombarding her body to this day.

Martland paused in his work, thinking hard. Thinking not just of Sarah but of her sister, Marguerite, and of all the other girls he had seen in Dr. Barry's office. Thinking of the fact that, as he later said, "There is nothing known to science that will eliminate, change, or neutralize these [radium] deposits."

For years, the girls had been searching for a diagnosis, for someone to tell them what was wrong. Once they had that, they believed faithfully, the doctors would be able to cure them.

But radium poisoning, Martland now knew, was utterly incurable.

Following the results of his tests, Martland shared the proven cause of Sarah's death. "There is not the slightest doubt," he wrote, "that she died...following the ingestion of luminous paint."

Perhaps it was this proof that prompted Dr. Drinker to step up at last. Ignoring USRC's threats to sue him, in the summer of 1925, he finally published his long-concealed report. Though USRC had tried its hardest to keep everyone in the dark—the Department of Labor, the medical community, and the women they had doomed to die—the light, at last, was flooding in.

At the Department of Labor, Commissioner Andrew McBride dramatically announced that he would close the factory if the firm did not protect its current workers.

Meanwhile, Martland was more concerned about those workers who had long since left the firm. In July 1925, he carried his testing equipment back into St. Mary's. It was Marguerite Carlough's turn to be measured for the radium that the doctor believed was lurking in her bones.

She was in a terrible condition on the day he ran the tests, with her mouth, as it had always been, the thing that was most agonizing. The alpha particles of the radium, Martland now believed, were slowly drilling those holes into her jawbone.

Despite the pain, Marguerite put the breathing tube into her mouth and blew. Just as her sister had done before her, she breathed, as steadily as she possibly could. *In...out.* On the day Martland ran her tests, the normal leak was 8.5 subdivisions in fifty minutes. (The "normal" number changed depending on the humidity and other factors.) When he checked Marguerite's results, they showed 99.7 subdivisions in the same time.

At least, she thought, it would help her legal case.

She had more reason than ever to want to win now. Following her sister's death, the Carloughs had added Sarah's claim to the litigation. USRC was now fighting three cases: for Marguerite, Hazel, and Sarah. Marguerite was the only one of those three left alive. So she wanted to do everything she could to help the case, not only for herself but for her sister. That was something to live for, to strive for, to battle through the pain for. While she was in St. Mary's, her lawyer interviewed her, even as she lay in bed. He took her formal testimony so that whatever happened, he would have it to fight the girls' case.

Yet Hazel, Sarah, and Marguerite weren't the only girls afflicted. That summer of 1925, former dial-painters were told to contact Dr. Martland for a formal diagnosis.

By that stage, Katherine Schaub had been troubled by her ailments for a long time. She had seen what had happened to Irene. She had read what had happened to Sarah. She wasn't stupid. She knew what Martland thought he would find. To her sister Josephine, she said slowly, "It must be that I have radium poisoning."

She tried it out in her mind, like slipping on a new dress. It clung to her, skin-tight, giving her nowhere to hide. It felt most peculiar, not least because Katherine was doing well that summer. She did not appear ill anymore. Her jaw wasn't troubling her, and all the infections in her mouth had cleared up. Her stomach, following her operation, was much improved, and her general health was good. She couldn't have what the others had; she couldn't. They had all died, and here she was, still living. Yet there was only one way to be sure. There was only one way to *know*. Katherine Schaub duly made an appointment with the county physician.

She wasn't the only one. Recently, Quinta McDonald had become more and more concerned about her own condition. She could barely walk anymore on her lopsided legs, while her teeth had started falling out spontaneously. And alongside Quinta was her old friend Grace Fryer, who now had no jaw trouble at all, who was apparently in good health, but whose back hurt worse with every passing day.

One by one, they came. Katherine. Quinta. Grace. They weren't ill like Sarah or Marguerite or Dr. Leman. They weren't at death's door. They stayed still as Martland scanned their bodies with his electrometer, asked them to breathe into a tube, and tested them for the telltale anemia that would betray what was happening inside their bones.

To each, he said the same. "He told me," Grace remembered, "that my system showed the presence of radioactive substances."

"He told me," Quinta said, "that my trouble was all due to the presence of [radium]."

He told them that there was no cure.

A deep breath was needed for that news. *In...out.*

Yet for Katherine, the diagnosis brought relief. "The doctors told me that [my tests] showed positive radioactivity," she remembered. "I was not as frightened as I thought I would be. At least there was no groping in the dark now."

Instead, there was light. Glowing, glorious light. Shining, stunning light. Light that led their way into the future. "The county medical examiner's diagnosis," commented Katherine Schaub with characteristic cleverness, "furnished perfect legal evidence for a lawsuit."

For too long, the women had waited for the truth. The scales, at last, were tipping against the company. The girls had just been given a death sentence, yet they had also been given the tools to fight their cause—to fight for justice.

The diagnosis, Katherine Schaub said, "gave me *hope.*"

PART TWO

POWER

17.
THE LIST
OF
THE DOOMED

There was much to be done. Even before the summer was out, Dr. Martland had given his support to Katherine Wiley's campaign to add radium necrosis to the list of compensable diseases. Yet the desired legal change was only part of it. The girls now understood how unforgivably careless the company had been with their lives. So the real question was how the firm's executives could have considered them expendable. Why didn't their basic humanity make the company stop lip-pointing long ago?

Grace Fryer, for one, was filled with anger as her clever mind raked over what had happened. For she recalled all too well a fleeting moment in her memory that sealed the company's guilt.

"Do not do that," Sabin von Sochocky had once said to her. *"You will get sick."*

Seven years later...here she was in Newark City Hospital.

Now she realized: von Sochocky had *known*. He had known all along. But if he had, why had he let them slowly kill themselves with every dial they painted?

Grace had an opportunity to put that question to the man himself—immediately. When Martland tested her and Quinta for radioactivity in July 1925, he wasn't the only doctor present. Von Sochocky sat quietly beside the technical equipment as the girls were told that they were going to die. And as Grace listened to the words fall from Martland's mouth—*"all your trouble...presence of radioactive substances"*—the memory of that warning came rushing into her mind.

Still reeling from the news, Grace nonetheless jutted out her chin and looked levelly at her former boss.

"Why didn't you tell us?" she asked simply.

Von Sochocky must have bowed his head. He stuttered out something about being "aware of these dangers" and said he had "warned other members of the corporation." His colleagues had supposedly stopped any attempts to change the girls' lip-pointing technique.

He now said to Grace, "The matter was not in [my]

jurisdiction but Mr. Roeder's. Since the matter was under his supervision, [I] could do nothing."

Well, there was nothing the girls could do now about their fatal illness, that was for sure.

From the very start, Grace bore her diagnosis bravely. She had a courageous spirit and refused to let Martland's verdict affect her life. So she tucked the diagnosis away in her mind and then carried on. She didn't stop work, and she didn't change her habits. She kept swimming, she kept socializing with her friends, and she kept on going to the theater. "I don't believe in giving up" was what she said.

Almost as soon as they received the news, Grace, Quinta, and Katherine Schaub hoped to bring a lawsuit against USRC. It wasn't just the principle of the matter; they needed money to pay their crippling medical bills. But instantly, there was bad news. Their action was barred by the statute of limitations (a law that placed a time limit on how long the girls had to file suit). Unlike the Carlough sisters, who had been recently employed by USRC, all these women had left the firm long ago. Grace, for example, hadn't worked for USRC since 1920. She was now trying to start a lawsuit more than five years later. That was three years too late according to the federal law, which gave workers two years from the time they were hurt to file suit. That law held, even though Grace's symptoms hadn't started until 1922 and she hadn't received a diagnosis of radium poisoning until a few weeks before.

It was frustrating to say the least. The women tried desperately to find a lawyer who was prepared to fight for them, but the attorneys all refused to take the case. Part of the lawyers' reluctance was likely due to the power of USRC. The girls' opponent in court would be a hugely wealthy, well-connected company. USRC had government contacts and enough money to prolong the legal fight for as long as it took.

Another problem, too, was just how new the disease was. Could it *really* be true that radium, the wonder element, had hurt the girls? Perhaps, as Roeder had said, the girls were trying to palm off their illnesses on the firm. Perhaps these women were liars and cheats.

Now the effects of the company's cover-up of the Drinker report really made themselves felt. Thanks to that concealment, published studies on the link between radium and the women's illnesses had been available for only a matter of weeks. None of the lawyers had ever heard of radium poisoning. No one knew anything about it. No one, that is, except for Harrison Martland.

Martland was in direct contact with the girls over that summer, offering what assistance he could. One day, Katherine Schaub went to his lab to discuss something very important. She had always wanted to be a writer and that day, she and

Martland wrote something together. Its topic was dark. In time, it would come to have its own name.

The List of the Doomed.

Martland wrote it out on the back of a blank autopsy report. He sketched out a series of penciled lines to create a neat chart and then picked up his fountain pen and wrote in flowing black ink, on Katherine's direction:

Miss Molly Magia [sic]
Miss Irene Rudolph
Mrs. Hazel Kuser
Mrs. Maillefer
Miss Marguerite Carlough...

The list went on and on. Slowly, methodically, Katherine supplied him with as many names as she could recall. She gave him the names of those girls she knew were ill or had died, as well as those who weren't yet sick. She recalled some fifty former coworkers.

In the years to come, the doctor was said to retrieve the list from his files whenever he heard of the death of a dial-painter. With chilling foresight, he would find her name on the list, written there back in the summer of 1925, and carefully write a neat red D beside the woman's name.

The handwritten List of the Doomed.

D is for death.

Katherine was at that time in fair health. But as her formal diagnosis sank in, she found that she could not stop thinking about that prediction. *D is for death.* She had already been made nervous by Irene's passing. Now, every ache became a symptom that could lead to her own sudden death. "I know I am going to die," she said. She stressed it, trying it on for size. "Die. DIE. It doesn't seem right." When she looked in the mirror, it wasn't the same Katherine who stared back at her anymore. "Her face, once usually pretty," a newspaper wrote of her at this time, "is now pinched and drawn with suffering. The suspense and worry have undermined her spirit."

That was the thing. The *worry*. It brought her so low

and made her so anxious. Her former company put it more harshly. They called her "mentally deranged."

"When you're sick and can't get around much," Katherine herself said, "things are different. Your friends aren't the same to you. They're nice to you and all that, but you're not one of them. I get so discouraged sometimes that I wish...well, I don't wish pleasant things."

She became very badly ill and consulted a nerve specialist countless times. But Dr. Beling couldn't stop her spiral of thoughts nor halt that flickering movie reel of ghost girls playing in her head. Katherine had always been lively and sociable before. But now, her sister said, "She is not the same girl at all."

Before the year was out, Katherine Schaub would be admitted to a hospital for nervous disorders. It was little wonder, given the trauma she could see her friends enduring. The real surprise was that more dial-painters weren't affected in this way.

In December 1925, Martland published a medical study about the dial-painters. It confirmed that the radium paint *had* poisoned them. In time, the article became a classic example of a medical mystery solved. But it was not accepted as fact by everyone when it was first published. Because, controversially, Martland didn't just discuss the dial-painters in his study. He also warned that swallowing radium in *any* form was dangerous, meaning not just radium paint, but also the radium pills and radium chocolate that people could buy. Shockingly, Martland said radium wasn't a wonder element at all.

He was instantly attacked. The doctor was discrediting a hugely profitable industry, and the radium manufacturers simply wouldn't stand for it. Swiftly, they tried to discredit him in return.

Yet it wasn't just those who made money from radium who had their doubts about Martland's declaration. Even the American Medical Association—which in 1914 had formally included radium on its list of "New and Nonofficial Remedies"—was skeptical. Such widespread doubts made the girls' claims look increasingly suspicious to the lawyers they contacted for help.

But while the scientists publicly fought over the cause of the girls' disease, there was one woman who was in its clutches, still fighting for all she was worth. Marguerite Carlough had been "half dead" for weeks. Her X-rays showed that the radium had eaten away her lower jaw to a mere stump. Yet she managed to make it home for Christmas, to spend it with her mom and dad. It was two years since that Christmas Eve when she'd had her tooth pulled and all this trouble had begun. It was six months since her sister, Sarah, had passed away.

In the early hours of December 26, 1925, at the age of twenty-four, Marguerite died too.

Two days later, for the second time in six months, her parents laid to rest a daughter in the peaceful quiet of Laurel Grove Cemetery. Yet Marguerite had not died quietly. As the

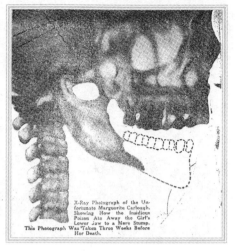

X-Ray Photograph of the Unfortunate Marguerite Carlough. Showing How the Insidious Poison Ate Away the Girl's Lower Jaw to a Mere Stump. This Photograph Was Taken Three Weeks Before Her Death.

X-ray of Marguerite Carlough's jaw from December 1925. It had been eaten away to a mere stump.

first dial-painter to file suit, the first to show it was even possible to fight back against the corporation that killed her, she went out with a roar.

It was a sound that would echo long afterward: long after she died, long after she was buried, long after her parents made their slow way home from her funeral and closed their door against the world.

18.

DEAD END

All she wanted, Grace Fryer thought as she flicked through the local paper in May 1926, was a bit of good news. There had been only one piece of it so far that year. Katherine Wiley's new law, to her and the dial-painters' delight, had been passed. Radium necrosis was now a disease for which workers could claim compensation. In many ways, it had been a lot easier to get it through than Wiley had anticipated.

Other than that, however, it had not been a great spring. Grace's jaw problems had started back up again. She had now lost all but three teeth in her lower jaw. Her back was incredibly painful too. She hadn't had it looked at by a doctor in a while, though. It was too expensive. Nonetheless, despite her troubles, Grace still commuted daily to her office. She commented simply, "I feel better when I am working." Indeed, she was said to meet people cheerfully in the bank.

Yet there was another reason to keep on with her job. Grace had run up medical bills of some $2,000 ($26,800), and she had no idea where she might find the money to pay them... well, no idea but one. By now, she had spent almost a year pursuing different attorneys. Faced with lawyer after lawyer turning down the case, the other girls seemed to have given up.

Nobody even saw Katherine Schaub anymore. After being released from the hospital, she stayed at home and refused to go out. "While other girls are going to dances and the theaters and courting and marrying for love," Katherine said mournfully, "I have to remain here and watch painful death approach."

As time went on, the girls started to doubt that a lawsuit was the right thing to do. Perhaps it wasn't fair to blame the company? Katherine had recently consulted Dr. Flinn—at the doctor's invitation. She didn't know that he was employed by USRC. His self-proclaimed "unbias[ed] opinion" was that "radium could not and had not harmed her." With a question now raised over the company's guilt, a lawsuit was the last thing on the women's minds.

The last thing on the other girls' minds, maybe, but it

remained a high priority for Grace Fryer. Still reading the local newspaper, she turned the pages slowly, deep in thought. And then, to her astonishment, she noticed a small piece buried within the paper. Scarcely able to believe her eyes, she read: *"Suits Are Settled in Radium Deaths."*

She quickly read on and found the headline did not

Suits Are Settled In Radium Deaths

A key newspaper article about Marguerite's case.

lie. USRC had settled the lawsuits of Marguerite Carlough, Sarah Maillefer, and Hazel Kuser. The women had beaten the corporation and gotten money for what the firm had done to them. Grace could barely believe it. Surely, that was an admission of guilt? Surely, this opened the door for her and her friends to bring a lawsuit? She read on in excitement: "Mr. Carlough [the girls' father] received $9,000 [$120,679] for the death of Marguerite Carlough and $3,000 [$40,226] for the death of Mrs. Maillefer, and Mr. Kuser received $1,000 [$13,408] for the death of his [wife]."

Grace was galvanized into action. *This* was the good news she'd been waiting for. Just two days after she'd read about the settlements, the wheels of her own claim were set in motion. A lawyer said he was willing to help now that the firm seemed in the mood to pay out. He wrote to USRC to tell them that Grace would sue if they did not reach an out-of-court settlement for her too. He told them she would accept $5,000 ($67,000).

It wasn't a gigantic sum of money. It would cover the medical bills that Grace had already run up, plus provide a nest egg to pay the future expenses that would undoubtedly be required. Grace wasn't a greedy person, and she didn't really want to start a big lawsuit. If the company would simply make her a fair offer, she was prepared to take that compensation and be done.

USRC took just one week to respond. They refused to do anything for Grace unless she took them to court. They probably knew how impossible it had been for her to launch a lawsuit so far, and they clearly felt she had no hope of ever successfully doing so.

Grace's heart must have sunk when she heard. She must have been confused too. Not only had the company agreed to pay money to her former colleagues just a few weeks before, but Miss Wiley had put that new law in place. Didn't that change anything?

But as it soon became clear, it did not. For a start, no one injured before 1926 could claim compensation. As Wiley's judge friend had warned her long ago, the new law applied only to workers who were hurt *after* the law had been passed. Yet that wasn't the only problem. In addition, as the new law became part of the existing state legislation, it automatically had a five-month statute of limitations attached. This was a length of time that would never be long enough for radium poisoning to show itself in *any* dial-painter, no matter when she was hurt. Finally and most crucially of all, the new law covered *only* radium necrosis, specifically jaw necrosis, of the aggressive kind suffered by Mollie Maggia and Marguerite Carlough. None of the other medical conditions arising from the women's poisoning—their life-sapping anemia, bad backs, shortening legs, even simply their loosening teeth—was valid for compensation. Wiley had found it relatively easy to get her new law passed. Now, suddenly, it became obvious why. The law, as written, was drafted so that no one would ever collect compensation.

Wiley soon realized her mistake. The Consumers League began campaigning to get radium *poisoning* into the law books. However, this fight would take them much, much longer before any changes were made.

There may also have been another reason that the company didn't want to settle Grace's claim. The firm might not have been making quite as much money as it once had. Part of the problem was finding staff. Its remaining employees were nervous and new workers scarce. Before the year was out, USRC would cut its losses and shut down the Orange plant, putting the site up for sale.

Even so, it wasn't down-and-out completely. The firm simply moved its business to New York.

Grace Fryer wasn't down-and-out either. But once it became clear the company wouldn't pay her any money, her lawyer dropped her case. Yet Grace felt more determined than ever to battle on. She was her father's daughter, and this child of a union rep would not back down so easily from a fight against a guilty firm. "I feel we girls should not give up all hope," she said.

So she went on to consult at least two other lawyers, but still without success. Part of her problem was that USRC was now benefiting from expert publications that said radium poisoning was *not* to blame for the girls' illnesses. This was just what Arthur Roeder had planned. The most high-profile of these new studies was authored by Roeder's favorite expert, Dr. Flinn. It was published in December 1926.

"An industrial hazard does not exist in the painting of luminous dials," Flinn wrote plainly. He said the girls' problems were due to a bacterial infection. Hoffman dubbed the report "more bias than science."

Yet it went way beyond bias. Flinn was lying through his teeth. For a start, his published conclusions blatantly contradicted his privately stated opinion to Dr. Drinker. He had written to Drinker in January 1926, "I cannot but feel that the radium mixture in the paint is to blame." Yet his deceitfulness was actually worse even than this.

In June 1926, six months *before* his study was published, Flinn discovered two radium-poisoning cases at the Waterbury Clock Company in Connecticut. The importance of these cases cannot be overstated. These Waterbury cases *proved*, once and for all, that it wasn't a bacterial infection that had been passed around a single studio. *It was the women's profession that had killed them.*

Despite knowing of the Waterbury cases for so long, Flinn didn't correct or withdraw his report. Instead, he allowed it to be printed. This gave USRC expert evidence to draw on in their continued denial of responsibility. Later, Flinn did say that he regretted his decision. But from his future behavior, one can assume, not *too* much.

Because Flinn wasn't finished with the New Jersey girls. In July 1926, he manipulated his way into examining Grace herself. Flinn, accompanied by another man whom Grace did not know, carefully took her blood and an X-ray. When the results were in, he announced with a smile, "Your blood picture [is] better than mine!"

"He told me," Grace later remembered, "I was in better health than he was and there was nothing wrong with me."

But that was not what Grace's body told her, day after day.

UNTIL DEATH DO US PART

Ottawa, Illinois
1926

The bells of St. Columba pealed out joyously across Ottawa. A wedding seemed to happen every other week these days as the dial-painters got married. Many were bridesmaids for each other. Marie Becker got engaged to Patrick Rossiter, while Peg Looney and Chuck Hackensmith eventually made plans to marry in June 1930. Charlotte Nevins—who hadn't worked for Radium Dial since 1923—was also one of those falling head over heels, with a man named Albert Purcell. Before the decade closed, Charlotte became the latest bride walking down the aisle of St. Columba.

One of its few parishioners not caught up in this maelstrom of marriage was Catherine Wolfe. A young man at church *had* caught her eye, however. His name was Thomas Donohue.

He was thirty-one to Catherine's twenty-three. Tom was a small man with bushy eyebrows and a thatch of dark hair. He had a mustache and wire-frame glasses. Like Catherine, who said a rosary every day with

Charlotte Nevins Purcell and her husband, Al.

her own set of beads, Tom was religious. "They were both very quiet people," recalled their niece. "Very shy people."

Perhaps that was partly why they wouldn't marry until 1932.

It's possible that Catherine told her desk mate at Radium Dial, Inez Corcoran, about Tom. Inez, a dark-haired nineteen-year-old, had her own story to share, for she was engaged to Vincent Lloyd Vallat. They were due to marry later that year.

Not all the married dial-painters quit their jobs. It seems the studio didn't want to lose its highly skilled workers. So the company became a pioneer in offering part-time terms to working moms. "I quit ten, twelve times," one girl recalled. "They always took me back; it took too long to train new ones." The company needed to keep hold of its best girls because business was still booming. Westclox hit a new production high of 1.5 million luminous watches in 1926, and Radium Dial painted all of them.

The new husbands noticed something strange in their households when their wives came home from work. One later wrote, "I remember when we were married and she hung her smock in the bedroom: it would shine like the northern lights. The first time I saw it, it gave me an eerie feeling—like a ghost was bouncing around on the wall."

Like someone else was in the room with them, just watching and waiting for the right time to strike.

There was no indication that the good times were ever going to end. No Ottawa women had fallen ill. Yet Radium Dial had not forgotten the holdup in business suffered by their competitor in New Jersey. They probably noted with concern, too, that USRC had recently been forced to pay out money to its former employees when it had settled the Carlough and Kuser lawsuits. Mr. Reed's invention of his glass pen had duly been supplied to the Ottawa dial-painters. No explanation was given as to why.

The Ottawa girls knew nothing of what was happening out east. The news piece about Marguerite Carlough's settlement was hidden inside a local paper eight hundred miles away. Dr. Martland's dramatic study from the year before was hotly debated...but only in the specialist medical press. Although his findings were reported by the general media of New York and New Jersey, such findings barely caused a ripple in the Great Lakes of the Midwest. Girls who lived in Ottawa didn't read the *New York Times*.

To be fair to Radium Dial, therefore, they didn't *have* to implement the change. The girls were not laying down their brushes in protest, and it wasn't as though there was any outside pressure to alter the working practices. Swen Kjaer's conclusion in his national study that radium dial-painting was dangerous had had no consequences. No organization had intervened on the national stage to keep workers beyond Orange from being harmed.

But although Radium Dial introduced glass pens, which were intended to put a stop to lip-pointing, it doesn't appear that they were fit for use. From the girls' perspective, they were not a success. Catherine Wolfe thought them awkward and clumsy to handle. And because the brushes weren't removed when the pens were launched, the dial-painters continued to lip-point to clean up the runovers. And those runovers were now plentiful due to the clumsiness of the new instruments.

The girls conceded, "We were watched very closely at first to see that we didn't try to go back to the brush." But it was a watchfulness that didn't last long. "Supervisor wasn't too observant," another girl later said.

Using brushes instead of pens to dial-paint was supposed to get you fired. But it wasn't a rule that was enforced.

Gradually, after just a few months, the glass pens fell out of use. Catherine Wolfe remarked, "We had our choice to use the glass pencil or Jap art brushes, whichever we found the most efficient to use."

Well, if *that* was the criterion, there was no contest. Some commentators later criticized the women for returning to the brush, calling them greedy, since the girls made more money that way. But they were not the only ones to profit from the choice they made. Radium Dial did too. And once it became clear that the glass pen didn't work, the company allowed the girls to go back to lip-pointing. After all, with 1926 bringing that new Westclox production high, it was not the ideal time for the firm to insist on a new method of production, particularly one that was so hopeless.

"The company left it up to us whether we used glass brushes or not," Catherine Wolfe remembered. "I preferred the hair brushes, as the others were awkward. I didn't think there was any danger in placing the brush in my mouth."

So she and Inez and Ella Cruse—another of the

Inez Corcoran Vallat.

original dial-painters in Ottawa—still lipped and dipped all day throughout that year of 1926. Catherine pointed the brush on every single number she painted.

Toward the end of the year, she laid down her brush to say a special goodbye to her friend Inez, who worked beside her. It was her colleague's last day on the job before a very special event. On Wednesday, October 20, 1926, Inez Corcoran married Vincent Lloyd Vallat. Together, the happy couple stood at the altar and made their solemn vows. They were vows that would see them through their future: through every dream, every day, every delightful thing to come.

Their voices echoed lightly around the cool church walls. "Until death do us part..."

20.

MAKE OR BREAK

Orange, New Jersey
1927

race Fryer limped into Dr. Humphries's office, trying not to cry out with pain. Humphries was shocked at the change in Grace. He hadn't treated her for some time. She'd been sent to him by Dr. Martland, who was worried about her spine.

Dr. Martland and Dr. Hoffman had both tried to help her, Grace mused, as Humphries rushed her straight to radiology for a new X-ray. Hoffman in particular, she thought, had been very kind. He'd noticed the recent, sharp decline in her health. So he'd written to USRC president Arthur Roeder on her behalf, appealing to him to help Grace "in a spirit of fairness and justice."

Hoffman had been surprised by USRC's response: "Mr. Roeder is no longer connected with this corporation."

It seems the firm hadn't appreciated being put in the position of having to settle lawsuits. Roeder's fingerprints were all over the company's questionable handling of the Drinker report too. Perhaps it was felt it was best all around if he left the firm. He had resigned in July 1926. But while he was no longer the public face of the company, he remained a director on the board.

Despite the change at the top, the company's attitude toward its stricken former employees hadn't changed one bit. The new president immediately rejected Hoffman's appeal for assistance. When Hoffman wrote to Grace to let her know, he added, "You must take legal action at once."

Well, Grace thought, she was *trying*. Despite her poor health, she had not stopped looking for a lawyer. Even now, she was waiting to hear back from a firm that the bank had recommended. In the meantime, she had come to see Humphries to find out what was wrong with her back.

It is difficult to imagine how she might have reacted to the news he had to share. The X-ray showed that Grace's spine had been shattered by the radium, with her medical notes recording the "obliteration" in her body. In her foot, meanwhile, the bones had been destroyed.

Humphries could do nothing but try to find a way to help her live her life. And so, on January 29, 1927, he fitted

Grace Fryer, then twenty-seven, with a solid steel back brace. It extended from her shoulders to her waist and was held in place by two crossbars of steel. She had to wear it every single day and was permitted to take it off for only two minutes at a time. Grace had no choice but to follow her doctor's orders. She later confided, "I can hardly stand up without it." She wore a metal brace on her foot too. Some days, she felt the braces were the only things keeping her together, helping her to carry on.

She needed them more than ever when, on March 24, she finally heard back from the latest set of lawyers: "We regret to say that in our opinion the Statute of Limitations barred your right of action against [USRC] two years after you left the[ir] employ."

A medical report on Grace Fryer's
destroyed spine and foot.

It was another dead end.

Grace had just one final card to play. "[Dr. Martland] agrees with me," Hoffman had written, "that it is of the utmost importance that you should take legal steps at once. [H]e suggests that you see the firm [Potter & Berry]."

She had nothing more to lose. She had everything to gain. Grace Fryer, now aged twenty-eight, with a broken back and a broken foot and a disintegrating jaw, made an appointment with the firm for Tuesday, May 3, 1927. Maybe this Raymond H. Berry would be able to help where no other attorney had.

There was only one way to find out.

———— ≋ ————

Grace dressed carefully for the appointment. This was make-or-break time. She'd had to change her wardrobe after the brace had been fitted. "It's awfully hard," she revealed, "to get clothes that don't make it show. I can't wear the sort of dresses I used to wear at all."

She styled her short, dark hair smartly, then checked her appearance in the mirror. Grace was used to dealing daily with well-to-do clients at the bank. She knew from experience that first impressions count.

And it seems her potential new lawyers thought the same. Potter & Berry, despite being a small law firm, had its offices

Raymond H. Berry.

in the Military Park Building, one of Newark's earliest skyscrapers; it had been completed only the year before. The lawyer she was meeting inside it, Grace soon realized as he introduced himself, was just as fresh-faced as his office.

Raymond Berry was a youthful lawyer, not even in his thirties. He had blond hair and blue eyes. And behind his baby-faced good looks was a brain as sharp as a tack. He had only recently graduated from Yale, yet he was already a junior partner.

That day, Berry took a lengthy statement from Grace. And it seems she may have shared his details with her friends. Just three days later, Katherine Schaub also called on him. By May 7, Berry had decided to take their case.

His tack-sharp brain had been working hard on the statute-of-limitations problem. His theory was this. The girls could not possibly have brought a lawsuit until they knew that the company was to blame. Of course, USRC had actively covered up the link between the girls' work and their illnesses when it chose to conceal the Drinker report. Because of that concealment, there had been a long delay before the girls knew that the company was responsible for their health problems. Berry believed strongly that the firm should not be allowed to use that delay, which it had caused, as a defense. The girls' *certain* knowledge of the link came only with Martland's formal diagnosis in July 1925. Therefore, in Berry's view, the two-year clock did not start ticking until that moment.

It was now May 1927. They were just in time. On May 18, 1927, Grace's lawsuit was filed against USRC. She was suing them for a cool $250,000 ($3.4 million).

From the very start, the radium girls' case attracted heart-rending headlines. *"Her Body Wasting, She Sues Employer: Woman Appears in Court with Steel Frame to Hold Her Erect,"* declared the *Newark Evening News* after Grace's first court appearance. Such coverage, combined with the friendship

> I hereby retain Messrs. Potter & Berry, as my attorneys to bring action in my behalf against the United States Radium Company for injuries sustained by me as an employee of the United States Radium Company, and I agree that for their compensation they shall receive one fourth of whatever sum shall be recovered in said action, I to pay costs of suit.
>
> Grace Fryer
>
> Dated: May 7 , 1927.

The contract Grace Fryer signed to appoint Raymond Berry as her attorney.

networks of the girls, soon led
to other dial-painters coming
forward, including Mollie
Maggia's sisters, Quinta and
Albina. Both women had
been crippled by the radium.
Quinta's hips had fused so
stiffly that she could not bend
over, while Albina's left leg
had shrunk to become four inches shorter than her right.

**Her Body Wasting.
She Sues Employer**

Woman Appears in Court
with Steel Frame to Hold
Her Up

Radium Substances - Blamed

Newspaper headlines
about the radium
girls' court case.

And someone else was suffering too. Edna Bolz Hussman, the "Dresden Doll," had been consulting doctors for the past year after her shrunken left leg had spontaneously fractured. She'd spent a whole year in a plaster cast, but it hadn't helped. Lately, her right shoulder had become so stiff that she couldn't use her arm.

Yet until recently, Edna had been sure that she didn't have radium poisoning. Hadn't that company doctor, Dr. Flinn, told her she was in perfect health just a year or so ago? She'd believed him. She'd had hope. That was until one night in May 1927 when she caught sight of her reflection.

In the dead of night, in the dead of dark, a ghost girl glowed in the mirror.

Edna screamed and fainted. She knew exactly what her

shining bones foretold, shimmering through her skin. She *knew* that glow. Only one thing on earth could make that glimmer. *Radium.*

After that, she knew the truth. In June 1927, only a month after receiving her formal diagnosis, Edna Hussman hired Raymond Berry too.

There were five of them now. Five girls crying out for justice. Five girls fighting for their cause. Grace, Katherine, Quinta, Albina, and Edna. The newspapers went mad, inventing notable nicknames for this new quintet. In the summer of 1927, it became official.

The Case of the Five Women Doomed to Die had begun.

21.

"FRAUD OF FRAUDS"

The company executives were taken completely by surprise by the five lawsuits. They had been certain that the girls would never be able to solve the statute-of-limitations problem. That was partly why the firm had been so confident in rejecting all their previous pleas for mercy. But now, faced with Berry's clever interpretation of the law, the executives were left scrambling for their defense.

It was, perhaps, inevitable who they would blame: the girls. The firm said the women hadn't taken due care and precaution for their own safety. And the corporation went further. It denied that the girls were ever instructed to lip-point. It denied any woman in the studio did. It even denied that the radium powder clung to them. The company admitted only one thing: it gave no warning. That was because it "denie[d] that radium was dangerous."

Such denials (such outright lies, one might say) formed USRC's written response to the girls' lawsuits. Yet that was only the start of the firm's attempt to take control of the situation. Faced with the women squaring up to it in court, it fought back behind their backs. USRC paid private detectives to follow the five girls. They were told to look into the women's personal lives. The firm was hoping the detectives might find something scandalous: evidence it could present in court to make the women seem untrustworthy.

They had another plan too. USRC had not forgotten that Grace had once proposed a $5,000 settlement. The firm now asked her if she would settle out of court. But Berry wrote back, "So far as settlement is concerned, [Grace] does not desire to make any [deal]."

In other words, we will see you in court.

Berry immediately threw himself into building his case. He quickly met the girls' allies—Wiley, Hamilton, Hoffman, Martland, Humphries, and von Sochocky—and spent a lot of time reading their notes and interviewing them. Berry immediately grasped how significant it was that USRC had covered up the Drinker report. So he wrote to Cecil Drinker to request that he give evidence to help the women. Drinker refused.

Berry would spend all summer trying to change his mind. In the end, he was forced to issue a formal court summons to get the doctor's evidence.

Though Berry was struggling to secure expert testimony to help the women, USRC was having no such problems. Flinn was still acting as its expert. And not just for them, as Berry soon discovered.

Berry had now learned of the Waterbury Clock Company cases of radium poisoning. Their existence proved that the girls' disease *was* caused by their job. Consequently, Berry wrote to the Workmen's Compensation Commission in Connecticut (the state in which the clock firm was based). He was hoping the commission would have some evidence of these Waterbury cases that he could cite in court.

But the commission's response was totally unexpected. They said no claims for compensation had been filed.

It was a puzzle. Connecticut law had a much longer statute of limitations of five years. That was just about enough time for a dial-painter to discover she had radium poisoning before bringing a lawsuit. At this point, at least three dial-painters had died in Waterbury, and others were ill. Had not *one* of their families filed suit?

They had not—and there was a very good reason why: Dr. Frederick Flinn. Through his company contacts, Flinn had enjoyed access to the Waterbury girls almost from when they began falling ill. "I [have] examined practically every girl now working in this industry," he once boasted. The girls not only knew him but trusted him. When he told them they were in perfect health, they believed him. And once radium poisoning *was* discovered, Flinn played a two-faced role. The dial-painters thought he was an independent medical expert. In fact, he was working on behalf of the company, and he persuaded the women to accept out-of-court settlements that silenced their complaints.

And that was the reason that not one case had been filed with the Workmen's Compensation Commission. Any claims that might have been raised had been quietly settled by the firm.

This was a very different approach from that taken by USRC. The New Jersey firm had tried their very hardest to avoid any settlements at all. The reason for the difference can be found in the Connecticut company's name. Waterbury was a *clock* company. It was not an out-and-out radium firm. USRC wanted to avoid settlements because people might think, if they agreed to them, that radium *had* harmed the girls. And if radium *was* dangerous—and people knew about it—what would happen to all the expensive radium products and all the profits the firm made from them? If the firm acknowledged the danger, it would likely mean an end to all that money. The clock company, on the other hand, had no such concerns. If it admitted radium was dangerous, there was no impact on its wider business. It didn't make its money from selling radium. It made money from selling clocks. So when its employees started dying, the Waterbury Clock Company simply settled any cases that came up, courtesy of Dr. Flinn.

"In these negotiations," wrote one commentator, "Flinn held the upper hand. He knew what he wanted and the women he dealt with were invariably young, unsophisticated, vulnerable, and without the benefit of legal counsel."

Had the Waterbury women taken some legal advice, they could have discovered what Berry well knew: under Connecticut law, many of them might have found justice thanks to the more generous five-year statute. However, the statute was five years only at the time of the discovery of radium poisoning. Following the emergence of the girls' cases, the law was rewritten in order to shorten it.

The clock company spent an average of $5,600 ($75,000) per affected woman in its settlements. But this figure is skewed by a handful of high payouts. Most victims received less than this average. Some, insultingly, were offered only two-digit sums, such as, in one shocking case, $43.75 ($606) for a woman's death.

RADIUM VICTIM DIES

Poisoning Contracted Four Years Ago Kills Bride.

By The United Press.
WATERBURY, Conn., March 19. —Mrs. Mildred Cardow, a bride of six months, died early today of radium poisoning which she contracted four years ago.

She is the third person to die here of the malady. Mrs. Cardow, who was 22 years old, was believed to have contracted the poison while working in a watch factory where she pointed brushes with her mouth while painting the faces of luminous watches and clocks.

Although no cure is known for radium poisoning, physicians believed she had a slight chance to live until yesterday.

Others who fell victims to the radium poisoning were Miss Elizabeth Dunn, who died January, 1927, and Miss Helen Wall, who died in July of the same year.

Newspaper article about the death of Connecticut dial-painter Mildred Cardow. Later, her husband was offered a $43.75 payout for her death.

If one squinted at the situation hard enough, one could say that Flinn did the Waterbury girls a favor. He certainly saw it that way: intervening to save them the trouble of bringing a lawsuit. But the company and Flinn held all the cards. Nor had Flinn finished with what Martland called his "double-dealing and two-faced" ways.

Flinn had now been forced to acknowledge the existence of radium poisoning. Yet that didn't mean that *all* the girls who fell sick suffered from it. So as Flinn continued to run his tests on the Waterbury women, he continued to find no positive cases of radium poisoning. Not one—not in 1925, not in 1926, not in 1927. Only in the fading months of 1928 would he concede, at last, that five girls *might* be affected. He told one worker, Katherine Moore, on eight separate occasions that there was not a single trace of radium in her body. She later died from radium poisoning.

Berry, hearing back from the commission, knowing nothing of Flinn's work at Waterbury, was completely stumped by the lack of evidence. But his new friend Alice Hamilton quickly realized what had gone on and filled him in. With the cases settled quietly by Flinn, of course there had been no evidence. There had been no publicity. No lawyers involved at all—just a tidy sum passed across a desk and a grateful woman who took it. It was all hush-hush.

None of it helped Raymond Berry.

From the beginning, Berry was very interested in Dr. Flinn. He had learned from the girls about his declarations of their good health—declarations that had confused them and made some of them doubt if they *should* file suit. Berry therefore decided as early as August 1927 to dig a little deeper into Dr. Flinn. His inquiries soon unearthed a shocking piece of news.

Dr. Flinn had been examining the girls: taking blood, reading their X-rays, arranging medical treatment. But when Berry asked the authorities to look into exactly who Flinn was, the New Jersey Board of Medical Examiners replied with the following information: "Our records do not show the issuance of a license to practice medicine and surgery or any branch of medicine and surgery to Frederick B. Flinn."

Flinn was not a medical doctor. His degree was in philosophy.

He was, as the Consumers League put it, "a fraud of frauds."

22.

IN THE SHADOW
OF
THE CHURCH SPIRE

Ottawa, Illinois
August 1927

Ella Cruse slammed the screen door of her house on Clinton Street and made her way down the few steps outside. She called goodbye to her mom, Nellie, as she went, but her voice was not as spirited as it once had been.

Ella didn't know what was wrong with her. She had always been healthy before, but now she felt tired all the time. She started walking to work. She took her bearings, as always, from the spire of St. Columba, which was only a block or two from her home. Ella and her family regularly attended services at the Catholic church, like most everybody she worked with.

Clinton Street was only a couple of blocks from the art studio too. So even though she could only walk at a snail's pace, Ella was soon there. She made her way up the school steps with all the other girls arriving for work. There was Catherine Wolfe, walking with that slight limp she'd recently developed, and Marie Becker, talking—as ever—a mile a minute. Peg Looney was already at her desk when Ella entered the studio, as conscientious as always. Ella said hello to them all.

Ella Cruse.

In 1927, Ella was twenty-four, the same age as Catherine Wolfe. Her glossy chestnut hair was cut into a fashionable bob, which ended daringly short at her cheekbones. The trendy haircut was finished with dramatic bangs that swept across her flawless skin. She had a shy smile that brought out a dimple in her left cheek.

She settled at her wooden desk and picked up her brush. *Lip... Dip... Paint.* It was a familiar routine by now, as she'd started working there when she was about twenty. She worked twenty-five days a month, eight hours a day, with no paid vacations.

Boy, she felt like taking a holiday now, though. She was tired and run-down, and her jaw felt sore. It made no sense. Ella had started seeing a doctor about six months back, but even though she'd gone to a couple of different physicians, none had been able to help. It was just like Peg Looney. She'd had a tooth pulled recently, but she said her dentist couldn't make it heal.

Ella looked up as she heard Mr. Reed come into their room. She watched as he paced up and down on one of his infrequent inspections. He had a certain swagger to his walk these days. But why wouldn't he? He now ran the joint, the superintendent at last, ever since Miss Murray had died of cancer back in July. Ella turned her attention back to her dials. No time to waste.

It was hard work today, though. All that summer, she had complained of pains in her hands and legs. It was tough to keep up with the delicate painting when her knuckles were so sore. She took a breather just for a minute and rested her head in her hands. But that also worried her. There was a hard ridge under her chin. She didn't know what it was or why it had suddenly appeared in the past few weeks, but it felt most peculiar.

Still, at least it was Friday. Ella wondered what the girls would be up to this weekend. Maybe Peg's boyfriend, Chuck, would have people over at the shack, or there'd be a plan to catch a movie at the Roxy. Absentmindedly, her finger stroked the small pimple that had appeared on her usually perfect skin a day or two earlier. It was on her left cheek, right by her dimple. When it had appeared, she'd picked at it, and it had started to swell. Now, she could feel pain and pressure under her fingertips. Hopefully, her skin would clear up before any parties started.

She tried to concentrate on her work all morning but found it harder and harder. No parties for her this weekend, that was for sure. In fact, she thought suddenly, no work either. She was done in, and she was done for today. She took her tray of dials up to Mr. Reed and said she had to go home sick. It was less than ten minutes before she was back on Clinton Street, as the St. Columba bells tolled the hour of noon. She told her mom she wasn't feeling well and probably went to bed.

"The next day," remembered her mother, Nellie, "we went to the doctor." That little pimple had swelled up on her daughter's face, and she wanted to get it checked. But there was nothing serious about her condition.

The doctor was in a jolly mood as he chatted with the Cruses. Ella told him that her mom had always been scared of her working at Radium Dial. He retorted with a hearty chuckle, "That's all bunk, there's not a cleaner place."

So Ella and Nellie went back to Clinton Street.

Ella may have skipped church on the Sunday. She certainly wasn't well enough for work come Monday morning. On Tuesday, August 30, her mother called out a physician again. He opened the pimple, but nothing came out. He then left them to it. It appeared that whatever was causing Ella's sickness was a mystery.

A mystery it may have been, but *not right* was what Ella Cruse knew it to be. That pimple, that little pimple, just kept swelling and swelling. It was incredibly painful. Nothing she or her mom or even the doctor did could halt it. It was an infection that was unstoppable. Her face became badly swollen. She had a fever too.

"The next day," recalled Nellie, "[the doctor] looked at her face [again] and ordered her to the hospital."

Ella was admitted to Ottawa City Hospital on August 31. But still that spot got bigger and bigger until you couldn't call it a pimple anymore. It wasn't even a boil. It went way beyond that. Ella's neat haircut still sprouted from her head, as fashionable as ever, but the girl below, in just a few short days, became unrecognizable. Septic poisoning set in, and her pretty face and head turned black.

"She suffered the awfulest pain," remembered her mother in horror. "The awfulest pain I ever saw *anyone* suffer."

Ella was her only daughter. Nellie kept a bedside vigil as long as the doctors would let her, even though the person in the bed didn't look like Ella anymore. But she *was* still Ella. She was still her daughter, and she was alive and she needed her mom.

Midnight, September 3. Saturday night slipped into Sunday morning, and Ella's condition declined. As she lay in bed—her system septic, her head swollen and black, her face unrecognizable—the poison in her body did its worst. At 4:30 a.m. on Sunday, September 4, her death came suddenly. She had been at work painting dials just the week before. All she'd had was a little spot on her face. How had it come to this?

On September 6, her parents traced the familiar path to St. Columba to bury their daughter. "Miss Cruse's death," reported the local paper, "came as a shock to all of her friends and family."

It was a shock. It left a hole—a hole in a family that could never be filled. Her parents said, many years later, "Life has never been the same since she went."

Ella's obituary mentioned only one other detail as it mourned this youthful Ottawa girl, who had lived there most of her life, who'd had friends, been popular, worn her hair in a bob, and lived her too-few days in the shadow of the church spire.

"She had been employed," the paper noted, "at the Radium Dial."

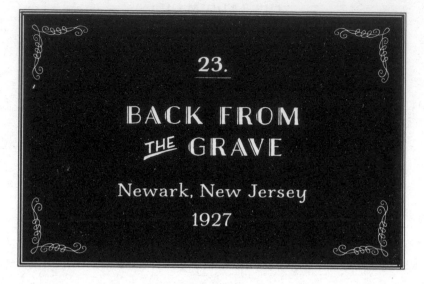

23.

BACK FROM _THE_ GRAVE

Newark, New Jersey
1927

he news of Flinn's nonmedical degree was shocking
to all. Katherine Wiley called him "a real villain."
But Flinn himself was not bothered by Berry's
discovery. In his eyes, he was still an expert in work-related
illnesses—just as Hoffman, a statistician, could also be called
a specialist in that field—and he had done nothing wrong. He
remained confident even as Berry reported him to the authorities for practicing medicine without a license.

But Berry soon had to put the Flinn matter to one side as
he prepared to meet USRC in court. The first hearing was set
for January 12, 1928. There was much to do before then. USRC
had already said that it wanted the girls to be examined by its
own company doctors. Berry anticipated that it was planning

to argue that the women were not suffering from radium poisoning at all. Berry's latest problem thus mirrored that of Dr. Martland in 1925. How could he *prove* it was radium that was hurting the dial-painters?

There was only really one way to do that, and it wasn't something Berry could ask of his clients. The only way to demonstrate decisively that radium was present in a person was to extract the radium from their bones. Yet the extraction process required burning the bones to ash and then boiling the ash in acid. This was nothing that Grace, or Edna, or Katherine, or the Maggia sisters could help with. Except...

Except for maybe *one* of the Maggia girls.

Mollie.

———— ≈ ————

It was shortly after nine a.m. that the men came to Rosedale Cemetery on October 15, 1927. They made their way through the rows of memorials until they stopped at one particular grave. They erected a tent over it and removed the headstone. Then they worked to uncover the coffin, heaving sodden earth out of the hole. Eventually, their efforts unveiled a nondescript wooden box with a silver nameplate. It was the coffin that held Mollie Maggia.

The family hadn't protested when Berry had suggested

raising Mollie from the grave. Not after he had explained his reasons. Her body could provide perfect supporting evidence for the dial-painters' fight in court. Even after all these years, she could still help her sisters.

The grave workers ran ropes under her coffin and attached stronger silver chains. Then they waited for the officials to arrive. There were thirteen of them in all, a mix of lawyers, doctors, and company executives. Only once they were all gathered around the grave did the men heave on the ropes and chains. Slowly, Mollie rose the six feet to the surface. Oddly, despite the dim fall day, her coffin seemed to glow with an unnatural light.

It was the light of the radium in Mollie's dead bones.

The top and sides of the glowing casket were removed.

Mollie Maggia's coffin being raised from the grave.

And there she was. There was Mollie Maggia, back from the grave. She wore a white dress and her black leather pumps. They were the clothes her family had dressed her in on the day she was buried in 1922.

The doctors removed her body carefully from her

coffin and took her to a local undertaking parlor. At 4:50 p.m., her autopsy would begin.

At 4:50 p.m., Mollie Maggia would finally tell the world the truth about her death.

———— ≋ ————

At the time Mollie passed away, the doctors had said she'd had a disease called syphilis. That was what had been written on her death certificate as her cause of death. Five years on, her autopsy was about to reveal if there was any accuracy to that claim.

The doctors started the autopsy by examining Mollie's upper jawbones. Carefully, these bones were removed in several pieces. The doctors had no need to do the same with her lower jaw. It was no longer present, having been lifted out in life.

There was a kind of ceremonial care in the doctors' steady tasks. They worked their way down her body, washing her bones in hot water and gently drying them. Some bones they put to the X-ray film test. Others, they ignited to ash that they then tested for radioactivity.

When they checked the X-ray films, days later, *there* was Mollie's message from beyond the grave. Her bones had made white pictures on the ebony film. Her vertebrae glowed in vertical white lights. They looked like rows of shining dial-painters, walking home from work. The pictures of her skull, meanwhile, with her jawbone missing, made her mouth stretch unnaturally wide. It looked as if she was screaming—screaming for justice through all these years.

There was, the examining doctors said, "No evidence of disease, in particular no evidence of syphilis." The report concluded, "Each and every portion of tissue and bone tested gave evidence of radioactivity."

It definitely *wasn't* syphilis. It was *radium*.

Berry added the significant results of Mollie's autopsy to his ever-enlarging file about the case. Just before the year ended, that file grew once again. But this time, with some unexpected news.

It concerned Ella Eckert, the fun-loving dial-painter who had once been great friends with Mollie Maggia. Berry had met her earlier in the fall, when she'd seemed in better health than any of his five clients. However, her arm had been noticeably swollen, from her shoulder down to her wrist. Though she'd had the usual symptoms of radium poisoning, such as anemia and a white shadow in her bones, Dr. Martland commented, "This case is very puzzling and not as clear-cut as the others."

On December 13, 1927, Ella Eckert died. Martland traced her name on the List of the Doomed. *D is for death*.

On the day she passed away, she had an operation. The

Headlines about the exhumation and investigation of Mollie Maggia's remains.

doctors had been mystified by what they found when they cut her open. A strange, hard lump had grown across her whole shoulder. Such a growth was new and unexpected to Martland—and to all the doctors. No dial-painter, so far as they knew, had ever presented such a thing.

Radium was a clever poison. It masked its way inside its victims' bones. It fooled the most experienced physicians. And like the expert serial killer it was, it had evolved its modus operandi: the *way* it killed the women. Ella had developed what was called a sarcoma, a cancerous tumor of the bone.

She was the first known dial-painter to die from such a thing. She would not be the last.

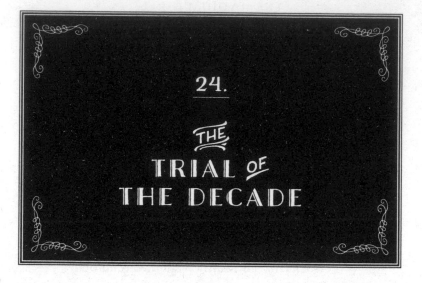

24.

THE TRIAL OF THE DECADE

O n January 12, 1928, the trial of the decade began. When the five radium girls arrived at court, they found themselves surrounded. Newspapermen crowded around them, flashing cameras in their eyes. As the women moved inside, the media followed. The journalists packed the seats in the public gallery.

The court was crowded, and not only with the media and supporters of the girls. USRC had assembled a huge team of lawyers. They were led by Edward A. Markley, a six-foot-tall gentleman with brown hair and eyes, which he framed with glasses. The son of a judge, he was six years older than Berry, with all the added experience and confidence that could give a man.

John Backes, the judge overseeing the USRC trial.

The judge overseeing the trial was John Backes. He was in his midsixties and wore a bushy mustache and glasses. Berry must have been hopeful for a sympathetic hearing from him, because Backes's own father had died after being injured at work. Certainly, he seemed to look kindly on Grace Fryer as she prepared to give her testimony on that very first day.

To her credit, she was calm. "Grace is so accustomed to talking of disease and decay that she can tell you of these deaths without flickering an eyelash," wrote a journalist of her remarkable composure. Still, there must have been a few butterflies as she sat in her chair on the witness stand. She shifted uncomfortably from time to time, her metal back brace chafing her skin. A fresh bandage clung to her jaw following a recent operation. Yet Grace took a deep breath and composed herself. This was her day in court.

"We were instructed to point the brush with our lips," she began, speaking clearly.

"Did [all the girls] do it that way?" inquired the judge.

"All I ever saw do it," she answered.

"Were you ever told at any time *not* to put the brush in your mouth?" asked Raymond Berry, cutting to the heart of the matter.

"Only on one occasion," she replied. "Dr. von Sochocky was passing through and when he saw me put the brush to my lips he told me not to do it."

"What else did he say?"

"He said it would make me sick."

Grace's answers were impressively succinct and informative. She and Berry had an instant connection. Question and answer flicked back and forth slickly as though their conversation was a choreographed routine. Yet Berry gave Grace space, too, to describe her suffering. He wanted everyone in court to hear what the company had done.

"I have had my jaws [operated on] seventeen times," said Grace, "with pieces of the jawbone removed. Most of my teeth have been removed. [My] spine [is] decaying and one bone in [my] foot [is] totally destroyed."

It was horrifying to listen to. Many in the courtroom were in tears. No wonder, when Markley made some smart comment, the judge snapped back at him, "If I find you guilty, I think you will be sorry."

After that warning, Markley approached Grace's cross-examination with some caution. He could doubtless see, too, that she was not going to be a pushover. And she certainly was not.

Central to the USRC lawyers' arguments was the statute of limitations and what the girls knew when. If they'd had information prior to July 1925 that their work had definitely made them sick, they should have brought a lawsuit at that time. And if a lawsuit *should* have been brought back then, it meant the *current* case was being filed too late, in which case the girls would lose automatically. No wonder Markley tried to push Grace into saying that she *had* known her work was to blame earlier.

"Did [your dentist] tell you he thought it was your work that was affecting you?" the lawyer asked cleverly as he stalked around the court.

"No, sir," she said bluntly.

The question was repeated.

"Why no," said Grace smartly. "I was working for the [bank] when I saw him."

USRC also quizzed her on all the different lawyers she had seen. And when they came to Berry, they asked her, "[Was he] the first one you had?"

"No, not the first one," Grace replied, locking eyes with her young lawyer. "The only one that ever brought suit."

Katherine Schaub watched the proceedings eagerly.

"Everything was going along splendidly, I thought," she wrote. "Tomorrow there would be another [day in] court, and the day after, still another. And so on until the entire case was heard. And then—the court would give its verdict. Then perhaps I could get away from everything and forget."

Still half listening to the proceedings, she started to picture her life afterward, how happy she hoped she would be. Just a few more days of these January hearings, she thought, and then it would all be over—one way or the other.

But it was not to be. "I was awakened from my dreaming," she later said, "by the sound of the [judge's] gavel hitting the desk. [Backes] was speaking. The next court day, he said, would be April [25]. I could have given way to tears, but tears would not do any good, I knew. I must summon all the courage I had—and fight."

The three-month delay was both frustrating and unexpected. But the time, in the end, passed quickly. Berry, who was concerned that little was being done for the girls medically, persuaded some New York doctors to admit the women to the hospital. All five spent a month in their care.

Many found that just being in the quiet calm of a hospital made a big difference to their mood. "I haven't had anything yet but a bath," Katherine wrote when they first arrived. "I enjoyed that because someone helped me to take it. A maid is a fine thing to have when you are sick."

There was one other bonus to being in the hospital. As Katherine wrote, they were at last "safe from intrusion [and] safe from the prying eyes of unwelcome advisers."

She probably had a particular "unwelcome adviser" in mind: Dr. Flinn. He had not stopped trying to get access to the girls, even though Berry had found him out. Flinn had recently told—and convinced—Dr. Humphries that he was a friend of the women. But the radium girls, now knowing Flinn to be a company man, had gone straight to Berry when they'd heard of this. They didn't trust Flinn one bit. So at their request, Berry wrote to the "doctor" to ask Flinn to stop harassing them. Flinn merely replied that he thought Berry rude.

But soon the women could not avoid Flinn. On April 22, three days before the trial was to resume, the girls were summoned to a compulsory physical examination by the company doctors. Flinn was one of those who conducted the tests. He was joined by other specialists, including one who was a close friend of USRC's vice president, Howard Barker.

Grace flinched when they pricked her with a needle to take her blood. She was afraid of anything that might result in cuts or bruises because her skin no longer healed. Some dial-painters had paper-thin skin that was so delicate, it would literally split open, even if simply brushed by a fingernail.

A week later, Grace realized she had been right to worry. In the place where the doctors had pricked her, the flesh surrounding the puncture mark was black.

During the examination, radioactivity tests were also conducted. But the equipment was deliberately positioned so that the table was between the women's bodies and the instruments. Flinn also held the equipment several feet away from the girls, which allowed the radiation to dissipate. Unsurprisingly, the company's verdict was that none of the women were radioactive.

But the girls' case was not finished yet. In three days' time, they were back on the stand for the fight of their lives.

25.

ON THE STAND

Katherine Schaub was first up. She cast her mind back to February 1, 1917, the day when she had excitedly made her way to the studio for her first day on the job. "The young lady instructed me," she recalled, "told me to put the brush in my mouth."

Berry took her through her suffering. She revealed she had grown "very nervous." The USRC lawyers likely saw her mental-health issues as a weakness. That was probably why they gave Katherine such a hard time.

She had just said that she lip-pointed "sometimes four or five times [per dial], perhaps more than that," when Markley stood to begin his cross-examination.

"Sometimes more," he began.

"Yes, sir."

"Sometimes less."

"Yes, sir."

"Sometimes you wouldn't put the brush in your mouth at all, would you?" he exclaimed, spinning around to deliver the line. She must have hesitated. "You don't *know*?" he said disbelievingly.

"I am trying to remember," replied Katherine nervously.

"Depend on your brush too, wouldn't it?... The brushes were supplied there, weren't they?"

"They were supplied, yes, sir."

"You could get all the brushes you wanted."

"No."

"You would go to [the forewoman] when you wanted a brush, wouldn't you?" he asked, closing in.

"Yes, sir," Katherine replied, "but you were not supposed to waste them."

"Of course you weren't supposed to waste them, but you were supplied amply with them, weren't you?"

The questions came thick and fast. Markley didn't miss a beat. He would have his next line of attack prepared even as Katherine stuttered out her answer.

As they had done with Grace, the company lawyers questioned Katherine extensively about her initial dental treatment. They wanted to know whether any connection had been made in the early 1920s between her illness and her job. Under such heated cross-examination, the nervous Katherine slipped up. She talked about the meeting that she and some of the other girls had had in Dr. Barry's office in January 1924. At the time, the women's disease was suspected to be phosphorus poisoning. And Katherine revealed, "There had been some talk about industrial disease..."

Markley seized on it. "What do you mean, 'There had been some talk'?"

Katherine realized her error. "I had never connected myself with it in any way," she said hurriedly.

But Markley wasn't going to let it go that easily. He brought up her cousin Irene, who had died in 1923. "You know Dr. Barry told her he thought it might be industrial disease, don't you?"

"Well, he had a slight suspicion that something was wrong," Katherine admitted weakly.

"He *told* you he had a slight suspicion?" Markley asked.

"He never told me that directly... I only know what my folks told me."

"When was it that they told you that?" Markley jumped in. He was probably hoping for an answer that would kill the case dead.

"Well, I don't know," retorted Katherine, back on track. "My cousin was ill so long and *I don't remember.*"

It seemed never to end. She felt worn down by it. Perhaps it showed. Judge Backes, who was keeping an eye on this vulnerable witness, interrupted Katherine's testimony at one point to ask, "Are you tired?"

But Katherine replied firmly, "No." She added, "I try to sit up as straight as I possibly can, because my spine is a little weak."

She would have been pleased to note that the gathered reporters scribbled down that detail of her suffering.

As it had been at the January hearing, the courtroom was packed with journalists. In fact, there were even more than before. The women's story was beginning to go international. The reporters would later write moving descriptions of the women's testimony, as Katherine, Albina, and Quinta all gave evidence that day. The press called them a "sadly smiling sorority" and said they "maintained an attitude of almost cheerful resignation."

Their composure was in direct contrast to those observing the trial. The spectators in the courtroom frequently mopped at their faces with handkerchiefs, crying tears "of which they seemed unashamed."

How could anyone not cry as Berry took Quinta McDonald through the fate of her friends?

"Were you ever acquainted with Irene Rudolph?" he asked her.

"Yes, sir, while I worked in the radium plant."

"Hazel Kuser?"

"Yes, sir."

"Sarah Maillefer?"

"Yes, sir."

"Marguerite Carlough?"

"Yes, sir."

"[Ella] Eckert?"

"Yes, sir."

"Are all these people dead?"

"Yes, sir."

It seems Grace may have indicated to Berry that she wanted to speak again. She retook the stand. She had a very good reason to want to do so. Grace had been staring across the courtroom at the gathered USRC executives, and her sharp memory had snagged on one of their faces in particular.

"Miss Fryer," Berry began after a quick consultation with Grace, "you were examined in the summer of 1926 by Dr. Frederick Flinn and there was another doctor who you did not know who was present at the examination. Have you seen that assisting doctor since that time?"

"Yes, sir."

"Is he here in the court today?"

Grace looked across at the executives. "Yes, sir."

Berry pointed at the man she had specified. "Is that the gentleman, Mr. Barker?"

"Yes, sir," said Grace assuredly.

"Do you know he is the vice president of the United States Radium Corporation?"

"I didn't know it then," she said pointedly.

Barker had been there on the day that Grace had been told by Flinn she was in better health than he was. He had stood by as Flinn had issued the diagnosis there was nothing wrong with her. Barker's presence showed just how involved the company was with Flinn's activities. Its own vice president had attended the girls' medical tests.

After lunch, the doctor who'd conducted Mollie Maggia's autopsy took the stand. He gave his important testimony that radium, not syphilis, had killed her.

Markley tried to get all evidence regarding Mollie struck out. But he was unsuccessful. "I will hear it," announced Backes firmly.

———— ≈ ————

The following day, the trial continued. Distinguished doctors testified that it had been common knowledge since at least

1912 that radium could do harm. And Berry admitted into the court record a host of literature to support the doctors' words, including articles published by USRC itself. Though Markley tried to weaken the impact of these documents by discussing the supposed healing powers of radium, it was apparent there were holes in his arguments.

Then Berry called on someone very special to testify for the girls. Harrison Martland took the stand—the brilliant doctor who had invented the tests that proved the existence of radium poisoning. The doctor who had provided a diagnosis to the women where all other doctors had failed.

On the stand, Martland was a superstar. No other word for it. When the company lawyers tried to suggest that radium poisoning couldn't exist because "out of two hundred or more girls, these girls [suing] are the only ones that had this trouble," Martland replied frankly, "There [are] about thirteen or fourteen other girls that are dead and buried now who, if you will dig them up, will probably show the same things."

The company lawyers also claimed there were "no other reported cases" beyond Orange, horribly ignoring all the Waterbury girls who had sickened and died. But Martland set them straight.

Berry could not be happier with how the case was going. And the next day promised to be even better. Dr. von Sochocky was going to take the stand. Berry couldn't wait to question him on the warnings he had given to Grace and the corporation about the paint being dangerous. Arthur Roeder had reportedly ignored those warnings, leaving von Sochocky feeling powerless to take any further action as the dial-painters had been Roeder's responsibility. Such powerful evidence, Berry felt, would seal the verdict once and for all, and surely in the girls' favor.

The next morning, toward the end of von Sochocky's testimony, Berry posed the killer question.

"Isn't it true," he said, his blue eyes bright as he turned to face the doctor, "that you said [you hadn't stopped lip-pointing] because the matter was not in your jurisdiction but Mr. Roeder's?"

"I object to this, Your Honor," interrupted Markley at once.

But before the judge could rule, the company's founder answered.

"Absolutely not."

Markley and Berry both stared at him, open-mouthed. And then Markley confidently retook his seat, crossing his long legs. "All right," the corporate attorney said easily, gesturing for the witness to continue.

"Absolutely not," repeated von Sochocky.

Berry could not believe it. For not only had Grace and Quinta told him about this, Martland and Hoffman had too. And they had all heard it from the doctor's own mouth. Why was he now lying? Perhaps he was concerned about how he would appear. Or

Sabin von Sochocky.

perhaps something else had happened. Unknown to Berry, a USRC memo from July 1927 had noted "We should get a line on what [von] Sochocky is doing and where he is." Perhaps there had been a secret conversation between the company and its founder that had led to the doctor switching sides.

Berry quizzed him on his wartime warning to Grace too. Perhaps here, at least, he could make some progress.

"Well, Mr. Berry," von Sochocky replied, "I don't want to deny that, but I don't recollect that very distinctly... There is a possibility I told her that, which would be the perfectly natural thing to do, passing by the plant, seeing the *unusual* thing of a girl putting a brush to her lips; of course I would say ['Do not do that']." He added bluntly, "[The danger] was unknown to us."

Berry was bitterly disappointed. Publicly, in court, he called von Sochocky a "hostile witness."

Berry recalled Grace to the stand as soon as von Sochocky's testimony was over, "not to discredit [the doctor]," Berry explained, "but to show actually what he did say." But Markley objected to Grace's evidence at once. Unfortunately, this time, the judge was forced to side with Markley, seemingly against his will. "Strike out the answer," Backes commented. "These rules of evidence have been invented to prevent people from telling the truth."

There were only a handful of other witnesses, including Katherine Wiley and Dr. Flinn, who was there as a paid witness for USRC. At 11:30 a.m. on April 27, 1928, Berry rested his case. For the rest of the day and in the days to follow, USRC would have an opportunity to tell its side of the story. And then—*then*, the girls thought nervously—the verdict would be given.

Markley stood up, his long body sliding out of his chair effortlessly. "I was wondering," he said smoothly to John Backes, "we may be able to shorten this if we have time for a conference?"

There was a discussion off the record. Afterward, as the judge's gavel banged, Backes made an announcement.

"The hearing is adjourned to September 24."

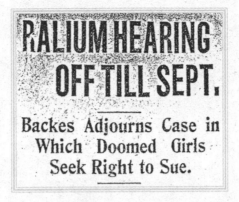

Newspaper article reporting
the delay in the trial.

September was five months away. *Five months.* To put it bluntly, it was time that the girls, in all likelihood, probably didn't have.

The delay, cried Katherine Schaub, was "heartless and inhuman."

But the law had spoken. Nothing further would be done until September.

The girls were devastated. Even Grace Fryer, who for so long had stayed incredibly strong, couldn't bear it. She flung herself onto the couch in her living room and burst into tears.

Her mother tried to calm her. She gently touched her daughter's metal-bound back, trying not to bruise her thin skin. "Grace," she said, "this is the first time you have failed to smile."

But Grace could not believe what had happened. Markley had claimed it would not be worthwhile for him to begin his case with only half the day remaining. So the case had been postponed until there was enough time in the court calendar to hear the USRC defense. It was a very long delay because the company intended to present approximately thirty expert witnesses, which required days and days of free court time.

Immediately, Berry fought the delay. He found two lawyers who had a case scheduled for the end of May and were willing to give up their court slot so the girls' case could be heard instead. Backes agreed to the new timing, but USRC would not. They said it would be impossible for them to proceed in May. Their experts were allegedly going abroad for several months and would not be back until after the summer.

USRC had several good reasons to fight hard to get their way. First, the company was back on track financially. Just one single order it had recently received was for $500,000 (almost $7 million in today's money). Business was booming. It did not want to lose this case.

Yet there was a darker reason too. Berry suspected that USRC's real motivation for delaying the court case was the girls' fragile health. Perhaps the company hoped they would die before a verdict could be given.

But in bad news for the company, in Berry's own words, he was "far from finished in this fight." In fact, Berry drew on his clients' feeble health to fight their cause. He asked four different doctors to swear to the following statement: "These girls are all becoming progressively worse. It is very possible that all or some of these five girls may be dead by September 1928."

It made for horrendous reading for the women. Yet it was the kind of move that Berry instinctively knew would get results, and he was right. The media were up in arms and their supportive articles had an immediate effect. "Everywhere, people were asking why justice was being denied these five women, who...had but a year to live," said Katherine Schaub, almost in disbelief. "What had once been a hopeless case, unheeded and unnoticed, now flashed before the public."

And the public was transfixed. "Letters came pouring in from all corners of the earth," Katherine remembered. Seemingly overnight, the girls became famous. Berry immediately made the most of their new celebrity. As the month of May 1928 unfolded and every day seemed to bring forth another call for justice from the press, Berry ensured that the girls were center stage. In media interviews, they shared the details of their lives. How Quinta had to be carried to her hospital appointments. How Edna's legs were fused into an awkward crossed position. How Katherine felt such terrible pain. She said in one interview, "Don't think I'm crying because I'm downhearted—it's because my hip hurts so. Sometimes it seems as though a knife was boring into my side."

The public, shocked and saddened, took the girls to their hearts. Berry soon realized how much the coverage was helping, because USRC fought back with everything it had. Predictably, the firm wheeled out Dr. Flinn. He told the media that his tests showed there was no radium in the women. He was convinced, he said, that their health problems were caused by nerves.

Yet the press preferred to report on the girls. "I couldn't say I'm happy," Grace Fryer admitted in one

Five Women, Facing Death By Radium Poisoning, Plead For Justice While They Live

Just one example of a newspaper headline supportive of the radium girls.

interview, "but at least I'm not utterly discouraged. I intend to make the most out of what life is left me." And when her time was up, she said she wanted to donate her body to science so that doctors might be able to find a cure. The other girls would later do the same. "My body means nothing but pain to me," Grace revealed, "and it might mean longer life or relief to the others, if science had it. It's all I have to give." She gave a determined smile. "Can't you understand why I'm offering it?"

The public was completely won over. As a result, the momentum in the case was in the women's favor. Soon, Berry found that the justice system was willing to support them too. No matter the response of the radium company, the trial was scheduled to go ahead at the end of May.

Nothing was going to stand in the way of justice. Of that both Berry and the girls were sure. Carried along on a swell of public favor, it seemed they would soon be home and dry.

Berry was in his office, preparing for the case, when his telephone chimed.

Judge Clark was on the line.

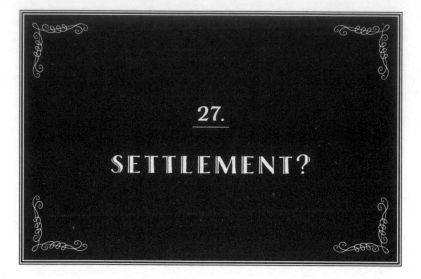

Judge William Clark was a hugely respected man. He'd had a very privileged background, living on a family estate called Peachcroft with a senator for a grandfather. Thirty-seven years old, he had auburn hair, gray eyes, and a large nose. And once upon a time, he'd been Raymond Berry's boss.

"To Judge Clark's office," read Berry's diary for May 23, 1928, "and talk re: radium cases with him." The judge had a suggestion to put to him.

Why not settle the lawsuits out of court?

Berry professed to reporters that he was not even considering a settlement. But privately, he soon began to wobble. It wasn't that he didn't think he could win the case. It was whether any verdict would come in time to benefit the girls. Berry wanted them to get justice, but most of all, he wanted them to be comfortable in their final days. Perhaps, he thought, he should give Clark's suggestion due consideration, as long as any settlement was fair.

His mind was made up just a day or so later when Katherine Schaub collapsed in church. "Pains like streaks of fire through my whole body!" she cried out. "I can't go on this way. I wish I wasn't going to live another month."

To Berry, it seemed inhuman not to try to get these suffering women a settlement if an offer might be forthcoming. Any legal case could take years to fight. And as Berry well knew from the doctors' sworn statements in his files, the women might not live until September.

On May 30, Judge Clark was reported as an unofficial mediator. It was a development that provoked considerable comment within the legal profession. After all, the judge was interfering in a case over which he had no power. Clark, however, said he resented criticism: "Just because I am a federal judge, does that mean that I cannot have a heart?" His motives, he said, were entirely humanitarian.

The following day, USRC held a board meeting to discuss possible terms. The company now seemed keen to settle. From the firm's perspective, settling this famous case out of court would make all the negative publicity immediately go away. Yet there was another reason too. It meant the firm could choose *when* to fight its battles in court. Inevitably, there would be future lawsuits from other dial-painters, because more and more former employees were sickening all the time. The firm hoped it might stand a better chance of winning its case in a few years' time, when Grace Fryer and her friends were not still plastered all over the papers. A settlement suited the company just fine.

A meeting between Berry and the firm's lawyers was held the next day, Friday, June 1, at 4:00 p.m. in Judge Clark's chambers. Two hours later, Clark made a quick statement to the excitable press waiting outside as he ran to catch his evening train: "There is no definite news but I am confident that the matter will be definitely settled at a conference [on] Monday."

Everybody seemed happy—everybody but the girls. *"Radium Victims Reject Cash Offers: Will Push Cases; Parleys Now Off!"* yelled one headline. The firm had offered them $10,000 ($138,606) each in settlement, but all the girls' medical and legal bills were to be deducted from that sum, leaving only a pittance.

"I will not grab at the first thing that comes along," exclaimed Grace fiercely. "I will not knuckle down to them now after all I've suffered."

No, the women said, *we do not accept*. Grace, as ever, seemed to lead the fight. She declared that she would "absolutely refuse to accept the company's offer." Instead, after discussion with the girls, Berry pitched alternative terms to USRC. The women wanted $15,000 ($208,000) as a cash lump sum for each of them, plus a pension of $600 ($8,316) a year for life, plus past *and future* medical expenses, and USRC to cover all court costs. The firm would have the weekend to think it over.

Monday, June 4, would prove a hectic day. At 10:00 a.m., negotiations continued, with the world's press camped outside. When, after forty-five minutes, the lawyers left Clark's chambers, they had to use a rear stairway to escape the massed media.

They were leaving to draw up formal papers. That afternoon, Berry summoned five brave radium girls to his office. They dressed up for the occasion. All wore fashionable cloche hats, while Grace slipped a fox fur around her shoulders. But better than any outfit, more dazzling than any jewels, were the smiles that wreathed all their faces. For they had done it. Against all the odds, after a phenomenally hard battle—fought while they were in the most fragile health imaginable—they had nonetheless held the company to account.

They spent three hours with Berry. In that time, the women signed the settlement papers. The company had kept

From left to right: Quinta McDonald, Edna
Hussman, Albina Larice, Katherine Schaub,
and Grace Fryer on June 4, 1928.

the lump sum in the final agreement at $10,000, but it agreed to all their other terms. It was a quite extraordinary achievement.

The media flashbulbs glared as the women posed for a photo to mark the moment. Quinta, Edna, Albina, Katherine, and Grace. They stood all in a row: the dream team. The "smiling sorority." And, for this one day, they were not sadly smiling but beaming, false teeth and all, in pure delight and not a little well-deserved pride.

The formal announcement of the settlement came from Judge Clark himself at 7:00 p.m. By then, a crowd of perhaps three hundred had gathered, and all the corridors were absolutely crammed. Clark fought his way through the crowds to a good vantage point from which he could break the news. He cleared his throat and asked for silence. It fell in a soft hush, broken only by the pop of flashbulbs and the papery whisper of pen on pad. Once he had the full attention of the press, the judge announced the exact terms of the deal. "You can say, if you want to," he added, "that the judge did a good job."

The settlement specified that the company admitted no guilt. The firm added, "[USRC] hopes that the treatment which will be provided for these women will bring about a cure."

And this was a crucial part of the settlement. The company had insisted that a committee of doctors be set up to examine the girls regularly. If a majority of these doctors ever decided that the girls were no longer suffering from radium poisoning, the payments would stop.

It was obvious to Berry that it was a plot. The company intended to get out of paying the pension and expenses as quickly as it could.

Nor was that the lawyer's only concern. Though he thought his former boss an honorable man, he now heard rumors that Clark was friends with some of the USRC directors. Worse than that, he learned that Clark was also possibly a stockholder in USRC or had been until very recently.

"I have," Berry said anxiously, "a great fear in the situation."

In the Essex County courthouse in Newark, its elaborate murals are dedicated to four things: wisdom, knowledge, mercy...and power. In this case, the last seemed cruelly apt.

Clark himself wrote to the women, "I want to express to you my very great personal sympathy, and my earnest hope that some way will be found of helping your physical condition." And it was the women, at the end of the day, for whom this settlement was everything. They had come out on top. They had never thought they would live to see the day.

"I think Mr. Berry, my lawyer, has done wonderful work," Edna enthused gratefully, speaking the thoughts of all five women.

Katherine simply said, "God has heard my prayers."

It was really only Grace who expressed a muted response. She said she was "quite pleased" with the settlement. "I'd like to get more, but I'm glad to get that. It will help in so many ways; it will alleviate some of the mental anguish."

She added, of their courage in bringing the lawsuit in the first place and of what they had achieved so publicly, "It is not for myself I care. I am thinking more of the hundreds of girls to whom this may serve as an example." She closed her statement not with a victory speech but with a warning. "You see, it's got us—so many more of us than anybody knows yet..."

28.

THE CHILL OF FEAR

Ottawa, Illinois
June 1928

The New Jersey settlement made international headlines—and the front page of the *Ottawa Daily Times*. "*More Deaths Raise Radium Paint Toll to 17!*" screamed the paper.

The girls in the Radium Dial studio were petrified. It wasn't as though they didn't have anything to worry about. Ella Cruse had *died* last summer, and several former workers weren't well, including Inez Vallat, Catherine Wolfe's old desk mate. The Ottawa paper, which the girls pored over with increasing panic, said the first sign of radium poisoning was decay of the gums and teeth. Peg Looney, whose tooth extraction from last year still hadn't healed, must have felt sick to her stomach.

"The girls became wild," remembered Catherine Wolfe.

"There were meetings at the plant that bordered on riots. The chill of fear was so depressing that we could scarcely work—scarcely talk of our impending fate."

The studio became a silent, still place. The girls slackened in their work, hands no longer lifting brushes to mouths at breakneck pace. Because they could scarcely work, production declined rapidly. So Radium Dial took action, calling in experts to run medical tests.

Marie Becker Rossiter watched proceedings with a beady eye. She noted that "they separated the girls. Some of the girls they took upstairs, away from the other ones. They tested both groups, but separately." The women didn't know why. Was it to do with those other tests the company had run, back in 1925? But those results had never been shared with the girls, so they did not know.

Divided into their groups, the women apprehensively went to meet the doctors. The physicians checked to see if the girls had radioactive breath, using the tests the Newark doctors had devised. They also took X-rays and blood.

Catherine Wolfe was tested, as were Peg Looney and Marie Rossiter. Reassured that the firm was looking after their best interests, the dial-painters then returned to their desks. They waited patiently for the results that they hoped would set their minds at ease.

But the results never came. "When I asked for a report on the examination," Catherine recalled, "I was told that this information could not be given out."

She and Marie conferred about it. Didn't they have a right to know? Marie, who was always forthright, determined that they shouldn't take it lying down. Full of fear and indignation, she and Catherine confronted Mr. Reed.

Their manager adjusted his glasses awkwardly and then opened his arms in a seemingly friendly way. "Why, my dear girls," he said to them, "if we were to give the medical reports to you girls there would be a riot in the place!" He almost seemed to make a joke of it.

That response clearly didn't settle the girls' nerves. But Catherine later said, "Neither of us then realized what he meant."

Mr. Reed, seeing their uncertainty, continued, "There is no such thing as radium poisoning."

"Are the workers in danger?" Marie demanded.

"You don't have anything to worry about," the superintendent repeated. "It's safe."

Nonetheless, the girls continued to devour the newspaper daily. It was full of horror stories from the east that shot bolts of fear right through them.

Three days after the announcement of the New Jersey

Statement by the
Radium Dial Company:

The full-page newspaper ad that Radium Dial placed on June 7, 1928.

girls' settlement, tensions in the Illinois studio were still running high. But that day, something appeared on page three of the local paper that changed everything. The women all pointed it out to one another and read on with ever-lightening shoulders.

It was a full-page ad placed by the Radium Dial Company. And it completely supported the superintendent's statements. More importantly, it was here, at last, that the girls learned the results of their recent tests.

The advertisement stated that the tests had been conducted by "technical experts" familiar with the symptoms of "so-called 'radium' poisoning." The company statement revealed: "Nothing even approaching such symptoms...has ever been found by these men."

Thank God. The results were clear. *They were not going to die.*

And the firm reassured them further, saying they would have stopped work in the studio if they'd thought dial-painting was dangerous. "The health of [our] employees is always foremost in the minds of [company] officials," they promised.

The ad concluded:

All the distressing cases of so-called "radium" poisoning reported from the east have occurred in establishments that have used luminous paint made from mesothorium... Radium Dial [uses] pure radium only.

That was why Mr. Reed had said "there was no such thing as radium poisoning," the girls now realized. This was why radium was safe—because it wasn't *radium* that had hurt the women out east. It was mesothorium.

Mr. Reed proudly printed bulletin notices with the company's statement. He posted them prominently in the studio and deliberately called the girls' attention to them. "He said that we should take particular notice of this advertisement," Catherine recalled.

And he used his charm to reassure the girls. "Radium will put rosy cheeks on you!" he told Marie with a grin.

The women continued to read the paper but continued to read only good news, as the company reran its advertisement over several days. In addition, the newspaper itself wrote an article in support of the community employer. It said the firm had been "ever-watchful" of its employees' health. The whole town was happy. Radium dials were one of Ottawa's leading industries, and it would have been an awful shame to have lost the business. But with the company's reassurances now given, it seemed there was no need for alarm.

In light of all this, the girls returned to work, their panic set at rest. "They went to work, they did what they were told to do," said a relative of Marie, "and that was the end of it. They never questioned it [anymore]."

What was there to question? The test results were fine. The paint contained no deadly mesothorium. These were simple facts—printed in the paper, pinned up on the noticeboard—that were as certain as the sunrises that bled each morning across the wide Illinois skies. Back up in the studio, the old routine continued anew. *Lip... Dip...*

Only one family, it seems, was unconvinced by the company.

The day after the ad ran, Ella Cruse's family filed suit against Radium Dial.

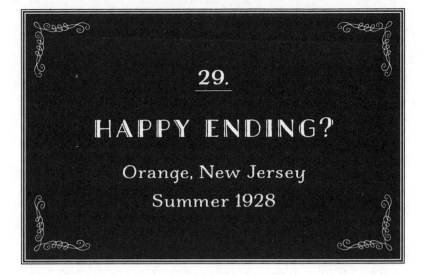

29.

HAPPY ENDING?

Orange, New Jersey
Summer 1928

For those five New Jersey dial-painters who had triumphed over their former firm, life was sweet. Katherine wanted to live "like Cinderella as the princess at the ball." She declared, "Today was mine." The budding author bought a typewriter and went on a shopping spree. "I bought the kind of coat I had always wanted," she enthused, "and a tan felt hat to match."

Edna, who had always loved music, invested in a piano and a radio. Many of the women bought cars so they could get around more easily. Yet the girls were also financially astute, investing in building and loan shares.

"Not a cent of [the settlement money] has ever entered this house," Grace informed a reporter. "To me, money doesn't mean luxury. It means security. Those $10,000 are safely invested."

"What for?" asked the journalist.

Grace smiled enigmatically as she answered. "For the future!"

Nor was the money the only blessing. Dr. Martland now offered some hope. He had observed that there had been no deaths for some years of the type suffered by Mollie Maggia and Marguerite Carlough. So he theorized that there were now two kinds of dial-painter cases: early ones and late ones. The early cases had suffered from the severe anemia and jaw necrosis that had eventually murdered Mollie. But the late cases did not have (or had recovered from) these devastating illnesses. Martland thought the shorter half-life of mesothorium perhaps explained the difference. Those girls who had been poisoned by mesothorium were under attack ferociously for the first 6.7 years. But

Edna Hussman and her husband,
Louis, with the car she bought
with her settlement money.

once mesothorium moved to its next half-life, the attack reduced enough to spare the girls' lives. Although the radium was still bombarding their bones and still poisoning them, radium was less aggressive than mesotho-rium. Martland now theorized that if the late cases "survived the early maladies, they had a fair chance of surviving radium poisoning altogether"—although they would always have those painful, moth-eaten bones. "I am of the opinion that the girls we are seeing now," he said, "while they may be permanently crippled, have a considerable chance of beating the disease."

That prognosis, bleak as it sounded in some ways, gave the women the most precious commodity: *time*. "Someone may find a cure for us, even at the eleventh hour," Grace said brightly.

More hope, too, came from the fact that all dial-painters nationwide would surely soon be protected. The public outcry at the New Jersey cases led to a national conference on radium poisoning being scheduled for the end of the year. In addition, Swen Kjaer began a much more detailed federal study into radium poisoning. "There is no question that this is an occupational disease and that there should be a reinves-tigation," commented Kjaer's boss, Ethelbert Stewart. He was asked why some firms were still using the old brush applica-tion method when other ways had been invented. He replied shrewdly, "The new methods probably were too slow for the greatest profit to the manufacturers."

Soon, Katherine Schaub, who spent the entire summer

away from Newark, experiencing "real country life," felt so much better. She declared her summer "splendid." "I loved to sit on the porch in the sun," she wrote dreamily, "and look out over the wide stretches of woodlands and hills."

While sitting on that porch, she wrote to Martland to thank him: "I am writing to express my sincerest appreciation for your great assistance in bringing it all to a happy ending."

A happy ending...if only that could be. Behind the scenes, Raymond Berry was most concerned that Katherine's "happy ending" was as fictional as a fairy tale.

Following the settlement, USRC had immediately launched into damage-limitation mode. By settling with the girls, it had crucially not admitted any guilt. It still denied any hazard existed in dial-painting. Now, to strengthen that argument, it asked the board of doctors that had been set up to examine the radium girls to get going with their work. USRC appeared confident that the board would soon give all five women a clean bill of health.

In the fall of 1928, Katherine, Grace, Edna, Quinta, and Albina were summoned to a New York hospital for the first committee examination. Naturally, USRC had chosen doctors who were pro-radium and who denied the existence of radium poisoning. Yet the tests were run without manipulation, so they proved that the women were radioactive.

The board of doctors refused to accept the results. They suggested the girls had somehow faked them. They insisted on *another* round of tests and this time invited doctors who were close to USRC to run them.

Luckily, there were also a couple of independent doctors present. They declared emphatically, "All five patients *are* radioactive."

The verdict was a genuine blow for USRC. Not least because every day they seemed to receive another new lawsuit from yet another former dial-painter. They'd wanted to have these famous radium girls deemed free of radium to help them fight the other suits.

Berry himself was representing one of the new cases. He won a battle partway through the new war when the judge ruled that Dr. Flinn was not allowed to conduct examinations of his client on behalf of USRC. Only a qualified physician could do it. It was a small victory, because nothing had come of Berry's complaints to the authorities about Flinn. The lack of action left the "doctor" free to publish. Flinn next blamed the girls' "improper diet" for their "tendency to store radium in their bones."

No one knew what Sabin von Sochocky's diet was, but improper or not, that November, he lost his own battle against radium poisoning. The careless way he had handled radium

Ethelbert Stewart, commissioner of the U.S. Bureau of Labor Statistics.

in his laboratory had finally caught up with him. Martland said, "He died a horrible death."

It meant he wasn't present at the national radium conference, held in December 1928. All the key players were there: Hamilton, Wiley, Martland, Humphries, Ethelbert Stewart, Flinn, and the radium company executives.

No one invited the dial-painters.

It was a voluntary conference, organized by the radium industry in an attempt to claw back some control. Really, it was just a piece of fluffy PR, which was designed to make it look as though the industry was doing something about the radium-poisoning scandal. The conference chairman acknowledged that it had no power to make the firms protect their workers. It was, as Wiley's boss later put it, "a whitewash."

The executives strongly argued that no further action was needed. They said only New Jersey cases had come to light, so radium poisoning wasn't a nationwide problem. Flinn, of course, had silenced the Waterbury girls. As a result, Ethelbert Stewart could discuss only one formally documented case outside USRC: the Ella Cruse lawsuit in Illinois. But hers was only a suspected case and not proven. Ultimately, there was no hard evidence of a widespread problem. It meant the girls' supporters were powerless to push through any proposals to protect current dial-painters, even though Wiley's boss called it "cold-blooded murder in industry."

The conference didn't confirm that radium poisoning existed or even that radium was dangerous. It simply agreed that further study should continue via two committees. Yet there is no record those committees ever met. As the New Jersey girls' stories became yesterday's news, no one was championing the dial-painters' cause anymore. "The Radium Corp. is playing a game," Berry wrote in frustration. And it seemed the radium companies were winning.

There were two other delegates worthy of mention at the national radium conference: Joseph Kelly and Rufus Fordyce of Radium Dial. They were the executives who had recently signed their names beneath the company statement in the Ottawa paper. They listened as one specialist said, "My advice to anyone manufacturing watches today would be to cut out the brush because you can paint on in another way." They listened as the New Jersey girls' deaths and disabilities were debated. They listened as the industry got away with murder.

And then they went home.

30.

MIDNIGHT MACHINATIONS

Ottawa, Illinois

1929

On February 26, 1929, radium-poisoning investigator Swen Kjaer made his way to the LaSalle County courthouse in the little town of Ottawa. He was surprised by how quiet it was. That day, there was a hearing in the Ella Cruse case. Given the high profile of the radium lawsuits out east, Kjaer had expected more fuss. Yet nobody was around. Not an eyelash flickered in the sleepy town.

Inside the courthouse, during the hearing, it was equally undramatic. Unlike in New Jersey, there were no throngs of journalists, no star witnesses, no dueling attorneys. All that happened was that the Cruse family's lawyer, George Weeks, simply stood to request a postponement. Kjaer was surprised that he wasn't pushing the case through more quickly, given the momentum provided by the New Jersey lawsuits.

Afterward, when Kjaer questioned Weeks, he discovered why he wasn't. The lawyer had needed to ask for postponements several times because he knew nothing about radium poisoning. Nor could he find any physician in Ottawa who could give him information. The family was claiming $3,750 ($51,977), which wasn't greedy, but at this rate, they would not see a cent. Weeks couldn't find anyone to tell him what radium poisoning was, let alone if Ella had died from it. Her parents were informed that the only way to get proof would be to dig up her body for an autopsy. But it would cost $200 ($2,772), money they simply didn't have. The case was left high and dry.

Kjaer continued on his pilgrimage around town. He called on the doctors and dentists who had promised to alert him should any dial-painters present symptoms of radium poisoning. As before, they all reported no cases.

He also visited the Radium Dial studio. It was still bustling, filled with women painting dials. He met the manager and asked to see the company test results. Radium Dial was now conducting regular medical exams of its employees, though the girls had noticed, as before, that they were separated prior to being tested. Catherine Wolfe even remembered, "Only once [was I] called to report for a physical examination [in 1928], whereas other girls apparently in good health were examined regularly."

Catherine was not in especially good health. She still had a limp, and just recently, she had started suffering from fainting spells. Concerned, she'd asked Mr. Reed if she could see the company doctor again. But he'd refused. She told herself she was worrying over nothing. The company had assured her that expert tests showed she was healthy. In addition, they had vowed to close the studio if there was any hazard, yet it was busier by the day. As time passed after the fuss in New Jersey, orders swiftly rose again to 1.1 million watches a year. Business was back on track.

However, Kjaer's inspection of Radium Dial troubled him. Two lab workers from Chicago showed changes in their blood, demonstrating that the firm's safety precautions were not good enough. The girls were also still eating in the studio without washing their hands. Kjaer concluded, "Further steps should be taken to protect the workers."

He met with Joseph Kelly. The company president promised him that the firm's "intention" was "to assist you in every way possible." Having seen the test results, Kjaer wanted to discuss two employees in particular. One was Ella Cruse. Kjaer declared, "I feel that this case should not be left out [of my study]." He requested further information on both girls.

Yet when Kelly sent him the data, all he enclosed were employment dates—not very helpful. Kjaer's time was limited, so he didn't question the company further. He thought he had enough to go on anyway.

So in his report, which was never seen by the Radium Dial girls, he wrote:

One dial-painter, ML, a twenty-four-year-old female, employed in a studio in Illinois, had been found radioactive in 1925 by electroscopic test. In 1928, another test was made, and she was found still radioactive... Complete information was not obtainable, and the firm protests against calling the diseased condition radium poisoning, but it seems well indicated by the test.

ML. *Margaret Looney*. She had been told by the firm she had "a high standard of health." She had been told that her tests showed nothing to worry about.

She had no idea what was coming.

———— ≈ ————

Peg Looney smiled up at Chuck Hackensmith from the red metal wagon in which she was sitting. Chuck smiled back as he bent to lift its handle and then patiently pulled the wagon along. Peg was now too sick to walk sometimes. Chuck's solution? Seat her in the wagon as though it was a shiny

Peg Looney.

limousine and then chauffeur her around the neighborhood.

But no matter how broad Chuck's grin was as he pulled that wagon, no matter how determined he became to put a brave face on what was happening, he couldn't conceal his true feelings. "He was devastated with the whole thing," recalled Peg's niece sadly.

The entire family felt the same. By the summer of 1929, red-haired Peg Looney was not at all well. The teeth extractions that never healed had only been the start of her troubles. She'd developed anemia, and then this pain had settled in her hip so that now she could barely walk—thus the little red wagon. Chuck was so kind to pull her around in it. He loved her fiercely. They were going to be married next June.

Chuck and his red wagon couldn't be there all the time, though. When Peg went to the radium studio, she had to walk. Her sister Jean remembered the way that she and all the Looney siblings would look out for her coming home.

"We'd all be sitting out on our porch just watching for her because she looked so bad walking," said Jean. "[She'd be struggling] all the way home. We'd run to meet her, each one would have an arm to help her."

When she reached home, borne along by her siblings, Peg could no longer assist her mother with the housework as she once had. She would simply have to lie down and rest. Her mother felt terrible watching her daughter's decline. Peg was wasting away, and her family watched in horror as she pulled teeth and parts of her jaw from her mouth. In the end, her parents scraped together the money to take her to a doctor in Chicago. The city physician told her she had a honeycombed jaw and that she should change employment.

Perhaps Peg planned to look for a new job when she felt better. But Peg was smart. She knew she *wasn't* getting better. Though the Ottawa doctors seemed clueless—one, who treated her in June 1929, simply put an ice pack on her chest—Peg herself seemed to divine what was happening. "She knew she had to go," recalled Peg's mother sadly. "You could see her slowly dying. There was nothing you could do."

"Well, Mother," she used to say, "my time is nearly up."

It wasn't just her hip or teeth that caused her agonizing pain. It was her legs, her skull, her ribs, her wrists, her ankles... Though she'd been ill for months, every day she still went to work to paint those dials. To the end, she was a conscientious girl.

Because of Kjaer's inquiries about her test results,

Radium Dial was aware that Peg was a special case in whom the government was particularly interested. So the company watched her very closely. They knew she had tested positive for radioactivity in 1925 and 1928. They knew from their own medical tests exactly what was wrong with her. So when Peg collapsed at work on August 6, 1929, Mr. Reed made arrangements for her to be admitted to the company doctor's hospital.

It was so lonely for Peg in that distant place, far from her home by the railroad tracks. The girl who had nine brothers and sisters and slept with them all in one tiny room, three to a bed, was completely on her own. Her siblings weren't permitted to visit. Her sister Jane went one time, but the doctors wouldn't let her into Peg's room.

Peg displayed symptoms of the disease diphtheria and was promptly quarantined. In her weakened condition, she also came down with pneumonia. Radium Dial, in a show of concern, paid close attention to her progress—and to her decline.

At 2:10 a.m. on August 14, 1929, Peg Looney died. This girl, who was to marry Chuck next year, who had once had dreams of being a teacher and was well known for her giggling fits, was no more.

Her family, though isolated from her, were still in the hospital when she died. One of the relatives present was Peg's brother-in-law Jack, an imposing man who worked as a car oiler for the railroad. He was the type of man who stood up for the right thing to be done. Which was why, when the company men came in the middle of the night and tried to take her body to bury it, Jack protested.

"*No*," he said firmly to them. "You will not [take her body]. She's a good Catholic girl and she'll have the whole Catholic funeral and have a mass."

"I think it was probably a good thing he was there," commented Peg's niece shrewdly, "because I do not know that the rest of the family—with everything that was going on—I don't know if they'd have been able to stand up to the company and the doctor. But Jack was more forceful. He told them, 'That's not going to happen.'"

The company men tried to argue with him. "They wanted the whole thing done with—just gone," Peg's niece went on. "It was like a big cover-up." But Jack stood his ground and would not allow them to take Peg's body.

Radium Dial lost that particular battle but did not give up. It seems the firm was very concerned that Peg's death would be identified as a case of radium poisoning. That would scare all the girls at the studio and possibly lead to lawsuits. The executives needed to take control of the situation. What did the family think, they asked, of having Peg autopsied?

The Looney family was already suspicious, given the Chicago doctor's comments, that it was her work that had killed Peg. They readily agreed on the condition that their own family doctor could be present, because they wanted to find out the truth. Their condition was all-important. After the firm's midnight machinations, they did not trust them.

The company agreed easily. Yes, yes, they said, no problem. What time?

When the family doctor arrived at the appointed hour, bag in hand, he found the autopsy had been performed an hour before he got there.

So he hadn't seen the multiple fracture lines on Peg's ribs, nor the way "the flat bones of [her] skull showed numerous 'thin' areas and 'holes.'" He didn't examine the radium necrosis that was found "very strongly" in the skull vault, pelvis, and at least sixteen other bones. He did not witness the widespread skeletal changes that were evident throughout Peg's battered body.

He was not there when the company doctor secretly removed the remains of Peg Looney's jaw.

He took her bones. He took the most compelling evidence.

The family was not sent a copy of the autopsy report, but Radium Dial received one. It was an incredibly intrusive record for them to have of Peg's last moments. It told them what she was like inside: the weight of her organs, their appearance, whether she was "normal." When it came to her bone marrow and her teeth, according to the company doctor, *she most certainly was.*

"The teeth are in excellent condition," read the official autopsy report. "There is no evidence of any destructive bone changes in the upper or lower jaw."

Her death certificate was duly signed. Diphtheria was the cause of death.

Though her family may not have been given a copy of the report, Radium Dial made sure to issue the local paper with a summary of it. So in Peg Looney's obituary, the following information was included, possibly at the request of the firm:

> *The young woman's physical condition for a time was puzzling. She was employed at the Radium Dial studio and there were rumors that her condition was due to radium poisoning. In order that there might be no doubt as to the cause of death [there was] an autopsy... Dr. Aaron Arkin... said there was no doubt that death was caused by diphtheria. There was no visible indication of radium poisoning.*

There was a curious final comment, perhaps suggested by a company executive with a bright idea of how to win support in the community. "Miss Looney's parents," read the piece, "appeared well pleased with the result of the autopsy."

They were not "well pleased." How could they be? They were grief-stricken. They were numb. They were devastated by their daughter's death.

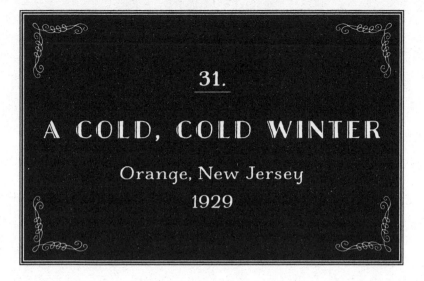

K atherine Schaub rebuttoned her blouse after her medical examination and waited for the committee doctor to speak. He'd said he had something important he wished to discuss. To her astonishment, he proposed that the radium company should stop paying her medical bills. Even though, in the settlement, they had agreed to cover them for life. He wanted her instead to accept a one-off lump sum.

Less than a year after the New Jersey settlement had been reached, USRC was attempting to wriggle out of the agreement.

The idea of paying a lump sum came from company vice president Barker. Yet it had the full support of the board of doctors. One of them said bluntly, "These women are not going

---

KATE MOORE

to die." In an attempt to persuade Katherine to accept the smaller payment, the doctor told her that USRC was close to bankruptcy.

This was a lie. The firm was simply fed up with paying the bills. The women, crippled and in agony, were regularly consulting doctors and buying painkillers. But of course all those bills soon added up.

To the firm's frustration, its plot to have the women deemed free of radium poisoning was not working out. Even though the board of doctors kept asking the women to do test after test, the results were always the same. The women *had* been poisoned.

As for the girls themselves, they were just doing their best to get through it all. They were forced to endure experimental treatments and tests. Edna's beautiful blond hair turned snow white with shock. All the girls looked far older than they were, with faces that had curiously slack skin around their chins, where their jawbones had been removed. Only Grace seemed better than she had the year before. Although she had now had twenty-five operations on her jaw, they hadn't broken her habit of smiling. She was said to be the happiest of the five by far. When she'd received the settlement, she'd said with determination, "People are now asking me if I am going to stop working: I do not intend to do anything of the kind. I'm going to keep right on at my job as long as I can, because I like it."

224

She still commuted daily, with the bank being understanding about the time off she needed for her tests.

Though the examinations happened often, the girls never learned the results. "The doctors don't seem to tell [me] anything," complained Katherine. "I would like to know if I am getting any better."

In fact, in many ways, Katherine *was* better. She now lived quietly in a rural convalescent home set on a hilltop, which she called "the jewel of the east." She wrote that the setting inspired her to get better so she could enjoy "hollyhocks and rambler roses and peonies and sunshine." She enjoyed that summer, which was just as well, because a cold, cold winter was coming.

———≈———

Black Tuesday they called it. October 29, 1929. The day a financial nightmare rocked Wall Street and "paper fortunes... melted away like frost under a hot sun." It was the day of the Wall Street crash, when a panic gripped the stock exchange and sixteen million shares were traded in a single day. The panic led to billions of dollars of losses and the collapse of the American economy.

More than a hundred blocks north of a stricken Wall Street, Quinta McDonald lay in her room at the New York Memorial Hospital. She was bedbound, but battling to stay alive. Come December 6, it seemed as though she might just have won her fight. Her husband, James, visited that day, and they chatted about Christmas. Despite her illness, Quinta said she hoped that she might be able to go home for the festivities. She wanted to give her two young children, Helen and Robert, a Christmas they would never forget.

Quinta McDonald.

Midway through the conversation, however, she suddenly sighed and said she felt tired.

James was not surprised. He bent to give her a kiss, being careful not to touch her leg. It was peculiar, but she had a swelling of some size at the top of her thigh. It gave her a lot of pain. Quinta asked James to leave early so that she could rest, and he did so, departing with no sense of foreboding.

That swelling on Quinta's leg... If Dr. Martland had seen it, he might have recognized it. It was a sarcoma—the kind of bone tumor that had killed Ella Eckert on a cold December day almost two years before.

On December 7, 1929, Quinta McDonald died too.

Her friends were completely devastated. The former dial-painters had become a tight-knit unit: the five of them against the company and against the world. Quinta was the first of them to fall. Her sister Albina collapsed when she heard the news. Katherine Schaub was greatly shaken too. Katherine chose not to attend the funeral but returned to her country home to find forgetfulness. "For a time," she said, "I succeeded in losing myself entirely in…my writing."

For the girls remaining in Orange, there was no such forgetfulness. In a way, they wanted to remember: to remember Quinta. On Tuesday, December 10, Edna, Albina, and Grace arrived at St. Venantius Church for her funeral. The difference in the radium girls' health was clear for the waiting reporters to see. Grace walked briskly, without help, while Edna seemed to be suffering the most. As for Albina, this was the second sister she had lost to radium poisoning. Even attending the funeral was a struggle. Yet she was determined to pay her respects. There was a long flight of stairs leading to the church door. Albina fought her way up every single step, even though she was apparently near collapse. But this was more important than her comfort. This was for Quinta.

It was a brief service. Quinta's children, who were ten and six, "kept close to their father, both too young to realize their loss, yet sensing." In the weeks to come, they would indeed have a Christmas they would never forget.

Quinta had made one final request. She wanted her death to be of service to her friends. So Martland conducted an autopsy. He discovered that Quinta had died from the same rare sarcoma that had killed Ella Eckert. Quinta's tumor may not have been on her shoulder, but it was the same thing. It was just that the radium had chosen a different target in her bones. Martland gave a statement about this new threat. "The bones of the victims," he revealed, "had actually died before they did."

One might have thought that after learning of Quinta's death, USRC might at last have softened its position. But one would be wrong. Raymond Berry did manage to win a settlement of $8,000 ($113,541) for his new client in the new year, but there was a catch. The only way USRC would pay his client any money, they said, was if Berry himself was included in the deal. The firm had decided he was far too effective an opponent to be left off a leash.

So Raymond Berry, the pioneering attorney who had been the only lawyer to answer Grace's call for help, found himself forced into signing his name to the following statement: "I agree not to be connected with, directly or indirectly, any other cases against the United States Radium Corporation."

Berry was gone. He had been a serious fighter against USRC. An annoying thorn in its side. But now it had plucked him out and banished him.

It was two settlements down, but USRC was winning the war.

32.

TIME-BOMB TUMORS

In the summer of 1930, Katherine Schaub placed her walking stick gingerly on the low step in front of her. She could now walk only with the aid of a cane or crutches. To her great disappointment, she'd been forced to return to live in Newark. After spending large sums of money trying to regain her health, she was entirely dependent on her $600 ($8,515) pension. But it didn't provide enough income for a rural home. She hated being back in the city, where she felt her health declined.

She started up the low step but slipped and came down hard upon her knee. It would have been painful for anyone, but Katherine was a radium girl: her bones were as fragile as china. She felt the bone fracture. Yet when Dr. Humphries examined

Katherine Schaub
with her cane.

her X-rays, he had worse news to tell her than the broken bone.

Katherine had a sarcoma of the knee.

She was admitted to the hospital for ten long weeks while they treated it with X-rays. It seemed to reduce the swelling, but Katherine was utterly depressed. Encased in plaster for months, she was eventually told that the bone hadn't healed as it should. So from now on, she would have to wear a metal leg brace. She cried when the doctor fitted it.

The board of doctors was, as ever, on hand to "help," but Katherine now refused their treatments. "They say you do not know a person," she wrote assertively, "until you have lived with them. I have lived with radium ten years now and I think I ought to know a little bit about it. So far as [the suggested] treatment, I think it's all bosh." She would not bend to their demands.

The doctors were angry about this—and not just about Katherine's stubbornness but also increasing boldness from all four remaining women. Yet in standing up for themselves, the girls were playing a dangerous game. After all, the committee controlled the purse strings for their medical care. The company began questioning every bill as though the women were trying to cheat them. It wasn't long before Grace was told she could no longer call on her usual doctor.

The year 1930 flowed fluidly into 1931. At the turn of the year, Katherine was still in the hospital. But her tumor was shrinking, thanks to Humphries's attentions. It currently measured 45 centimeters wide. Come February, she was still unable to do much in the way of walking, but it seemed she had beaten the worst of it.

The spring of 1931 found Grace Fryer in good spirits too. She was still determined to be as positive as she could. "I work and I play and I 'dance' a bit," she said. "I go motoring. I even swim—but I can stay in the water only two minutes at a time. I can't leave the brace off my back any longer than that."

In the hospital in Orange, however, there were no such diversions for the latest patient wheeled through its doors. A woman named Irene La Porte, who had worked with Grace during the war, now followed her friends to Dr. Humphries's office.

It was the summer of 1930 when she'd first noticed something was wrong. Her husband, Vincent, took her to Dr. Humphries, who diagnosed a pelvic sarcoma that was then about the size of a walnut. Despite the doctor's efforts, her decline was very fast. Irene was admitted to the hospital. But by March 1931, the doctors said there wasn't very much they could do for her.

In April, they called in Dr. Martland. "I found a bedridden patient extremely emaciated and filled with a huge sarcoma," he remembered. His diagnosis was immediate and absolute.

"He told me definitely," remembered Vincent La Porte, choking up, "that she did [have radium poisoning] and she had about six weeks to live."

They did not tell Irene, wanting to spare her. But the world was widely informed about what was happening to her body. By then, Martland had seen enough cases to be able to describe these time-bomb tumors to the press. He explained that a dial-painter could often remain healthy for years after her exposure to radium. But eventually, these big, cancerous sarcomas would take over her body. They were the new phase of this terrifying poisoning.

Importantly, they also proved, once and for all, that poisoning from radium-226 was just as fatal as poisoning from mesothorium. It may not have been as aggressive, and the girls' declines may not have been as swift. But slowly, steadily, and unstoppably, radium would ultimately cast its cruel, cold curse.

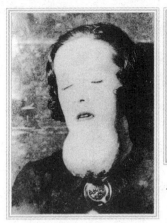

A dial-painter with a radium-
induced sarcoma of the chin
(front and side views).

Martland could reach only one conclusion. "I am now of
the opinion that the normal radioactivity of the human body
should not be increased; [to do so] is dangerous," he wrote.
It had to be, for each week, another dial-painter presented
another sarcoma, each in a new location—her spine, her leg,
her knee, her hip, her eye...

Irene's family couldn't believe how fast she was fading.
But she still had grit in her. On May 4, 1931, as she lay dying in
the hospital, she filed a claim for damages against USRC. She
was willing to settle.

But the company was just about done with settlements.
Since they had muzzled Berry, they were not too concerned
about the opponents to follow.

Only a month later, after fighting such a hard, hard battle
that she was destined never to win, Irene died on June 16, 1931.

At the time of her death, Martland said her tumor had become enormous. He reported, "You couldn't take the whole mass out together without taking the woman apart. The whole mass was larger than two footballs." That was how Irene La Porte was killed.

Her husband, Vincent, was filled with an intense rage. It was red hot at first, searing him with pain and grief. But as time went on, it cooled into an icy desire for vengeance. And Vincent La Porte would fight on for his wife. He would fight on through the courts—through 1931, and '32, and '33 and even beyond.

Irene La Porte's case against USRC would be the one that finally led to a judgment for all the New Jersey girls. Vincent didn't know it when he started, but that fight was going to take years yet. The company was in no rush.

Then again, neither was he.

Martland had one final statement to give on the sarcomas—on the insidious time bombs that he now knew were lurking inside every dial-painter who had ever lifted a brush to her lips.

"I believe," he said, "before we get through, the number will be appalling."

33.

A VERY BIG MISTAKE

Ottawa, Illinois
August 1931

Catherine Wolfe paused for a moment on her way into work, stopping at the corner of East Superior Street to catch her breath. It was normally a seven-minute stroll to the studio from her house, but these days, it took her much, much longer. As she limped down Columbus Street, the sight of St. Columba lifted her spirits. The white church was like a second home to her. It was where she had been christened and baptized, where she took communion, and where she would marry one day...

She had lots of blessings, she thought to cheer herself as she made her way along, counting them off as though they were the beads of her rosary. There was her health: Catherine, despite the limp, was in okay health otherwise. There was her fiancé, Tom Donohue: the couple were due to be married in January 1932. And there was her job. Six million Americans were currently unemployed but Catherine earned $15 ($233) a week, and she was grateful for every cent.

She tried not to think about those who were less fortunate. Like her former desk mate, Inez Vallat. Aged twenty-four, Inez was no longer able to work due to her mysterious illness. She'd lost twenty pounds, her pelvis ached, and her teeth had started coming loose. Catherine tried not to think about poor Peg Looney either, who was dead and buried in her grave.

Catherine made it, finally, to Radium Dial. As she made her awkward way over to her desk, she felt the other girls' eyes on her. Her limp, she sensed, was causing talk. But Mr. Reed never criticized the quality of her work, so she tried not to let the gossip bother her.

Catherine was no longer a full-time dial-painter. The change in her duties had been directed by the studio bosses because of her ill health. Radium Dial knew that she was lame and—as they had done with Peg Looney—they were keeping a close eye on her. Catherine's job now was to weigh the radium for the other women and to scrape the radium remnants from the used dishes, often simply using her fingernails. As was to be expected, her bare hands became luminously bright. And since she often ran her fingers through her hair, her whole head would glow fiercely. When she peered at herself in a mirror in a dark bathroom, she often thought that the new job got her even more covered in radium than the old one had.

She dial-painted now only when an emergency order required an extra pair of hands. Then Catherine would slip her brush between her lips, dip it in the powder, and paint. The girls all still did it that way at Radium Dial. Their instructions had never changed.

That day, Catherine had just begun weighing the material when the girls nearest the window sent the message around that Mr. Kelly and Mr. Fordyce had come on a visit. The president and vice president of the firm, all the way from Chicago! The girls straightened their blouses, and Catherine ran a nervous hand through her dark hair. Then she pushed herself up from her desk and limped across the studio to the stockroom.

She was partway there when Mr. Reed and the executives came into the studio. Mr. Reed began pointing out various aspects of the work. But Catherine had this funny feeling that the visiting officials were looking only at her. She got what she needed from the stockroom and made her slow way back to her desk, conscious of her limp. By this time, she'd asked Mr. Reed on several occasions if she could be examined by the company doctors. But he always refused. She'd recently gone to a local physician instead. He'd told her the limp was caused by rheumatism. Catherine felt she was too young for that—she was only twenty-eight—but she didn't know what else it could be.

Mr. Reed and the other men were still standing there, having an inaudible conversation under their breath. She felt inexplicably anxious and turned to face the windows, lit by the August sun.

The sunlight was blocked by a shadow.

"Mr. Reed?" asked Catherine, looking up from her work.

He wanted her to come to the office. So she slowly made her way there. Mr. Kelly and Mr. Fordyce were also in the office. She fiddled with her hair again.

"I'm sorry, Catherine," said Mr. Reed suddenly.

Catherine looked at him in confusion.

"I'm sorry, but we have to let you go."

Catherine felt her mouth drop open, suddenly dry. Mr. Reed was firing her. *Why?* she wondered. Was it her work? Had she done something wrong?

Mr. Reed must have seen the questions in her eyes.

"Your work is satisfactory," he admitted. "Everyone is talking about you limping. It's not giving a very good impression to the company."

Catherine hung her head, though whether with shame or anger or hurt, she was not quite sure.

"We feel..." Mr. Reed broke off for a moment to make eye contact with his bosses. They gave him a nod; they were all in this together. "We feel it is our duty to let you go."

Catherine felt stunned. Shocked, wounded. "I was told to go," she remembered later. "I was told to go."

She stepped out of the office, left the radium men behind. She picked up her purse and limped back down the stairs to the first floor. Everything around her was familiar. For nine years, six days a week, she had spent her life in this studio. The walls of the old high school seemed to ring for a second with the laughter of the girls she had known there. Of Charlotte and Marie. Of Inez, of Ella, of Peg.

No one was laughing now.

Catherine Wolfe, fired for being sick, swung open the glass door at the entrance of the studio. It was six steps down to the sidewalk, and on every one, she felt her hip ache. Nine years she had given them. It had meant nothing.

No one watched her go. The men who had fired her got on with their day. The girls were too busy painting to put down their brushes. Catherine knew as she reached the final step what they would all be doing inside. *Lip... Dip... Paint.*

No one watched her go. But Radium Dial had underestimated Catherine Wolfe.

The firm had just made a very big mistake.

34.

THE
END OF
THE ADVENTURE

Orange, New Jersey
February 1933

K atherine Schaub bit down hard on her lip to keep from crying out, her eyes squeezing shut with the pain.

"All done," the nurse likely said reassuringly, having changed the dressing on Katherine's knee.

Katherine opened her eyes warily, not wanting to look down at her leg. All through the past year, doctors had been keeping tabs on her tumor. It was 45 centimeters, they told her, then 47.5, then 49. Its earlier reduction had been reversed. In the past week or so, the bone tumor had broken through her paper-thin skin. Now, the lower end of her thigh bone was sticking out of the wound.

She tried to focus her mind on happier things. Before

she'd been admitted to the hospital, she had spent some time at a private hospice, Mountain View Rest, for her nerves. That had been quite wonderful.

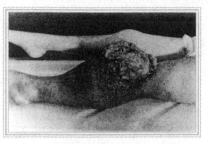

A dial-painter with a radium-induced cancer of the knee.

She had finished writing her memoir, had even had an extract from it published in a magazine. She, Katherine Schaub, was a published author. It was what she had always longed to be. "I have been granted," she wrote with peaceful pleasure, "[a] priceless gift—I have found happiness."

If only she could have stayed in the mountains. She felt so much brighter there. Yet it had become impossible financially. As her health grew worse, she had to travel into Orange more and more often to see Dr. Humphries. Each visit involved an expensive taxi fare. And the board of doctors had become outraged at the bills. In fact, they'd had enough of the women's expenses altogether.

The previous February, in 1932, Katherine, Grace, Edna, and Albina had all received a no-nonsense letter from the committee doctors. It informed them that USRC would no longer pay for certain medicines, routine doctors' visits, or home nurses. The latter was a service the women increasingly relied on to help clean and dress themselves. The board was acting, it said, to prevent "exploitation" of the radium company.

There had been consequences following the committee's decision. Katherine became even more determined not to submit to their experiments. The doctors merely dismissed her as a "highly hysterical woman."

However, Katherine's suspicion of medical men had a downside for her too. It seems it made her wary of accepting *any* therapeutic advice. In time, Dr. Humphries recommended she have a leg amputation in order to get rid of the cancerous sarcoma in her knee. But she refused. And Katherine could be stubborn when she wanted to be. It was perhaps partly why she had been one of the five girls who'd won a settlement from USRC in the first place.

The committee's letter from 1932 mentioned "the very depressed state of business" as a reason why the company was refusing to pay their expenses. Inevitably, sales of luminous watches had declined along with everything else in the country after the Wall Street crash. But it wasn't only the struggling economy that was sucking the dollars from the firm's bank account. It was the case of Eben Byers.

It had been all over the papers in March 1932. Byers was a wealthy industrialist who raced horses. He was high-profile and important. Back in 1927, Byers had been injured. His doctor had

An advertisement for Radithor, a brand of radioactive water.

prescribed the radium tonic Radithor. Byers was so impressed with it he consumed several thousand bottles.

When his story made the news, the headlines read, *"The Radium Water Worked Fine until His Jaw Came Off."* Byers had died of radium poisoning on March 30, 1932. But before he died, he gave evidence to the Federal Trade Commission (FTC) that Radithor had killed him.

The authorities reacted with much more speed than they had in the cases of the dial-painters. In December 1931, the FTC stopped production of Radithor. The U.S. Food and Drug Administration would go on to declare radium medicines illegal. Finally, the American Medical Association removed the internal use of radium from its list of "New and Nonofficial Remedies," where it had remained even after the discovery of the dial-painters' deaths. It seemed wealthy consumers were much more worthy of protection than working-class girls. After all, dial-painting was still going on, even in 1933.

Katherine had read the stories about Byers with sadness for the victim but also an overwhelming sense of vindication.

Radium *was* a poison. The girls knew that intimately. But until the Byers case, public opinion had swung the other way. Indeed, with four of the famous radium girls still alive— almost five years on from their court case—there had been much muttering that their lawsuit had been nothing more than a fraudulent scheme to get money from the company.

For that company, the Byers case was a disaster. USRC supplied the radium for many of the products that had now been banned. The whole radium industry collapsed. It may or may not have been connected, but in August 1932, having failed to find a buyer for the old Orange plant, the firm had it bulldozed to the ground. The dial-painters' studio was the last building to come down.

The women had mixed feelings, seeing it gone. It was a bittersweet triumph of sorts. Except for them, erasing the studio and all it had done was not as simple as covering the site with anonymous asphalt. Lying in her hospital room in February 1933, Katherine Schaub forced herself to look at what the radium had done to her. Her leg was a mess. Finally, after much consideration, she decided to have it amputated.

It was a decision for her future. "It is my ambition to continue writing," she said. She could do that, she thought, with or without a leg.

But Humphries had bad news for her. Katherine and

her leg had recently worsened, and both were now in far too serious a state for such a major operation. Soon afterward, Katherine became even more unwell. On February 18, 1933, she died at the age of thirty. It was the end of her "adventure," as she herself put it.

Katherine Schaub was just fourteen when she'd started work with the radium company on that long-ago February day. She had dreamed of writing and of fulfilling her potential, and she did publish her work and she did fulfill that potential. It was just that her destiny was not quite the one she'd dreamed of as a girl. In taking on the company, she became a celebrated example of standing up for your rights.

35.

BRAVE UNTIL ᴛʜᴇ LAST

I t could be worse, Grace Fryer thought. It really could be a lot worse.

Just lately, in July 1933, Grace had become bedridden. But as she kept telling herself, it really could be a lot worse. "I feel better when I'm at home," she said brightly. "I guess it's because I like home better than anything else."

Grace's friend Edna shared her feelings about that. "Home always makes me feel better," Edna commented. "I have my good and bad days, but I can endure them when I'm home."

Edna was doing very well, all things considered. Despite her fixed, crossed legs, she still managed to move about with the aid of a cane, calling on friends and even hosting bridge parties. She'd taken up crochet too. It was something she could do for hours on end without leaving her chair. Although her spine was now affected by the radium, she kept her spirits up. She even believed she would live quite a few more years yet.

Grace Fryer.

Edna declared she never thought about her illness being fatal. "What good would that do?" she exclaimed.

Like Edna, Albina found that her spine had become affected. She now wore a steel corset. But she was able to hobble about with mouse-size steps as long as she had a cane. Though she was only thirty-seven, Albina's hair, like Edna's before her, had turned entirely white. Nevertheless, she was much happier these days than she had once been. "I know they say," Albina said shyly, "there is no hope of being cured—but I'm trying to hope there is."

By September 1933, Grace was clinging to the same hope. But it seemed to fade with every passing day. Though her mother kept her at home as long as she could, Grace was eventually admitted to the hospital under the care of Dr. Humphries.

He was worried, he said, about the growing sarcoma in her leg.

"I am not going to live much longer," Grace had once said. "No one has ever been known to recover from this trouble. So, of course, I will not either. But why worry?"

"It was not death of which Grace was afraid," said her mother. "It was the dread of the suffering—the eternal suffering—the years of torment. She was brave, until the last."

The last came on October 27, 1933. She died at 8:00 a.m., as the doctors were starting their day. Dr. Martland attended her autopsy, conducting his final, careful consideration of this most special of patients. Grace's death certificate stated she was killed by "radium sarcoma, industrial poisoning." It was a fact in black and white. It was the radium industry that killed her. It was the company.

Grace was buried in Restland Memorial Park. Her grave was marked with a stone that had a gap beneath her name. When her mother passed away, fourteen years later, her name was added to her daughter's so they could both rest in peace.

Grace Fryer's death was reported by the local papers. The family supplied a photograph of her to accompany the news. It was a picture from before the poisoning had set in. She looked forever young: her lips smooth and shining, her eyes piercing, as though she could see into souls. She wore a conservative set of pearls and a lace-shouldered blouse. She was beautiful and bright and unbroken, and it was how she would always be remembered by those who'd loved her.

"The family all just seemed so sad," her nephew Art recalled. He was born after Grace died. He was the son of her little brother Art, who used to take her to her hospital appointments. "My father really did not talk about it. But I think he was affected his whole life by this. This was his big sister, who was a beautiful girl."

And Grace Fryer was not just beautiful. She was brilliant. She was smart. She was determined and forthright and strong and special.

Her little brother did once speak of her, when his grandson had asked him to. "I will never forget her," he'd simply said. "*Never.*"

And Grace Fryer was never forgotten. She is still remembered now—*you* are still remembering her now. As a dial-painter, she glowed gloriously from the radium powder. But as a woman, she shines through history with an even brighter glory. Stronger than the bones that broke inside her body. More powerful than the radium that killed her or the company that shamelessly lied through its teeth. Living longer than she ever did on earth, because she now lives on in the hearts and memories of those who know her only from her story.

Grace Fryer: the girl who fought on when all hope seemed gone. The woman who stood up for what was right, even as her world fell apart. Grace Fryer, who inspired so many to stand up for themselves.

Yet even as Grace was laid to rest, her story was not over. For her spirit lived on, eight hundred miles away, in the women who came after her. When Grace died, no radium company had been found guilty for killing its workers. No firm had been found at fault. Now, as Grace rested peacefully, others would take up her torch. Others would follow in her footsteps. Others would battle on as they continued the fight. For recompense. For recognition.

For justice.

PART THREE

———

JUSTICE

36.

CONSPIRACY?

Ottawa, Illinois
1933

he executives of the Radium Dial Company had confirmed knowledge of radium poisoning since at least 1925, less than three years after their studio first opened in Ottawa. That was the year Marguerite Carlough first filed suit in New Jersey and Martland devised his tests. The executives had read Kjaer's studies, attended the radium conference, and seen the Eben Byers story. They *knew* radium was dangerous.

When their employees found out about the New Jersey cases in 1928, the company lied. They placed a full-page advertisement in the paper. It said the girls were safe, and their medical exams proved it. It said the paint was safe, because it was made purely from radium. When Peg Looney died, the company lied. There was "no visible indication of radium poisoning"—but only because her jawbone was no longer visible to anyone, having been cut from her after death.

With these assurances plastered across the papers, the town supported the company. After all, the executives had promised they would close the studio if there was *any* danger. No wonder the town was behind them, when they apparently took such good care of their employees and seemed willing to put people before profits. It must be really, *really* safe to work there, everyone thought.

Because eight years on from Marguerite's lawsuit, Radium Dial was still trading daily in the little town of Ottawa.

———— ≋ ————

Oh no, the local doctor said, it was definitely *not* radium poisoning that Catherine Wolfe Donohue had. She limped out of the consulting room, still no wiser as to the cause of her illness, and made her slow way home to East Superior Street. She did not walk alone. She pushed a stroller in which lay her baby son, Tommy. He had been born in April 1933, just over a year after she'd married Tom Donohue. "God has sure blessed me," Catherine wrote, "with a grand husband and [a] lovely child."

She and Tom had been married on January 23, 1932, in St. Columba. It was a modest wedding with only twenty-two guests. Catherine's uncle and aunt had both passed away by then, and Tom's family did not approve of the union because of the bride's poor health. Defiantly, he'd married her anyway. The local paper deemed it "one of the prettiest weddings of the mid-winter season."

The house where Catherine Donohue and her family lived.

Today's appointment had been the third doctor Catherine consulted. But he was as useless as the rest. "They were just guessing," commented one dial-painter's relative about the town's physicians. "They had no idea [what the trouble was]— especially any doctors in Ottawa."

It was certainly true that the local physicians were not the most knowledgeable. Some of their cluelessness was apparently due to ignorance, despite the fact that by this time, Dr. Martland had published many articles on radium poisoning.

Catherine thought over her appointment. Mindful of the dial-painters' deaths out east, she had asked the doctor today if she might have radium poisoning. But he'd said clearly that he didn't think so. However, he'd added that he didn't know enough about it. No one in Ottawa seemed to know anything. Certainly, Ella Cruse's family had gotten nowhere with their lawsuit.

Every time she went to church, Catherine was aware of the Radium Dial studio just across the road. It was a much quieter place these days. The economic downturn had the little town of Ottawa firmly in its grip. Many dial-painters had been laid off. Those who remained no longer lip-pointed, perhaps because of the Eben Byers case. Some were using their fingers instead. This doubled the amount of paint each woman handled. But given the financial hardships, the workers would paint any way they could. Those lucky enough to have a job were fiercely loyal to the firm. There was a feeling, in fact, that the whole town needed to support such a generous employer. There were very few of them around in these difficult times.

Though most of the original girls had been laid off or quit, their friendships had not faded. Catherine's close neighbors included Marie Rossiter and Charlotte Purcell, and the three women often spent time together. When they met, they talked. They talked of Catherine's tender jaw. Of Charlotte's achy elbow. Of Marie's sore legs. Marie and Charlotte had also gone to various doctors. The women soon realized they'd all had the same response.

Just like in Orange, mysterious illnesses were plaguing the radium girls of Ottawa. But there was no Dr. Martland here solving the medical mystery. The town's physicians seemed to think it a coincidence that the women had all been dial-painters. The conditions the girls were experiencing were completely unknown in this town.

Although...there *had* been that visit from the national investigator Swen Kjaer. He visited the local dentists and doctors—not once but twice. He told them what he was looking for and described the telltale signs of radium poisoning. Yet the doctors do not seem to have connected the dots. Nor did they notify the Bureau of Labor Statistics of these curious cases, as they once promised to do.

An oversight? Or was it as some of the dial-painters' relatives thought: a conspiracy to protect the company? "They were all bought off," claimed one.

"It was confusing," remembered Catherine's niece. "I only remember that no one seemed to know what was wrong. But we knew *something* was wrong. Really wrong."

37.

"VERY SUSPICIOUS"

n the end, the women were forced to look outside their town for help. Chicago, the nearest city, was eighty-five miles away, but Tom Donohue, Catherine's husband, traveled eighty-five miles there and eighty-five miles back. He brought a city doctor back with him: Charles Loffler. A blood specialist, Loffler was kindly looking with ears that stuck out. Yet even with his expertise, he still took months to confirm a formal diagnosis.

Come April 10, 1934, Charlotte Purcell could wait no longer. Over the past few months, a lump had been steadily growing in the crook of her left elbow. It was now the size of a golf ball. Frightened, she went to the Cook County Hospital. Its doctors told her that she had only one option. If she wanted to live, they would have to amputate her arm.

Charlotte was twenty-eight years old. What choice did she have? She chose life.

Charlotte
Purcell after
her operation.

They cut it off at the shoulder. "There was no way," a relative later said, "that they could use a prosthetic arm or a hook because they had nothing to attach it to." It was gone. Her limb, which had always been there—scratching her nose, carrying shopping, holding a watch dial—was gone.

Her doctors were mystified by the arm itself, with its huge sarcoma. After the operation, they preserved it in chemicals. They were fascinated by it because it was so odd.

A couple of weeks after Charlotte's amputation, a letter arrived for the Donohues at 520 East Superior Street. It looked innocent enough. But the news it held was anything but. Having assessed the results of all his tests, Loffler could finally confirm it: Catherine Donohue was suffering from radium poisoning.

"Tom was devastated," remembered his niece. "Just absolutely devastated. I don't know how the man functioned."

"After that," Tom himself said, "I took care of [Tommy] when [Catherine] could not do so."

Catherine herself never spoke publicly about how she

felt. She probably prayed, as did many of her friends. "I firmly believe," wrote one of her former colleagues, "that prayers is all that brought me through."

Yet just days after Catherine and Tom received that letter from Chicago, Catherine's disease took even the comfort of prayer away from her. On Wednesday, April 25, 1934, she hobbled the short distance to St. Columba. But she found herself unable to kneel in church. Her hips had become so locked that she could no longer bend her legs to pray. It was extremely distressing for Catherine, who was very religious.

Dr. Loffler tried to communicate with Radium Dial about his discoveries. He telephoned company vice president Fordyce. "I told him from the cases I had seen, I thought it would be wise to investigate all the [other] cases," he said.

But Loffler's discoveries were not new to Fordyce. After all, the firm knew the results of the radioactivity tests that the Radium Dial workers had taken back in 1928. The results showed that of the sixty-seven girls tested that day, thirty-four were suspiciously or positively radioactive. Thirty-four women: *more than half the workforce.*

The company said in its press statement at the time, "Nothing even approaching symptoms [of radium poisoning] has ever been found." That declaration was not some mistake, caused by confusion. The data was clear. Most of the employees were radioactive—a telltale sign of radium poisoning. But though the women's breath betrayed the truth, the company had lied.

Radium Dial still had the women's names on its secret list of results. Each was numbered according to how radioactive she was. Ranked at number one for positivity: Margaret Looney and Marie Rossiter. Catherine's result was "very suspicious."

For almost six years, Radium Dial had known the women were radioactive. Yet it had covered it up, keeping the results from the women, because it did not want its business to suffer.

It meant that when Loffler's call came in, Fordyce was ready. He refused to do anything.

Yet Catherine, Charlotte, and the other girls were determined to make the company pay. In many ways, they had no choice but to sue. By that time, Catherine had spent thousands of dollars on medical bills. She and Tom were broke. To the women's relief, they managed to hire a Chicago lawyer, Jay Cook, who agreed to represent them pretty much for free.

Though the women never met him, he gave advice from the city. Cook told them they must inform Radium Dial of their diagnosis immediately. Under Illinois law, the company was then meant to provide medical care and compensation, since the women had been injured at work.

As instructed, Charlotte and Catherine telephoned and

wrote to the company. But by May 8, there had been no reply. So on the advice of Cook, the women took matters into their own hands. They headed back to Radium Dial to confront their old manager, Mr. Reed.

———— ≋ ————

It was a journey Catherine had undertaken so many times before. Turn right out of the house, walk straight to Columbus Street, turn left, and walk one block to Radium Dial. But it had never been a journey like this before. She felt nervous but knew she had to stand up for herself—and for all the other girls. They had agreed that she and Charlotte would be their spokeswomen.

Charlotte walked slowly by her side, keeping pace with Catherine's limp. It felt so strange walking now, Charlotte thought. She had never realized before how much you used your arms when you walked. Now, there was nothing but air by her left side.

Charlotte was a woman who didn't dwell on herself. "She never felt sorry for herself, *ever*," said a relative. Though she had said after her amputation, "I can't do housework," already she was finding ways to cope. She had managed to open and close her baby's diaper pins with her mouth. She'd discovered that she could wash up the frying pan if she set its handle under her chin. Her husband, Al, did everything else.

But he wasn't here now. It was just the two of them: Catherine and Charlotte. The women walked along, so different from how they'd been when they'd first entered the studio in 1922. Catherine hobbled up the six front steps and tried to straighten up as much as she could. They made their way inside and found Mr. Reed.

"I have received a letter from my doctor, who has been treating me for weeks," Catherine said formally to him. She had a sophisticated voice, and her words were sure. "He has come to the definite conclusion that my blood shows radioactive substance." She gestured at Charlotte to include her. "We have radium poisoning."

There it was: fact. Hard to say out loud, but fact. She paused to see if there was a reaction. But there was nothing from the man who had been her manager for nine years.

In spite of Mr. Reed's silence, Catherine went on, "[My lawyers] have advised me to ask the company for compensation and medical care. We have legal advice that we are entitled to compensation."

Mr. Reed looked over his former employees. Catherine had barely been able to get into the studio. Charlotte no longer had an arm.

"I don't think," he said slowly, "there is anything wrong with you."

The women were stunned.

"There is nothing to it at all," he said again.

"He refused," Catherine remembered angrily, "to consider our request for compensation."

She notified him about the condition of the other women, too, but he didn't back down. He didn't back down even when, two days later, another Ottawa dial-painter died.

After her death, the cover-up continued. Illinois death certificates include the question "Was disease in any way related to occupation of deceased?" But when the attending doctor completed the paperwork, he answered no.

The local doctors were not convinced there was a connection. Yet the women were absolutely sure of it. And they were ready to fight for that truth. So in the summer of 1934, a large group of them—including Catherine, Charlotte, Marie, and Inez Vallat—filed suit against Radium Dial for $50,000 ($884,391) each.

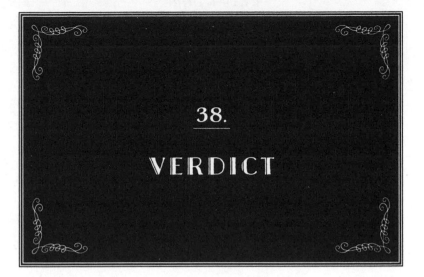

38.

VERDICT

As in New Jersey, the women's lawsuit acted like a stone in a lake, sending ripple effects all across the radium firm. In October 1934, Joseph Kelly, the president of Radium Dial, was forced out of his company.

But Kelly was not finished with Ottawa just yet. He soon opened a new dial-painting firm, Luminous Processes. And his managers persuaded many of the Radium Dial women to join.

It seems the workers weren't told it would be run by Joseph Kelly and Rufus Fordyce, who had been in charge of Radium Dial during the radium-poisoning scandal. They *were* told something extraordinary though. They were informed "that earlier dial-painters had died because they put brushes in their mouths, and since brush-licking was no longer permitted, exposure to radium would not be harmful." It was an admission of guilt, but the original dial-painters never got to hear of it.

The new studio opened just a few blocks over from Radium Dial in a two-story redbrick warehouse. Most of the dial-painters moved across, believing the new operation to be safe. They applied the paint using handheld sponges, wooden spatulas, and their fingers. They wore thin cotton smocks to give them some protection from the glowing dust.

Not every worker went, however. Mr. Reed stayed on as superintendent of the old firm. He remained loyal to the company he had served for many years.

As 1935 began, Jay Cook filed two separate claims for the women: one in the normal law courts and a second with the Illinois Industrial Commission (IIC). The lead case, Cook decided, would be that of Inez Vallat. "She was a living corpse," Catherine said sadly of her former desk mate, "hobbling around like an old woman."

Jay Cook told the dial-painters they stood a good chance of winning. Illinois law was progressive, and a pioneering act passed in 1911 had long commanded companies to protect their employees. But as the case got going, almost immediately the women ran into trouble. Radium Dial was being represented by a team of top lawyers. They found several legal loopholes, through which they now twisted the case. There was the loophole that had plagued Grace Fryer and her friends: the statute of limitations. Inez had filed suit years after she left Radium Dial, and her disability did not occur while she was employed. There was the fact that radium was a poison. Injuries caused by poison were *not* covered by the Occupational Diseases Act. And there was the law itself. Radium Dial claimed that its outdated wording was too vague for companies to know what they needed to do to protect their workers and was therefore invalid.

"When Attorney Cook filed his test case," the *Chicago Daily Times* later wrote, "Radium Dial did not even bother to deny the women's charges. In effect, the company's reply was, 'Even if it is true, what of it?'"

On April 17, 1935, a ruling was given. And the women lost, on a legal technicality. The judge ruled that the law that should have protected them was not written clearly enough. They could not believe it, yet they fought on. Cook, at his own expense, took the battle all the way to the Supreme Court, but to no avail.

It was shocking. The *Chicago Daily Times* called it "an almost unbelievable miscarriage of justice." But there was nothing the women could do. They'd had their day in court, and the law itself had been found inadequate.

Cook, reluctantly, had to drop their case, even though the girls still had a claim filed with the IIC and even though politicians now vowed to rewrite the lousy law. "I hated to have to [drop their case], but I simply couldn't afford to keep on," Cook later said. "If I had the money, I'd fight their case free. It's one of those things that should be fought through to a finish. I hope they get another lawyer."

But finding another lawyer was easier said than done. There were forty-one attorneys listed in the Ottawa town directory, but not one would help them. Nor was it only the local lawyers and doctors who were against the women's fight for justice. Their neighbors were too. With the United States in the middle of the Great Depression, the local community took the side of the firm that could give them work and wages. The women found they were disbelieved, ignored, and even shunned.

Meanwhile, the mortgage on the Donohues' house crept up to $1,500 ($25,000). "There are medicines that ease the pain," Catherine said. On these drugs, she and Tom were spending hundreds of dollars.

Nor had they given up looking for a cure. Catherine found herself trying various Chicago hospitals and dentists, each appointment bringing yet another bill to pay. Even though she frequently fainted these days, she pushed herself to get to the meetings and submitted to whatever tests the doctors asked her to complete. Catherine had more reason than ever to want to live. In November 1934, she had given birth to a baby daughter, Mary Jane. But distressingly, none of the doctors she consulted

Catherine with her son Tommy (middle) and daughter Mary Jane (right), who holds a doll.

could halt the destruction of Catherine's teeth and gums.

The women struggled on, each of them fighting a personal battle to survive. At the end of the year, word of another legal judgment reached them. It didn't necessarily affect their case, but it was still of considerable interest.

On December 17, 1935, the ruling finally came back on the Irene La Porte case in New Jersey. Her husband, Vincent, had been fighting it on her behalf for more than four years. *This* was the case USRC had chosen to see through to judgment.

The company, by this point, did not deny the cause of death. It simply cited the statute of limitations as the reason why it should not have to pay.

Several dial-painters testified at the trial. Many had their own lawsuits pending. All pinned their hopes on Irene winning her case, for if she did, the verdict would apply to them too. Everyone gathered to hear the judgment.

The judge began by expressing his sympathy for the girls. No one could hear their story and not be moved. He said frankly that now the world knew radium was dangerous, the lip-pointing technique used by USRC would be considered "not...merely [careless] but criminal."

But there was a "but." A big but. The judge continued: "This case *must* be decided on the facts as they existed in the light of the knowledge of 1917." Then he concluded bluntly, "The [case] must be dismissed."

USRC had chosen well. Seven years on from Grace Fryer's case, the company had the answer it was looking for: not guilty.

Justice had been denied to Irene La Porte, but not just to her. It had been denied to all those New Jersey dial-painters with lawsuits still pending. And to all those families who were battling for loved ones who had died. And there was another group, too, who had not seen justice: all those New Jersey women who had not yet found a worrying lump on their hip or their leg or their arm but who would in the future.

It had been, the USRC executives reflected, a very good day indeed.

39.

FIGHTING BACK

You fight and you fall and you get up and fight some more. But there will always come a day when you cannot fight another minute more.

On February 25, 1936, Inez Vallat died. She was twenty-nine. After eight years of agony, she finally died from a sarcoma in her neck.

The Ottawa doctors completed her death certificate. *Was death in any way related to occupation of deceased?*

No.

Inez's death, coming on top of the lawsuit defeat, was a blow that left the Ottawa women reeling. Many of the original girls were too ill to attend her funeral, no matter how much they wanted to say goodbye. Catherine Donohue, these days, seldom even left the house. She and Tom didn't want to face what was happening. "We never talk about it," confessed Tom. "We just go along as if we were all going to be together forever. That's the only way."

Catherine added, "As long as we're together, it doesn't seem so bad. We just pretend I'm the way I was when Tom married me." But every day, the evidence stacked up that she was not the same at all. The Donohues could play all the games of make-believe they liked. Cold, hard facts could not be wished away with magic. Inez's death was proof of that.

The girls couldn't even feel hopeful when the governor signed the new Illinois Occupational Diseases Act, which now *included* poisoning. The new bill was the direct result of the women's case. It would protect thousands of workers. But it would not become law until October 1936. Given how quickly the women were dying, they hadn't much hope they would be alive to see the day.

The same month the new law was signed, however, the girls were approached by a journalist. She lifted their sagging spirits somewhat. Her name was Mary Doty, and she was a leading reporter with the *Chicago Daily Times*. She gave the women a voice in a series of articles that ran in March 1936. "We'll always be grateful to the *Times*," the dial-painters would later say, "for helping us when everything was so black."

Doty knew just how to write to grab attention for the girls' cause: "They shoot to kill when it comes to cattle thieves in Illinois...but womenfolk come cheap." And she painted a picture of the women's conditions that

Catherine Wolfe Donohue and her family in 1936.

would haunt her readers: "Some [girls] creep along, unable to move beyond a snail's pace; another with an empty coat sleeve or a mutilated nose, withered hands, a shrunken jaw."

The girls posed for photographs, many with their children. Catherine's daughter, Mary Jane, looked absolutely tiny. At a year old, Mary Jane weighed only ten pounds and had match-thin arms and legs. "Her parents," wrote Doty, "hope against hope her mother's illness will not leave its permanent mark on her."

Catherine herself said to the press, "I am in constant pain. I cannot walk a block, but somehow I must carry on." When the journalist asked about her friend Inez, Catherine cried.

Charlotte Purcell was pictured with her daughter. She was gradually coping with having only one arm. In time, she would relearn how to make beds, peel potatoes, and even hang out washing, with the clothespins stuffed into her mouth. As she told reporters, though, she was haunted by the thought that the sacrifice of her arm had still not been enough. The radium ran right through her body, and she didn't know where it might strike next.

The women found the publicity got them motivated again. A few months later, Charlotte, Catherine, and Marie got a new attorney, Jerome Rosenthal, for their case before the IIC. They also approached the government for help. Their target was Frances Perkins, the secretary of labor, who was the first woman ever to serve in a presidential cabinet. It was Tom Donohue who contacted her, writing letters to the secretary and telephoning her. Whatever this quiet man said clearly made an impact. No less than three federal departments began investigating.

The case was snowballing, and Tom dug deep for the most important act of all. His wife had told him about the company tests. He judged that getting hold of the original data would provide powerful evidence in court, since it was clear Radium Dial had lied about the results. On May 20, 1936, he decided to ask Mr. Reed outright for his wife's results. He felt they should have been given to the women anyway or at least to him as Catherine's husband. He was only asking for what was rightfully theirs. "This day," Tom said, "I wanted to find out the name of them doctors, who was supposed to examine them women that was working there, that didn't give them a report."

Reed might have seen him coming. At any rate, the two met each other not in the studio but on the streets of Ottawa.

Tom started out calmly enough. "Why wasn't the report given to me?" he asked.

Reed, taken aback by Tom's direct question, did as he had always done and tried to ignore the situation. He brushed by him.

"I only have another question to ask you!" shouted Tom at the superintendent's retreating back. He ran to catch up with him. "I only want to help the women!"

Mr. Reed had had enough. Perhaps there was a guilt eating away at him that led to what happened next. "He started to swing at me," Tom remembered with some astonishment.

Tom, though small, had what his family called an "Irish temper." "I don't think anybody in our family," one of his relatives later said, "would go out of their way to cause a confrontation, but they wouldn't let one go if it came to them. I'm sure he'd have been angry. I'm surprised he stayed as level-headed as he did."

Mr. Reed kept hitting him. This was the man who had overseen his wife's slow murder. The same man who had then fired her when the poison's effects started to show. Tom dropped all pretense of civilized conversation. "I swang at him," he remembered with some satisfaction.

The two men brawled in the street. Tom found himself landing blows for Catherine, for Charlotte's lost arm, and for Ella, Inez, and Peg. Reed floundered under the attack, and the police were called. Even though Mr. Reed had started it, the respected superintendent of Radium Dial had Tom Donohue arrested. He brought charges of assault, battery, and disorderly conduct.

Tom was now in the hands of State Attorney Elmer Mohn, facing two criminal charges.

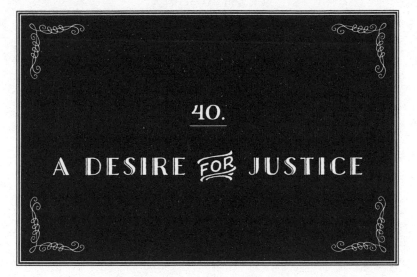

40.

A DESIRE FOR JUSTICE

ssault, battery, disorderly conduct...and insanity. The "controlling interests" in the affair now even tried to bring a charge of insanity against Tom. It was a move Tom's relatives said was "typical of a company with its back against the wall." "They know that they're gonna go down," said his niece. "They'll do anything. They'll try anything."

Fortunately for Tom, the police case against him was not reported to progress further than a handful of initial hearings, perhaps because there was no truth to the trumped-up charges.

Like all cowards with their backs against the wall, the company now chose to turn and run. In December 1936, Radium Dial abruptly closed its doors and left town. Mr. Reed followed the company out in the new year.

Radium Dial had been run out of business by Joseph Kelly's new firm, Luminous Processes. After more than fourteen years of the radium company operating in the old high school, the rooms fell silent. No chatter from the girls, no laughter from the darkroom. Just empty rooms, haunted by all that had gone on.

With Radium Dial vanquished, Joseph Kelly had a monopoly on radium dials in the little town of Ottawa. It may have been the Great Depression, but things were turning out rather well for the company president.

The same could not be said for the husbands of the former dial-painters. They had just about managed to cling to work through the Depression so far. But in 1937, their luck ran out. Workers were laid off from the local glass factory, and Tom Donohue and Al Purcell were among them.

For the Purcells, who had three children to feed, it became almost impossible to cope. Charlotte ended up serving them mustard sandwiches. "You took whatever you could get," remembered Tom's niece. "It was a very tough time."

Eventually, Charlotte and her family moved to Chicago. But even in the city, it was challenging. Charlotte's son recalled, "We used to go to a bakery and ask for day-old [bread]. We heated the apartment with a coal stove, and we used to walk around the [train] tracks in Chicago and pick up coal."

It was hard—but it was harder still back in rural Illinois.

With the house already mortgaged to the hilt, Tom Donohue was running out of ideas. "Tom was nearly bankrupt," remembered a brother-in-law. "Catherine was full of radium and dying by inches. She suffered agonies, and [he spent everything] buying medicines to try to relieve Catherine." The family now had debts of some $2,500 ($41,148). They needed help from the government just to have food to eat.

"They were on relief for a while," confided their niece. "[They felt] very ashamed. Not wanting people to know about it."

Yet they weren't the only ones needing help. Lines of desperate people formed outside the soup kitchens in Ottawa. Everyone was living hand to mouth. The Donohues had almost no thought of a lawsuit anymore. This was a battle for survival. By the spring of 1937, their lawyer, Rosenthal, had dropped the case anyway. The women were due to have a hearing before the IIC later that year, but as things stood, they had no attorney to represent them.

Time passed. On March 28, 1937, Catherine Donohue and her family marked Easter Sunday, one of the most important dates in the Catholic calendar. As a gift, someone gave a cuddly toy bunny to Mary Jane and Tommy, who were then aged two and almost four. Tommy liked to paint, just as his mother once had. He had a watercolor set that he played with often.

Catherine took her communion gratefully from the visiting

priest. She received it at home now, since she was unable to get to church. Easter Sunday was all about Christ being reborn: salvation, hope, the repairing of a broken body. It was all the more horrible, then, that this was the moment Catherine's body fell further apart. "Part of her jawbone," a friend recalled, "broke through the flesh and [came] out into her mouth."

"It was so horrible," remembered her niece. "[It] just dropped out. I mean it was just... You thought, Oh dear God. Can't even eat! Just so sad."

Tom Donohue was forced to watch his wife literally disintegrate before his eyes. It was horrifying. Yet on this celebration of renewal and rebirth, Tom found himself renewing one thing at least. His desire for justice. And he knew just who Catherine needed to help her now.

Her friends.

Tom chose wisely the friend he reached out to. Just down the road from the Donohue home, Marie Rossiter took a call from Tom. He asked her to call the former Radium Dial girls and find out if any of them might want to hire a lawyer.

Marie was someone who would always take the bull by the horn. If someone needed her help, she would give it willingly. "She was an organizer all right," said her relatives.

True to form, Marie launched straight into action, calling all the women. Charlotte Purcell was immediately on board, together with a handful of others.

That small band of girls now shot for the moon, using media publicity to appeal for a lawyer—*any* lawyer—to take their case. "*Radium Death on Rampage!*" cried the front page of the *Chicago Daily Times* on July 7, 1937. "*Walking Ghosts Jilted by Justice!*" The paper reported that the women had no lawyer for their upcoming hearing before the IIC. It was scheduled for July 23, sixteen days away. The hearing was "their last stand—their last hope of collecting damages." "Without a lawyer," the paper wrote, "the women fear legal trickery. Indeed, so hopeless is their outlook that many of them may stay away."

Catherine Donohue spoke up. "That's what the company's lawyers would like, I suppose," she said archly, "for all of us to stay away."

Front page of the *Chicago Daily Times* on July 7, 1937.

"The Radium Dial Company," the piece went on, "has closed its plant in Ottawa [and] 'skipped out from under,' leaving only a $10,000 [$164,595] bond posted with the Industrial Commission." It seemed that $10,000 was the sole pot of money available to the girls for compensation and medical care.

Radium Dial had fled to New York. Its new president, William Ganley, soon came out fighting. He announced, "I can't recall a single actual victim of this so-called 'radium' poisoning in our Ottawa plant." With these words, he continued the cover-up. With these words, he banished the memories of Ella and Peg and all the other dead girls who'd been killed by their work.

Radium Dial was not going down without a fight. That much was clear. The firm had won this case before in the courts when they had triumphed over Inez Vallat. They seemed supremely confident they would win again.

The company president's attitude underlined to the women just how much they needed an attorney. Yet as the clock counted down to the all-important hearing, no lawyer came forward. They were on their own. So despite their crippling illnesses, the girls decided it was time for them to go on a quest. It was time to take a trip to the big city.

41.

LEGAL CHAMPION

hicago: a land of steel and stone and glass, where a forest of skyscrapers stretched above the antlike actions of its citizens below. As the five women made their way through the city streets, Chicago's urban architecture dominated their view.

It was two days before the hearing. The women headed to North LaSalle Street, right in the heart of the theater district. Given the heat of the July day, they were glad when they reached the address they sought: number 134. So this was the Metropolitan Building...

Catherine Donohue had just about managed the journey. This was one outing she would never have missed. Catherine had been appointed chairman of the girls' new group, and it was essential she led this quest to find a lawyer.

She was wearing a stylish black dress with white polka dots. That morning, she'd slipped it on with nervousness—and some concern. That lump on her hip, she'd thought anxiously as the fabric slid over her increasingly thin body, was definitely a little bit bigger than before.

With her were four other dial-painters, including Marie. They had all dressed fashionably, many wearing tailored jackets. Hats straightened and dresses smoothed, the five women walked fearlessly into the lobby. Then they rode the elevator up to the office they required.

They immediately made eye contact with the dark-haired man standing behind the desk. He wore a three-piece tweed suit and glasses atop his large nose. He was somewhat full-figured, and he had kind eyes.

"Ladies," he probably announced, stretching a welcoming hand across the desk to greet them, "I'm Leonard Grossman."

Grossman was a lawyer who had always fought for the underdog. Forty-six years old, he was larger-than-life and charismatic, with a passion for helping those in need. That passion was such that he sometimes worked for free or for unusual objects such as shoes. Money wasn't what drove Grossman: his principles were his fuel.

When the dial-painters walked into his office, it was a perfect meeting of minds.

"We were at our wits' end when he came to our rescue," remembered Catherine Donohue. "He had no thought of money. He just wants to help us girls, to help humanity."

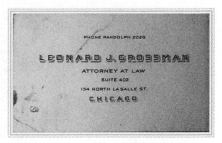

Leonard Grossman's business card.

As for Grossman, he declared to his new clients, "My heart is for you; I am happy to be in this fight for you."

At last, the women had a legal champion. And they'd found him not a moment too soon. In two days' time, Grossman and the girls had a hearing to attend before the IIC.

———— ≋ ————

Step by step, inch by inch, Catherine and the other girls made their slow way to the yellow-stoned LaSalle County courthouse on Friday, July 23. It was just four blocks south of St. Columba in Ottawa, so they did not have far to go. When they arrived, they were grateful to see that their story was being covered by the press.

It was a boost that Catherine in particular needed. In the short time since she'd been in Grossman's office in Chicago, another piece of her jawbone had come out into her mouth. Not knowing what to do with it, she had put it in a small paper pillbox.

Leonard Grossman in his Chicago office,
July 21, 1937, with Ottawa dial-painters,
including Marie Rossiter (first from left) and
Catherine Donohue (fourth from left).

The women's spirits were lifted further as they entered the courtroom and saw Grossman there, ready to do battle for them. They hoped that this time, they at least stood a fighting chance. Some of the women sat at the counsel table with Grossman as he prepared to open their case. Together, they surveyed the opposition.

Representing Radium Dial were the very same legal firms who had fought—and won—the Inez Vallat case two years earlier. The leading lawyer was Arthur Magid, a young-looking man with thick, dark hair and glasses. Another was Walter Bachrach.

Grossman's first job was to ask for a postponement to give him time to get to grips with the case. Magid readily agreed. The firm was in no rush for the trial to begin. The longer the legal process could be delayed, the weaker the women would be.

There was not much more to that first hearing, although Bachrach did reveal what the company's defense would be. He said he would claim "the paint was not poisonous and that none of the women actually were suffering from radium poisoning."

Not poisonous. Even from the little Grossman knew of the case, he realized that this position was the *opposite* of the arguments the same lawyers had used in the Vallat lawsuit. Then, the company had said radium *was* a poison, because poison was not covered by the law, and the court had to find against the girls. Now that the law had been rewritten to *include* poisons, the company had switched its position.

It was just the sort of slippery injustice that Grossman had fought against before. Inspired, he rose to the occasion. He stood center stage in the courthouse and exhibited his skills. Seeing him shine, many of the girls wept to realize that such an accomplished attorney was finally on their side.

"We should have laws," Grossman started in his somber, melodious voice, "that will do away with things that rack, ruin, and destroy bodies."

He turned and scanned his eyes across the crippled women sitting at the desk. He gestured at them with feeling.

"We do not need to have martyrs such as we have sitting around this table," he said, "and the many dead who worked with these girls." He paused dramatically and then went on. "With the help of God, we *will* fight to a finish!"

42.

A LONG *AND* LONELY FALL

Work began on the case immediately. That same day, straight after the hearing, Grossman and the women met for a conference so he could gather more information. Then he packed up his big brown leather briefcase and headed on back to Chicago. Soon, he was regularly working eighteen-hour days.

Grossman decided that he would lead his case with Catherine Donohue's claim. Catherine didn't necessarily have the most evidence behind her, nor was she the biggest character among the women. It wasn't even that she had the most fire in her belly for the fight. It was simply believed that she was the woman who would be next to die. "She hasn't long to live," said a friend quietly. "We want her to have her day in court."

While Grossman worked away in Chicago, it seemed a long and lonely fall to Catherine. That hard lump on her hip was growing undeniably bigger. Catherine became more and more ill. Nevertheless, she refused to give up hope. She told herself she just needed to hang in there. She still believed a cure would come.

Catherine was now unable to manage the stairs, so Tom brought her wrought-iron bed downstairs to the front room. He slept on a couch at the foot of it. He made Catherine's new sickroom as comfortable as he possibly could. Her crutches were set against the wall, ready for when she was helped to the bathroom. A makeshift lamp sat at the head of the bed, alongside a radio. Tom hung a large wooden crucifix above the bed, while the cuddly rabbit given to the children at Easter kept her company on the bedside table.

The room had two windows in the front and a window to the west. "It had good light," recalled Catherine's niece Mary, "but they kept the shades drawn; I suppose that was what she wanted." It made for a rather dim setting, but then Catherine had a light of her own.

"My body," she revealed numbly, "gives off a faint luminous glow when surrounded by darkness."

"You could see every bone in her body," remembered her nephew James.

The radium in her bones shone bright.

It seemed to eclipse everything, even Catherine herself. When the girls had played their games in the darkroom at work, they themselves had vanished so that all you could see was the radium. When people looked at Catherine these days, the same thing happened. They didn't see *her*. They saw only the poisoning that had taken over her body.

"People are afraid to talk to me now," Catherine confessed. "Sometimes it makes me terribly lonesome—they act as though I'm already a corpse. It's hard to have people around and still to be alone."

As the year drew toward its end, Catherine's isolation became even more intense. She spent her days and nights lying down inside and could only go out with Tom's help. "He used to carry her around in his arms," recalled James.

"I suffer so much pain," Catherine wrote to a friend, and she may not simply have meant her aching hip and jaw, "that at times I feel my life was pretty hard to bear."

Her isolation meant she had no idea what was happening in the court case. Grossman had been too busy to write. "This is the first of the Radium Dial cases," he later said, "and I can leave no stone unturned in reaching for all the light and truth and all the facts of record." He did, however, send the girls a festive card "with every good wish for a Happy Holiday Season."

And Catherine took his advice to make that Christmas a happy one. She and Tom and Tommy and Mary Jane might be poor, and Catherine might be sick, but they were together at Christmas. That was something for which she was simply very, very grateful.

———— ≋ ————

The new year, 1938, was all about preparing for the trial. The court date was set for February 10—six days after Catherine's thirty-fifth birthday. On February 5, Catherine and Tom struggled to make what was now an extremely difficult journey to Chicago. Yet they had to persevere. Catherine needed to undergo medical examinations by three physicians: Dr. Loffler, Dr. Dalitsch (a dentist), and Dr. Weiner, who took new X-rays of Catherine's bones. This trio of doctors had agreed to testify in court, and they would base their testimony on these exams.

They were shocked as Catherine staggered into their offices on that Saturday morning. She was pale and thin—weighing seventy-one pounds—and could only walk with the help of two people. Dalitsch found the destruction of Catherine's mouth went "right through the body of the lower jawbones" so that the bones themselves were fragmented. Her infected mouth was also full of smelly pus. Meanwhile, her white blood cell count was only a few hundred. Normal levels are about eight thousand. She was, Loffler thought, "near death from exhaustion caused by the lack of these [cells]."

Yet it was her X-rays that troubled the doctors most. That hard tumor on her hipbone was now the size of a grapefruit.

The doctors didn't share their findings with the Donohues. Catherine was a sick woman—she needed to get home to bed. But there was another reason they kept quiet too. They feared that if Catherine knew about her dire condition it would speed up her decline. Far better that she stayed hopeful and positive. That, the doctors believed, would help her fight this disease far more than knowing the facts.

So, unknowing, Catherine and Tom made the difficult journey back to Ottawa. Tom carried his wife into their front room and laid her gently on the bed. She needed to rest. In five days' time, she would have her day in court. Catherine Wolfe Donohue was holding Radium Dial to account for what it had done to her and her friends, and she was determined, no matter what, to make a difference.

43.

HER DAY IN COURT

Thursday, February 10, 1938, dawned as a cool and cloudy day. In the front room of their house on East Superior Street, Tom Donohue helped his wife to dress. He helped her slide on her knee-high nude stockings and lace her flat black shoes. Catherine had picked out her best outfit. Once again, the black dress with white polka dots slipped over her head. She slowly fastened its black belt around her shrunken waist. The dress hung so much more loosely than it had in July when she'd first met Grossman. But she wasn't going to think about that today.

Tom prepared to carry Catherine to court. Yet he could not do it alone; a friend helped. Catherine was seated on a wooden chair as they lifted her. Her skin bruised so easily and her bones were now so fragile that it was difficult for Tom to carry her in his arms, next to his chest. The chair was a safer choice. They carried her all the way to the courtroom and then went up to the fourth floor. Grossman greeted them, coming to assist.

As they helped her into one of the courtroom's chairs, Catherine gazed around at the unremarkable room. As it was a hearing before the IIC, it looked more like a meeting room than a court. It was, in fact, the office of the county auditor. It had a diamond-patterned tiled floor and was dominated by a large wooden table with sturdy legs. Chairs were set around it for the key players and then ranged in semicircles beyond that for spectators.

Catherine's friends were already there, including Marie. But the women weren't the only ones present. Just as the New Jersey girls' case had done a decade before, the women's suffering had captured the imagination of the nation. Reporters and photographers from across the country thronged the room.

Although the media had turned out for the trial, it seemed the Radium Dial executives had not. Neither had all its legal team. Only Arthur Magid was present, seated next to the arbitrator (judge) at the big table. There was no Walter Bachrach, no Mr. Reed, no President Ganley. No one but Magid to represent the firm.

Catherine looked closely at the judge. This was the man who would decide her fate. George B. Marvel was sixty-seven years old. He was a round-faced gentleman with white hair and glasses, which he wore positioned toward the end of his small nose. He'd been a lawyer and a bank president prior to joining the IIC. Catherine wondered what he would make of her case.

As she took in her surroundings, waiting for the trial to begin at 9:00 a.m., the press took in the sight of her. "Mrs. Donohue," the *Chicago Herald-Examiner* later wrote, "could hardly stand alone. Her arms were no larger than a child's and her face was drawn and pinched. Her dark eyes burned feverishly behind rimless glasses." The *Chicago Daily Times*, somewhat unkindly, called her a "toothpick woman" because she was so extremely thin.

Catherine sat at the main table, with Tom seated just behind her. She carefully pulled off her big fur coat and placed it neatly on her lap. But she kept her hat on, perhaps because she seemed to be cold all the time these days, frozen by the lack of fat on her body and by her failing heart. Feeling the pus starting to ooze again in her mouth, she pulled out a patterned handkerchief and kept it by her. She seemed almost constantly to have to hold it to her mouth.

Grossman checked with her to see if she was ready, and

she nodded briskly. The lawyer was dressed in his usual three-piece tweed suit, his eyes bright with anticipation. For more than half a year, he had worked tirelessly on the women's case. He knew both he and Catherine were well prepared.

"Human lives," Grossman said in his opening state-ment on the case, "were saved among our country's army of defense, because Catherine Donohue painted luminous dials on instruments for our forces. To make life safe, she and her coworkers [are] among the living dead. They have sacrificed their own lives. Truly an unsung heroine of our country, our state and country owe her a debt."

Right away, it was that unsung heroine's turn to speak. Seated at the central table, with Grossman by her side and Magid and Marvel opposite her, Catherine was the first to give evidence. She wanted desperately to appear strong. But her voice, speaking through her battered mouth, betrayed her. The papers commented on her "weak and muffled voice," which was "faltering." Her friends sitting right behind her could barely even hear her speak.

But speak she did, describing her work, the way the powder covered the girls all over and made them glow, the practice of lip-pointing. "That's the way this terrible poison got into our systems," she cried. "We never even knew it was harmful."

Grossman gave her an encouraging smile. She was doing

brilliantly. While Catherine took a quick drink of water, her lawyer now introduced into evidence the deceitful full-page ad that Radium Dial had printed in the local paper.

"Objection," Magid was reported to say, rising, but George Marvel allowed it.

"After those New Jersey people died from radium poisoning in 1928," Catherine continued, "we began to get alarmed. But shortly after that Mr. Reed called our attention to [this] advertisement. He said we did not have to worry."

Marvel nodded slowly, taking notes and reviewing every word of the notice. Catherine glanced over her shoulder at her friends, who sat in a row behind her, listening intently. "After Miss Marie Rossiter and I had been examined the first time," she continued, nodding at Marie before turning back to face the judge, "we wanted to know why we didn't get our reports. Mr. Reed said to us, 'My dear girls, if we ever give a medical report to you, there will be a riot in this place.' Neither of us then realized what he meant."

But they did now. As Catherine described the encounter in court, Marie paled. "Oh!" she cried aloud, the implication of her manager's words sinking in.

"That is the Mr. Reed," Catherine added pointedly to the judge, "who is still with the company in New York."

The press had found him there, overseeing the

dial-painters. He had "assumed responsibility for the opera-tion," which could well have been a promotion. The company, it seemed, rewarded loyalty from its employees.

Just at that moment, there was a disturbance. The chief security examiner of the commission came rushing into the room. He brought with him documents that Grossman had requested from the company. The girls' lawyer quickly flicked through the files. He could see at once that the women's test results from 1925 and 1928 were not included, as he had asked.

There were, however, some interesting letters. They revealed that Radium Dial had no insurance. Though they had tried to get it, no insurance firm was willing to cover them. After the New Jersey cases, it was clear that lip-pointing was unsafe. No insurance firm wanted to take that risk.

Nevertheless, Joseph Kelly had continued operations. On October 30, 1930, the IIC gave notice to Radium Dial that it had not complied with the Workmen's Compensation Act, which required insurance. In response, Radium Dial was forced to pay to the commission the $10,000 bond that Catherine and her friends were now hoping to share between them. The bond was intended to act as a kind of thin safety net in case any employees got hurt. But with so many workers injured, it meant the women were suing for a share of an incredibly small fund.

And there was no more money. Grossman had tried to

trace other Radium Dial assets for the girls to claim from but without success. Now that the firm had fled to New York, it seemed the IIC had no power to reach across state lines to access any of the company's cash.

It was financially disappointing, but in many ways, this case was not about the money. It would make a difference— Tom and Catherine in particular would be saved from poverty if they won—but it was more important to the women by far that what had happened to them was recognized. The girls had been told they were liars and cheats and frauds. They had seen the company literally get away with murder. The truth was what they were fighting for.

To the almost continuous objections of Arthur Magid, which were all overruled, Catherine told of her and Charlotte's visit to Mr. Reed after they'd been diagnosed. "Mr. Reed said he didn't think anything was wrong with us," Catherine whispered as angrily as her weakened voice would allow. "He refused to consider our request for compensation."

Marvel nodded, transfixed by Catherine. Her stick-thin body was trembling, but she didn't let it stop her.

"After two years," she said, remembering back to 1924, "I began to feel pains in my left ankle, which spread up to my hip. Fainting spells also occurred. At night the pain became unbearable."

She told of how her pains had spread, all across her body. She told of how she had become a bedridden invalid, unable to eat or care for her own children. And then, as her fingers twisted a scapular medal—a Catholic

Catherine identifying an exhibit for Grossman during the trial, with Tom and the girls behind her.

talisman—she told of no longer being able to kneel to pray. In heartbreaking detail, she described her suffering, and not just her own. Catherine told the court how her two children were also affected.

Shortly before her testimony ended, Catherine reached for her purse and withdrew a small jewelry box. She held it discreetly on her lap. She and Grossman had discussed this beforehand, so he asked her about the evidence she had brought.

Catherine bent her head to the box and lifted it up with her thin hands. The court leaned in, wanting to know what was inside. Slowly, very slowly, she opened it. And then, from within it, she withdrew two fragments of bone.

"These are pieces of my jawbone," she said simply. "They were removed from my jaw."

44.

TOO WEAK FOR TEARS

Catherine's friends, watching her hold up the pieces of herself, shuddered in the courtroom.

Her bones were formally admitted into evidence, along with several of her teeth. After such staggering testimony, Grossman allowed her to rest. She sat quietly in her chair, dabbing her handkerchief to her mouth and watching as Dr. Dalitsch came to the table to give evidence.

He was a clean-featured man, with a strong forehead, thick lips, and dark hair. He gave his expert opinion on the cause of Catherine's disease. "The condition," he said plainly, "is a poison from radioactive substances."

With the killer statement in the bag, Grossman began more quick-fire questioning.

"In your opinion," he asked, "is Catherine Donohue today able to do manual labor?"

The dentist looked across the table at Catherine, who was huddled in her chair, listening to him speak. "No," he said sadly, "she is not."

"Is she able to earn a livelihood?"

"No," said Dalitsch, refocusing on Grossman.

"Have you an opinion as to whether this condition is permanent or temporary?"

"Permanent," he answered swiftly.

Catherine dropped her head: *this is forever.*

"Have you an opinion," Grossman asked, "if this is fatal?"

Dalitsch hesitated and glanced meaningfully toward Catherine, who was only feet from him. Grossman's question hung in the air. Five days before, after the examinations in Chicago, Catherine's three doctors had indeed determined that her condition had reached its "permanent, incurable, and terminal stage." Yet the physicians, who in all kindness sought to spare her, had not told Catherine Donohue.

"In her presence?" Dalitsch now asked uncertainly.

But he had said enough. He had said enough in the way he had paused. Catherine sobbed, slipped down in her chair, and covered her face with her hands. At first, silent tears ran down her cheeks, but then, as though the full weight of what he hadn't said hit her, she screamed in hysteria. She screamed aloud as she thought of leaving Tom and her children, as she thought of leaving this life, as she thought of what was coming in her future. She hadn't known. She had had hope. She had had *faith*. Catherine had truly believed she was not going to die, but Dalitsch's face said otherwise. She could see it in his eyes. So she screamed, and the broken voice that had struggled to speak was now made powerful in her fear and distress. Tom broke down and sobbed at the sound of his wife's cries.

The scream was a watershed. After it, Catherine could not keep herself upright. She collapsed and was caught by a physician nearby. Dr. Weiner leaped to his feet to hold her up, and Tom rushed to Catherine's side as she lay slumped in her chair. While Weiner felt for her pulse, Tom's concern was only for Catherine. He cradled her head with his hand and touched her shoulder to try to bring her back to herself—back to him. Catherine was sobbing hard, her mouth wide open, showing the destruction inside: the gaps where her teeth should have been. But she didn't care who saw. All she could see was Dalitsch's face in her mind. *Fatal. This is fatal.* It was the first time she'd been told.

The press photographers wasted no time in capturing the moment. Tom was suddenly aware of them, suddenly aware that he wanted to get his wife away from all this. He summoned Grossman and Weiner, and together the three men lifted Catherine's chair and carried her from the courtroom.

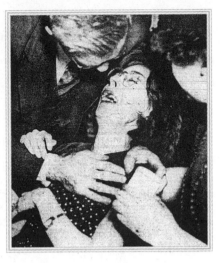

Catherine collapses on February 10, 1938; her husband, Tom Donohue, and others rush to her aid.

"The woman's sobs," a paper commented bleakly, "could be heard from the corridor."

As the judge called an immediate recess, Catherine was carried to the county clerk's office and laid out on a desk. Her fur coat was laid beneath her so she had something soft and pleasant against her skin. Books of birth records propped up her head as a makeshift pillow. Tom gently eased his wife's glasses from her face and stood helplessly by her side.

Catherine was unable to return to the hearing. "She is in total collapse," said an attending doctor. "She will not, cannot, live very much longer."

Tom was not there to hear his words. He had carried Catherine home to East Superior Street. Yet when the papers printed the pictures of Tom and Catherine the next day, they pulled no punches. Above a photograph of the stricken couple was the headline *"Death Is the Third Person Here."*

———— ≈ ————

The hearing resumed at 1:30 p.m. in Catherine's absence. Having settled his wife at home, Tom returned to the court- house, wanting to represent Catherine at this hearing that was so important to her. If she was not well enough to be there, he would stand for her instead.

The hearing picked up where it had left off as Tom sat numbly in a chair at the back of the room.

"Is her condition fatal?" asked Grossman of Dalitsch.

The doctor cleared his throat. "It is fatal in her case," he acknowledged.

"In your judgment," asked the lawyer, "what might be Catherine Donohue's reasonable [life] expectancy?"

"I don't think we can state definitely," Dalitsch began to bluster, perhaps conscious of her husband sitting in court, "depending on the care she had and so on—treatment..."

Grossman fixed him with a look. This was a courtroom, not a clinic, and it did not help Catherine's case to beat around the bush. Dalitsch straightened up under Grossman's glare.

"I would say...months," he stated bluntly.

Tom felt tears at his eyes again. *Months.*

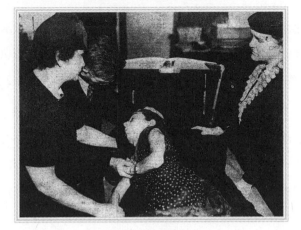

Catherine laid out on a
desk after collapsing.

"There is no cure in its advanced stages?" queried Grossman.

"No," said Dalitsch. "There is none."

As the afternoon wore on, the other doctors were questioned.

"She is beyond a doubt in the terminal stages of the disease," testified Dr. Weiner.

"She has but a short time to live," agreed Loffler. "There is absolutely no hope."

No hope. No cure. No Catherine.

Tom listened to it all with tears streaming down his cheeks. He endured it all. By the end of the afternoon, he was near collapse and had to be led from the courtroom.

The company lawyer, for his part, barely bothered to

cross-examine the doctors. Magid limited his questions to what Radium Dial considered the critical issue. Was radium a poison? But as slick as Magid was, no testimony was presented to support his arguments.

In contrast, the women had plenty to say. Catherine had by now recovered a little from her collapse, and she was determined to continue giving evidence. Her physicians pronounced her too ill to leave her bed. In fact, they said giving evidence might prove immediately fatal.

But Catherine was adamant. So Grossman suggested that the hearing be resumed the next day at her bedside. If she couldn't come to the courtroom, then Grossman would bring it to her. After considering the request, George Marvel agreed.

It fell to Grossman to inform the press. As he announced that a bedside hearing would be held the following day, he added a final comment that he knew would provoke the press into copious column inches.

"That is," he said darkly as he surveyed the gathered media, "in case she is alive..."

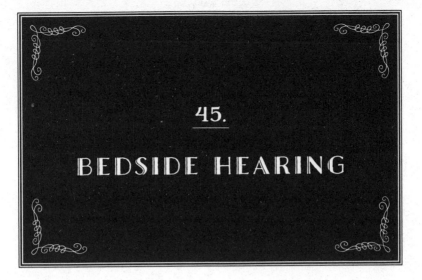

45.

BEDSIDE HEARING

When Friday, February 11, dawned, Catherine Donohue *was* still alive. The weather outside on East Superior Street was unsettled, but Catherine, despite her weakened condition, felt certain of what she had to do.

"It's too late for me," she said bravely, "but maybe it will help some of the others."

It had been agreed by Radium Dial that Catherine's would be a test case. If she won, then all the other victims would find justice as well. It made it all the more important to her that she fought on.

The mass of visitors arriving at the Donohue home that morning were directed to the dining room. There, Catherine

The bedside hearing at
the Donohue home.

lay on the sofa. Some thirty people in all crowded into the room—lawyers, witnesses, reporters, and friends.

Catherine barely had the strength to open her eyes to welcome them. Her friends greeted her with concern. They usually visited this place socially, but today was a very different occasion. The women sat on chairs lined up by the sofa. Charlotte Purcell, who had come down from Chicago, was closest to Catherine. Charlotte's health had declined rapidly of late. Only the week before, she had lost another tooth. She sat huddled in a thick gray coat, its left sleeve hanging empty by her side.

The hearing began. As Grossman questioned Catherine, he knelt by her side so she could hear him better. Catherine answered him through closed eyes. Only occasionally would she open them, and even then she didn't really seem to see.

"Show us," Grossman encouraged, "how you were taught to point [the brush], as you described in testimony yesterday." He held out a child's paintbrush toward her, taken from Tommy's watercolor set.

Catherine took it. She paused for a moment, feeling its barely there weight in her hand. Her fingers curled familiarly around it. "Here's how it's done," she croaked at last. Her voice sounded tired. "We dipped it in the radium compound mixture." Catherine dabbed the brush into an imaginary dish. Then, very slowly, she bent her stiff arm back and raised the brush to her lips. "Then shaped it," she said with emotion, "like this." She slipped the brush between her lips and twirled it. *Lip... Dip... Paint.* When she'd finished, she held it up with a shaking hand. The bristles now tapered to a perfect point. Seeing it, "a shudder ran through her trembling frame."

"I did this thousands and thousands of times," Catherine said dully. "That was the way we were *told* to do it."

"Did any official of Radium Dial ever tell you that the U.S. Government had condemned the use of camel-hair brushes in painting with radium?" Grossman asked.

Catherine looked shocked to hear it. "No," she replied. The girls sitting behind her exchanged looks of anger.

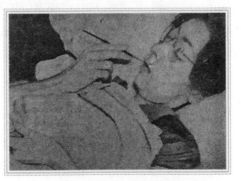

Catherine demonstrating lip-pointing during the bedside hearing.

"Was there any notice posted [about] the dangers of radium dial-painting with the hair brushes?" Grossman queried.

"No, sir," Catherine replied surely, "there was none. We even ate our lunches on the work tables near the luminous paint... All they told us"—she was panting now with the effort of speaking—"was to be careful not to get any grease spots on the dials."

Grossman touched her gently on the shoulder. She was exhausted, he could tell. He carefully took her through the remaining key points, including the way she had been fired for limping. Then he let her rest.

He called Charlotte Purcell to take the oath.

"Objection," called out Magid immediately. He didn't want the other girls to give evidence, saying this was Catherine's case alone.

"This is a test case, Your Honor," Grossman cut in smoothly, appealing to Marvel. "I don't know that I will have these girls with me at any future time." His eyes scanned the row of young women sitting alongside Catherine. "Not *all* of them," he added pointedly.

Marvel nodded. He permitted the women to be questioned, though the girls were not allowed to testify specifically about their own conditions.

Charlotte came to the table to take the oath. Then she too

twirled the brush in her mouth, showing her missing teeth as she did so. One girl's eyes filled with tears as Charlotte talked.

"Were you employed," Grossman asked her, "at the Radium Dial Company when Catherine Donohue was employed there, in the same room?"

"Yes, sir," said Charlotte.

"Did you have your left arm then?"

Charlotte swallowed hard. "Yes, sir."

"How long were you employed there?" he asked.

"Thirteen months," she said, almost spitting out the words.

He asked her about the confrontation she and Catherine had had with Mr. Reed. "Did you have your arm then?"

"No, sir," she replied bluntly.

"What did Mr. Reed say?"

"Mr. Reed," said Charlotte, her eyes burning angrily, "said he didn't think there was any such thing as radium poisoning."

One by one, Grossman called the girls to give evidence, which they did sitting alongside the lawyers at the Donohues' dining table. Marie Rossiter clenched and unclenched her fingers as she reported what had gone on.

"Mr. Reed said radium would put rosy cheeks on us," she remembered in disgust, "that it was *good* for us."

Grossman asked each of them in turn if the painting

demonstrations had been an accurate reenactment of the technique they'd been taught. Each nodded her head.

All the women testified on Catherine's behalf. As each woman stood up for her friend, she was mirrored by Arthur Magid, who continually objected to their evidence.

Throughout it all, Catherine herself lay mute on the sofa. Sometimes, she dozed to the lullaby of her friends' voices as they lilted around her. At last, it came to an end. Across the two days, fourteen witnesses had given evidence for Catherine. Now, Grossman rested his case. Everyone turned expectantly to Arthur Magid.

But the company lawyer presented no evidence and called not a single witness. The firm was standing solely on its legal defense that radium wasn't poisonous.

With no further evidence to hear, Marvel formally closed the hearing. He would give his verdict, he said, in a month or so. Before then, both sides would have the opportunity to submit written legal briefs, which would set out their arguments in full.

Then the hullabaloo of the court was over. Everyone departed, and Tom shut the door of 520 East Superior Street behind them. Somehow, the house seemed even quieter than it had before the hearing. Now, all he and Catherine could do was wait.

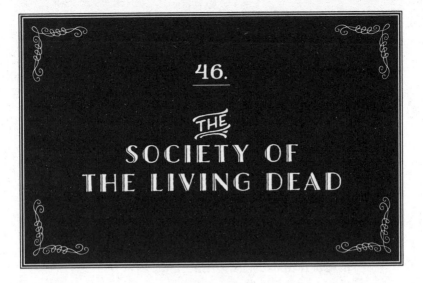

46.

THE
SOCIETY OF
THE LIVING DEAD

he women didn't let the time go to waste. They decided to form a society to fight for the rights of people who had been injured at work. On February 26, 1938, the society had their first meeting. They called themselves the Society of the Living Dead.

That first meeting happened the same day that Grossman delivered his first legal brief to Marvel. The timing was probably deliberate. It meant both events were covered by the press. And if it had been a trial by media, the girls would have won hands down. The papers called Radium Dial "criminally careless."

The need for the society was painfully apparent. The federal investigations that Frances Perkins had ordered into the women's poisoning appeared to have come to nothing.

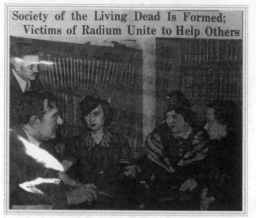

Society of the Living Dead Is Formed; Victims of Radium Unite to Help Others

The Society of the Living Dead is formally launched.

The government's focus was the Great Depression. It had other priorities than the dial-painters' cause.

Meanwhile, as the weeks passed and everybody waited for the verdict, Catherine's health got worse and worse. "Once that [stage of the] illness began," remembered her niece Mary, "it was just like a spiral down, down, down... It wasn't a gradual thing. It was fast."

All Catherine could do was lie weakly on her bed in the front room with the shades drawn. She lay under a blanket, with the tumor on her hip like a malignant mountain rising beneath. She was in so much pain.

"I just remember her moaning, moaning," remembered her niece quietly. "You knew that she was in pain, but she didn't have the energy to scream.

"I can't describe," she went on, "how *sad* that house was. You felt the sadness when you came in there."

It was a sad house. It was a house in which a mother knew

she was going to have to leave her children. Yet Catherine now took some small solace from an unexpected source. The public. They were heartbroken for her family too. Her story was emblazoned across the newspapers, and readers were horrified by it. Catherine received hundreds of supportive letters that came from coast to coast. "You have my sympathy and my greatest desire for a complete victory," read one. "And I know millions of people think the same."

On March 28, 1938, the final legal brief was filed. After consideration of this, Marvel would give his verdict. In it, Grossman did not mince his words. "I cannot imagine a fiend fresh from the profoundest depths of [hell] committing such an unnatural crime as the Radium Dial Company did," he wrote.

"[Their actions are] an offense against Morals and Humanity, and, just incidentally, against the law."

Grossman wrote powerfully. The judge had declared that he would not make a final

Grossman, Tom Donohue, and Charlotte Purcell pose for the media as Grossman delivers his final legal brief.

ruling until April 10, yet on April 5, the telephone rang in Grossman's office. He was summoned to the headquarters of the IIC.

The verdict was in.

———— ≈ ————

There was no time to tell the Donohues. Grossman managed to summon those few former dial-painters now living in Chicago, including Charlotte Purcell, and they alone were able to reach the hearing in time. They all crowded into the wood-paneled room to hear the verdict. George Marvel's judgment was read aloud by the chairman of the commission. Both Magid and Grossman stood to hear him speak.

"The Industrial Commission finds that...a relation of employer and employee existed between the company and the plaintiff...[and that Catherine Donohue's] disability *did* arise out of and come in the course of her employment."

He had found the company guilty.

Guilty of crippling Catherine—and, by implication, Charlotte too—but not just that alone. This verdict meant it was also clear the firm was guilty of killing Peg Looney, Ella Cruse, Inez Vallat...so many more. Those women's lives could not be saved. But their murderers were now unveiled in the cold light of day. The light of justice flooded in. The truth, after all these years, was finally out.

"Justice has triumphed!" declared Grossman.

It had been a long, *long* battle. In many ways, it was a battle that had begun on February 5, 1925, when Marguerite Carlough had first filed suit in New Jersey: the very first dial-painter ever to fight back. Catherine's triumph in court, thirteen *years* later, was one of the first cases in which an employer was made responsible for the health of its employees. What the girls had achieved was astonishing: a groundbreaking, law-changing, and life-saving accomplishment.

Marvel awarded Catherine her past medical expenses, her salary for the entire time she had been too sick to work, damages, and an annual life pension of $277 ($4,656) for the remainder of her life. It came to a total of some $5,661 ($95,160) and was the maximum possible award the judge could give.

It was the *Ottawa Daily Times* that claimed to break the news to Catherine. A reporter raced to 520 East Superior Street and found her lying alone in bed in the front room. Catherine was so ill, when the journalist told her that she'd won her case, she showed little emotion and did not smile. Tom would later confide that she "cries but rarely smiles; she has forgotten how to laugh."

"I am glad for the sake of my children and my husband," Catherine eventually whispered. Then she added, "The judge is grand... He's very fair. That means a lot."

As though the idea of fairness had triggered something in her, an anger blazed within her for a brief moment. "It should have been done a long time ago," she said, almost bitterly. "I've been suffering. I'll have to suffer more." She went on, "I wonder if I will live to receive any of the money; I hope so. But I am afraid it will come too late."

Yet Catherine had not put her life at risk for herself. She had done it for her family and friends. It was with tender hope that she said, "Now maybe [Tom] and our two children can really live again."

She added one final comment in a croaked whisper. It fell oddly flat in the quiet, stale-aired room, which held none of the jubilation of the courtroom in Chicago.

"I hope the lawyers don't upset it," Catherine Donohue said.

47.

ONE MORE DAY

wo weeks after the judgment, Radium Dial appealed the verdict. It was a severe blow to Catherine. "I only wish my case was through with," she said wistfully. "Lord knows I need the medical care."

That was an understatement. She suffered terrible, constant pain. Her jawbone continued to fracture into ever-smaller fragments. Each new break was more painful than the last. And with the new breaks came a new development. Catherine started bleeding from her jaw, losing approximately one pint of blood each time. She was admitted to the hospital, where her doctor issued a formal statement: "In my opinion any unusual stress such as a court appearance might prove fatal. I have advised and urged her to [avoid] any such activity."

But this was Catherine Donohue he was talking about. No matter what her doctor said, she was determined to fight Radium Dial tooth and nail. Released from the hospital by the start of June 1938, she was home just in time to hold a meeting at her house the day before the appeal hearing. Grossman and the other women were present and so was Dr. Loffler.

Catherine's thin body barely dented the mattress as Loffler took her blood. Whereas once Catherine had dressed smartly in her polka-dot dress for gatherings such as these, now she wore a white cotton nightgown. When she stepped onto the scales, Catherine knew at once that Loffler would not allow her to attend the next day's hearing. She weighed sixty-one pounds. She was not much heavier than her five-year-old son.

Catherine and Dr. Loffler at Catherine's home the day before the appeal hearing.

Although Catherine was unable to attend, Grossman and the other women stood up for her in court. The appeal hearing was held before a capacity crowd. Having seen Catherine's condition the day before, Grossman declared the case was a race with death. "If Mrs. Donohue dies before a final ruling," he said solemnly, "her estate under the law would receive nothing."

Perhaps that was why Arthur Magid immediately requested a postponement. But it was not granted. The appeal was heard that very afternoon.

To the women's shock, Radium Dial now alleged they were lying—about everything. As evidence of this claim, the firm submitted to the court a formal statement from Mr. Reed, the girls' former boss. It was itself, frankly, a pack of lies. He said he'd never told the girls that radium wouldn't hurt them. He said he did not instruct the women to lip-point. He even said he was not on the company payroll at the same time as Catherine—a lie quickly exposed by the local town directory. It listed Reed as an employee of Radium Dial through all the years Catherine had worked there. As for swearing that nobody told the girls radium wouldn't hurt them, there was a full-page ad signed by the company's president and printed in the local newspaper that had said exactly that.

The so-called evidence of Reed was the sole item submitted by the company in its appeal. So at 3:30 p.m., the hearing was closed. A five-man committee would judge the final verdict. They promised a decision by July 10.

Catherine just needed to hang on a little longer.

She prayed for a miracle. That was all the hope she had left. Desperate, she wrote to a Catholic priest on June 22, 1938:

> The doctors tell me I will die, but I mustn't. I have too much to live for—a husband who loves me and two children I adore. But, the doctors say, radium poisoning is eating away my bones and shrinking my flesh to the point where medical science has given me up as "one of the living dead."
>
> They say there is nothing that can save me—nothing but a miracle. And that's what I want—a miracle... But if that is not God's will, perhaps your prayers will obtain for me the blessing of a happy death.
>
> Please,
>
> Mrs. Catherine Wolfe Donohue

That "Please" said it all. Catherine was begging for help. She had no shame or pride now—she just wanted to survive. Catherine's own mom had died when she was six, so she knew exactly what it was like to grow up without a mother. She feared for her own children, suffering the exact same fate as she. Just one month longer was all she asked. Just one more week.

One more day.

Catherine counted each one as it passed. July 10 was not so very far away. She was living for her children, for Tom, but also for justice. She simply prayed it would be done.

The Donohue family: Tom, Catherine, Tommy, and Mary Jane.

And on July 6, 1938—four days early—her prayers were answered. On this date, the appeal of the Radium Dial Company was thrown out of court by the IIC. They upheld Catherine's award, and not only that, they added an additional $730 ($12,271) to it to cover the medical expenses she'd incurred since April. It was a unanimous decision.

Catherine wrote with happy pleasure, "It was a wonderful victory." And on July 17, the women held a reunion to celebrate their success. They had a "lovely time" toasting their incredible triumph. The other girls were full of plans for their own cases. Thanks to Catherine, they too could now bring claims before the IIC. Grossman said he would begin with Charlotte's case immediately. The women felt unfamiliar emotions: happiness and peace and hope. One of Catherine's friends said simply, "I live in the hope of living."

Catherine did the same, with the verdict in court seeming to buoy her. It gave her another hour, another dawn. One more day in which she could greet Tom in the morning, kiss Mary Jane good night, and see Tommy draw just one more picture with his watercolor paints. Catherine kept on living.

And then, on July 26, Radium Dial went above the IIC to file another appeal in the circuit court.

It was a shock: a stab to the happy balloon of hope that Catherine had been carrying. It was a blow from which she found she simply could not recover. "She had held on," Grossman said, "to a slim thread of life as long as she could, but yesterday's move to deprive her of what was legally hers was too much. She had to let go."

Catherine Wolfe Donohue died at 2:52 a.m. on Wednesday, July 27, 1938, the day after Radium Dial filed its latest appeal. She passed away at home, with Tom and the children by her side. She remained conscious until a short time before her death, and then just slipped away.

———————— ≋ ————————

As was required by Illinois law in cases of poisoning, an inquest was held into her death. Tom and Catherine's friends attended. Grossman was there too. He called her death "a cool, calculating, money-making murder."

As dramatic as Grossman's declaration was, it was Tom's testimony that proved most powerful. The inquest was held the day after Catherine died, and Tom's grief was fresh and raw. After giving evidence about his beloved wife, he left the stand in tears. The jury was instructed by the coroner that they had only to identify the cause of death and not apportion blame.

Newspaper headline about Catherine's inquest from July 29, 1938.

But they did anyway. "We, the jury, find that [Catherine Donohue] died of radium poisoning absorbed while she was employed in an industrial plant in Ottawa." At Grossman's suggestion, the name of the Radium Dial Company was added to the formal verdict.

Then Catherine's death certificate was formally signed.

Was death in any way related to occupation of deceased?

Yes.

———— ≈ ————

Catherine was buried on July 29, 1938. Hundreds of people

gathered to pay their respects to her. She had proved herself a most exceptional woman: a quiet, unassuming person who had only wanted to work hard and love her family but who had made a difference to millions in the way she responded to her own personal tragedy. She was carried to St. Columba by an assorted mix of Wolfe and Donohue relatives, this final journey, at last, causing her no more pain.

Grossman was not present. Even on the day of Catherine's funeral, he had to be in court, defending her claim. The company had been denied the right of appeal, but they were appealing even that. They appealed over and over and over. In fact, Radium Dial fought the case all the way to the Supreme Court.

Other lawyers might have dropped the case, citing lack of funds, because Grossman was paying the full cost of all legal proceedings. But Leonard Grossman had vowed to stand by the women, and he did not let them down. He was battling in Catherine's memory now, and that was a powerful motivator.

It drove him onward. And it was worth the fight. Ultimately, the Supreme Court dismissed the case, meaning Catherine Wolfe Donohue won. She won eight times in total. But the final victory came on October 23, 1939.

The papers described her battle for justice as "one of the most spectacular fights against industrial occupational hazards." Now, that battle was at an end—*finally* at an end. It was a pure, clean victory, with no clouds or contingencies to sully it. It was outright justice, plain and true. The women had been vindicated. The dial-painters had won.

And it was Catherine Wolfe Donohue, in the end, who had led them all to victory.

EPILOGUE

The radium girls did not die in vain. Although the women could not save themselves from the poison in their bones, in countless ways, their sacrifice saved many thousands of others.

Fifty days before the final triumph in Catherine Donohue's case, war was declared in Europe. Once again, there was enormous demand for those luminous dials used in military machines. Yet thanks to Catherine and Grace and their colleagues' bravery in speaking out about what had happened to them, the government was forced to protect the new generation of dial-painters. Safety standards were introduced, based entirely on knowledge gained from the bodies of those women who had come before. The standards were set not a moment too soon; seven months later, America joined the Second World War. The U.S. radium dial-painting industry exploded, with USRC alone increasing its personnel by 1,600 percent.

In addition, the radium girls protected workers employed on the most secret wartime mission of them all: the Manhattan Project. Atomic-bomb making used radioactive plutonium, which was biomedically very similar to radium, meaning it would settle into the bones of anyone exposed to it. Thanks to the girls, people now knew how very dangerous that was. So the project issued protective guidelines to its workers. They were based directly on the radium industry safety standards.

After the Allies triumphed—helped by the use of those very atomic bombs that the Manhattan Project built—the debt the country owed to the radium girls was acknowledged in full. An official of the U.S. Atomic Energy Commission (AEC) wrote, "If it hadn't been for those dial-painters, the [Manhattan] project's management could have reasonably rejected the extreme precautions that were urged on it and thousands of workers might well have been, and might still be, in great danger." The women had been, officials said, "invaluable."

Even after the war was over, the dial-painters' legacy continued to save lives as the world entered the age of atomic energy. Then the nuclear arms race began. Over the next decade, hundreds of aboveground atomic tests were conducted across the globe.

Each blast resulted in radioactive fallout drifting back to earth. It landed not only on the test site but also rained down upon fields of green grass, wheat, and grain, through which radioactive isotopes entered the human food chain. Just as radium had in the dial-painters, these isotopes—especially a dangerous, newly created one called strontium-90—began to deposit in human bones. "Every one of us," wrote the Consumers League in alarm, "is a potential victim."

The AEC dismissed the concerns. The risks, it said, were very small when compared to "the terrible future we might face if we fell behind in our nuclear defense effort." Yet its words were not enough to calm the troubled public. Not after they had seen what had happened to the radium girls. In 1956, growing public unease led the AEC to establish a committee to examine the long-term health risks of atomic tests, specifically the effects of strontium-90. But how, the researchers thought, could they possibly begin this study for the future health of humanity when they were dealing with such an unknown substance? All they really knew was that strontium-90 was chemically similar to radium...

The dial-painters were needed to help once more.

The AEC termed the women of "incalculable value." They seemed able to predict for scientists the likely long-term health effects of this new radioactive danger. Their suffering would provide "vital insight, with implications for hundreds of millions of people all over the world."

Medical studies began immediately, including in New Jersey and Illinois. Eventually, the Center for Human Radiobiology (CHR) was created, located in a multimillion-dollar clinic called the Argonne National Laboratory, based seventy-five miles from Ottawa. Here, special lead-lined vaults were constructed, buried under three feet of concrete and ten feet of earth. In these vaults, the dial-painters' body burdens (the amount of radium inside them) were measured. The research was designed to help future generations and called "essential to the security of the nation." "If we can determine the long-term effects of radium," one of the scientists said, "we're quite sure we can predict the long-term, low-level effects of fallout." Scientists were seeking to "give the world an exact guide on safe radioactivity by studying all dial-painters who can be found."

There were dial-painters still living—albeit with a time bomb ticking in their bones. Dr. Martland had already explained why they had survived thus far. Radium was known to settle in the girls' bones and known to cause sarcomas, but *when* such deadly tumors might begin to grow was the factor that remained mysterious, like a dark trick. Radium had not given away all its secrets just yet.

The hunt to find those living dial-painters now began. *"Wanted: Radium Workers of the Roaring Twenties"* read the headlines. Employment records were found and snapshots of those long-ago USRC picnics unearthed. The company photograph taken on the steps of Radium Dial became a vital source of clues. The scientists said, "Each of these persons is worth [her] weight in gold to science." The girls were termed "a reservoir of scientific information." In an eerie echo of the women's treatment when they sued their former firms, private investigators were hired to track them down.

Those they found were often willing to help. Even family members of the girls took part because scientists were concerned that the radioactivity in the women's bodies may have harmed their loved ones. Grace Fryer's little brother Art was tested. Though he was fine, it was a theory that was not exaggerated. Swen Kjaer's notes mentioned the death of a dial-painter's sister. She had never worked at a studio but had died of radium poisoning nonetheless. Kjaer wrote, "The source of contamination appears to have been her sister, the dial-painter, with whom she shared a bed."

Many of the original girls, of course, were no longer alive to help with the study. Edna Hussman had died on March 30, 1939, of a sarcoma of the thigh bone. Albina Maggia Larice died from the same thing on November 18, 1946.

Yet even the deceased dial-painters had something to offer the scientists. Dr. Martland had collected tissue and bone samples from the radium girls when he was making his groundbreaking discoveries in the 1920s, and these ended up in the studies' archives. Those contributing to the world's knowledge of radiation included Sarah Maillefer, Ella Eckert, Irene La Porte, and many more. The researchers even went to the Cook County Hospital and brought back Charlotte Purcell's amputated arm. They found it still in its chemical crypt, saved through the decades due to its never-before-seen symptoms.

In 1963, perhaps at least partly in response to the research on the dial-painters, President John F. Kennedy signed the international Limited Test Ban Treaty. This banned atomic tests aboveground, underwater, and in outer space. Strontium-90, it had been decided, was too dangerous for humanity after all. The ban undoubtedly saved lives and, very possibly, the entire human race.

Atomic energy remained part of the world. It is a part of our lives even today, when fifty-six countries operate 240 nuclear reactors and more still are used to power nuclear ships and submarines. Yet thanks to the radium girls, whose experiences led directly to the regulation of radioactive industries, atomic power is able to be operated, on the whole, in safety.

The study of the dial-painters did not end when the threat of nuclear war subsided. Experts said there was a "moral obligation to future generations, to learn as much as possible about the effects of radiation." So the dial-painters were studied for the rest of their lives.

Decade after decade, the radium girls came voluntarily to CHR to be tested. Even after death, some were autopsied, their bodies giving up secrets that the scientists couldn't learn in life. Thousands of women helped with the study, through their forties, fifties, sixties, and beyond. Their contribution to medical science is enormous. We all benefit from their sacrifice and courage, every day of our lives.

And among those women who submitted to examination for the good of humanity were some familiar faces, such as Marie Rossiter. Although for much of her life, Marie had "huge and spotty" legs from the radium, which forced her to walk with a limp, she refused to let it rule her life. She said, "I witnessed the bad times, but you get through them."

There was a friend of hers who'd gotten through the bad times too: Charlotte Purcell. She'd been told in the 1930s that she was the Ottawa dial-painter most likely to die after Catherine Donohue, but thirty years later, she was still living. Charlotte had had a sarcoma, back in 1934, but her courage in choosing to have an amputation undoubtedly saved her life. She lost all her teeth and had one leg shorter than the other, but like Marie, she refused to let it bring her down. When the scientists invited her to Argonne, she accepted. The doctors had told her that doing so would help others, and Charlotte Purcell was never a woman to turn down an appeal for aid.

As for the companies, eventually the law caught up with them. But by then, the damage had been done. In 1979, the U.S. Environmental Protection Agency (EPA) found that the former USRC site in Orange had unacceptable, environmentally hazardous levels of radioactivity: twenty times higher than was safe. The EPA ordered USRC's corporate successor (the company that had since taken over control of the radium firm) to perform the cleanup work, but it didn't. The courts were not forgiving. In 1991, the New Jersey Supreme Court found USRC "forever" liable for the contamination and declared the firm had known about the dangers at the time it operated there. Residents of contaminated homes sued the firm. After seven years, the cases were settled out of court, costing the company some $14.2 million (almost $24 million) in damages. It report-edly cost the govern-ment $144 million ($209 million) to clean up radium-contaminated sites across New Jersey and New York.

Charlotte Purcell with
her dog, Rags.

As for Radium Dial, despite the wartime boom, it went bust in 1943. The radioactive building it left behind in the center of Ottawa, however, had a legacy that lasted far beyond that. The building itself was knocked down in 1968. But its radioactive waste was dumped all around town, including alongside a school field. Later studies showed an above-average cancer rate near the old factory site, as well as across town.

Yet Ottawa officials did not address the problem. It was like a rerun of the community's disbelieving attitude toward Catherine and her friends. It was decades before the EPA stepped in. Only then were funds finally found to begin tackling the dangerous legacy of radioactivity that Radium Dial had left Ottawa. It was an operation that would take many years. In 2019, the cleanup was still going on.

———— ≈ ————

CHR studied the dial-painters for decades. Its scientists came to learn that radium was a sneaky element. With a half-life of sixteen hundred years, it had plenty of time to make itself known in those it had poisoned, causing its own special damage across the decades. As the researchers followed the women through the years, they witnessed what the long-term effects of internal radiation *really* were.

The dial-painters who had survived did not escape

unharmed—far from it. Some women were stricken early but then suffered for decades. One Waterbury girl was bedridden for fifty years. The older the women were when they dial-painted and the fewer years they worked, the less likely they were to die in the early stages. So they lived on, but the radium lived with them: a marriage from which there was no divorce.

Many suffered significant bone changes and fractures. Most lost all their teeth. There were unusually large numbers who developed bone cancer, leukemia, and anemia. The radium honeycombed the women's bones so that, for example, Charlotte Purcell later suffered a partial collapse of her vertebrae. Like Grace Fryer before her, she ultimately wore a back brace.

Marie Rossiter had at least six leg operations. Her swollen legs began turning black. In the end, she had her leg amputated, but it didn't slow her down. She was still the life and soul of the party, whizzing about in her wheelchair.

The CHR scientists had at first been looking for a magic level of radiation exposure under which no harm was done. But after studying the effects of radiation long-term, they ultimately came to agree with Martland. He had warned decades before that "the normal radioactivity of the human body should not be increased."

It is impossible to say how many dial-painters were killed by their work. So many were misdiagnosed or never traced that the records simply do not exist. Sometimes the cancer that former workers suffered later in life was never linked to the job they did in their teens, though it came as a direct result. And the deaths, too, were only one part of it. How many women were crippled as a result of their poisoning is also unknown.

Some women survived for forty years or more, but the radium always came calling in the end. The newspapers followed some of the deaths. *"Radium, Dormant Killer, at Work Again!"* screamed the headlines through the years.

Against all the odds, however, a few of the dial-painters had good, long lives. Charlotte Purcell lived to be eighty-two. She was adored by her grandchildren. "She was probably one of my most favorite people in the whole world," raved her granddaughter Jan. "She was one of the most courageous, loved and influential people in my life. What my grandmother taught me was: it doesn't matter what life throws at you, you can adapt.

"When I asked her to teach me how to jump rope, she said, 'Well, I don't think I can teach you because I only have one arm.' I suppose that was upsetting to me so she said, 'Well, wait.' She tied a rope to a chain-link fence and then she jumped rope with one arm and showed me how to jump rope."

Jan's brother Don added, "It was nothing out of the ordinary to me [that she didn't have an arm] because she made it that way."

The women didn't talk to their families about the incredible legacy they had given the world. And the radium girls did not simply set safety standards and contribute immensely to science; they left their mark in their country's laws too. In the wake of Catherine Donohue's triumph in 1939, Secretary of Labor Frances Perkins announced that the fight was "far from won" when it came to workers' compensation. Subsequently, building on what the women had achieved in life, further legal changes were made to protect all employees. The dial-painters' case and others like it ultimately led to the establishment of the Occupational Safety and Health Administration, which now works nationally in the United States to ensure safe working conditions. Businesses are required to inform employees if they work with dangerous chemicals. There are now processes for safe handling, training, and protection. Workers also now have a legal right to see the results of any medical tests.

When Marie Rossiter died in 1993, she donated her body to science, as many dial-painters did. Hers would not be the last Ottawa dial-painter corpse to be studied. Nor was it the first. That honor goes to Margaret Looney.

Peg's family had wanted her to be tested as soon as they'd heard about the postwar studies. At that time, however, research was limited to the living. That changed once CHR was established. Finally, someone was prepared to investigate what had really killed Peg.

Every one of her nine brothers and sisters signed the necessary forms. In 1978, researchers dug up Peg's body for testing. They discovered she had 19,500 microcuries of radium in her bones—one of the highest quantities found. It was more than a thousand times the amount scientists then considered safe.

They didn't just discover the radium. They discovered that the company doctor had cut her jawbone from her while she lay dead. That was probably how the Looney family found out about it.

"I'm *angry*," said one of Peg's sisters. "They knew she was full of radium. And then they lied."

"Every family has sadness and grief," another added steadily. "But Margaret's death was unnecessary."

That was the tragedy. Radium had been known to be harmful since 1901. Every death since then was unnecessary.

For a long time—too long—the legacy of the radium girls was recorded only in the law books and in scientific files. But in 2006, an eighth-grade Illinois student named Madeline Piller read a book on the dial-painters by Dr. Ross Mullner. "No monuments," he wrote, "have ever been erected in their memory."

Madeline was determined to change that. And when she began to champion her cause, she found that Ottawa, at last, was ready to honor the radium girls. The town held fish-fry fund-raisers and staged plays to secure the $80,000 needed.

On September 2, 2011, the bronze statue for the dial-painters was unveiled by the governor in Ottawa, Illinois. It is a statue of a young woman from the 1920s, standing on a clock face. She holds a paintbrush in one hand and a tulip in the other. Her skirt swishes as though at any moment, she might step down from her time-ticking pedestal and come to life.

"The radium girls," the governor announced, "deserve the utmost respect and admiration...because they battled a dishonest company, an indifferent industry, dismissive courts and the medical community in the face of certain death. I hereby proclaim September 2, 2011, as Radium Girls Day in Illinois, in recognition of the tremendous perseverance, dedication, and sense of justice the radium girls exhibited in their fight."

The statue is dedicated not only to the Ottawa dial-painters but also to "dial-painters who suffered all over the United States." This bronze radium girl—forever young, forever present—stands for Grace Fryer and Katherine Schaub, for the Maggia and Carlough sisters, for Hazel and Irene and Ella too. She stands for all the dial-painters, whether they lived and died in Orange, in Ottawa, in Waterbury, or anywhere else. It is a fitting and most deserving memorial. After all, there is so much to thank the women for.

The statue in
Ottawa dedicated
to the dial-painters.

"The studies of the radium-dial workers form the basis of much of the world's present knowledge of the health risks of radioactivity," wrote Dr. Ross Mullner. "The suffering and deaths of these workers greatly increased [scientific] knowledge, ultimately saving countless lives of future generations."

"I always admired their strength," said Catherine Donohue's great-niece, "to stand up and unite."

And united, they triumphed. Through their friendships, through their refusal to give up, and through their sheer spirit, the radium girls left us all an extraordinary legacy. They did not die in vain.

They made every second count.

POSTSCRIPT

We girls," said one worker, "would sit around big tables, laughing and talking and painting. It was fun to work there."

"I felt lucky to have a job there," revealed another girl. "The job paid top dollar for women in this area. All of us got along real good."

"We slapped the radium around like cake frosting."

The women wore smocks, washed once a week amid the family laundry. They drank open cans of soda through their shifts, which they bought from the machine in their studio. They worked with bare hands and painted their fingernails with the material "for kicks." They were allowed to take radium home to practice painting.

There was radium everywhere in the plant—and outside on the sidewalk. Contaminated rags piled up in the workrooms or were burned outside in the yard. Radioactive waste was emptied into the toilet of the men's washroom. Ventilation shafts discharged above a nearby children's play area. The women didn't clean their shoes before they left work, so they walked the radium all over town. Employees recalled that you couldn't work in the plant without getting covered with the stuff. "I'd come home from work at night and look in the mirror and see little specks of it glowing in my hair," recalled one dial-painter. The women's hands would bleed as they tried to scrub away that supernatural shine.

"The company," said one girl, "always led us to believe everything was under control and safe, but I don't think they cared."

She was right. Before too long, the workers started suffering. "I had to have a mouth operation," said one, "but now my teeth are so loosened that they are probably all going to fall out... I have a blood disease I can't seem to get rid of." The women noticed tumors appearing on their feet, their breasts, their legs. One woman recalled that the doctors kept cutting off parts of her colleague's leg, bit by bit by bit...until finally there was nothing more left to amputate. Ruth, the colleague, eventually died.

The women went to their supervisor, worried sick. "A man from the New York headquarters came out here," a radium girl remembered, "and told us [our work] wouldn't hurt us."

The executives blustered, "Employees are responsible for safety too."

But there were no warning signs in the workrooms. The women had been told that, as long as they didn't lip-point, they would be perfectly safe.

These women worked in a little town called Ottawa, Illinois. These women worked for Joseph Kelly's firm, Luminous Processes.

The year was 1978.

Safety standards only keep you safe if the companies you work for use them. Concerns had been raised about the Ottawa plant for decades, but it wasn't until February 17, 1978, that the dangerous studio was finally shut down. Inspectors found radiation levels were 1,666 times higher than was safe. The abandoned building became something of a bogeyman for Ottawa residents, who became afraid to walk or even drive past it. It was graffitied with the slogan *"Dial Luminous for Death."*

"A lot of us are dead," one Luminous Processes dial-painter stated bluntly. Of a hundred workers she mentioned, sixty-five had died. The cancer rate was twice as high as normal.

Yet Luminous Processes was unapologetic. It wriggled out of paying cleanup costs, contributing approximately

$62,000 ($147,500) to the multimillion-dollar bill. Meanwhile, executives used double-talk to put off the women when they demanded answers. Workers were offered just $100 ($363) in severance pay and had difficulty suing the firm. "They didn't have any respect for the health of the girls," one Luminous Processes worker spat. "They were just interested in getting the work out."

"Luminous Processes," declared the local paper, "seems to put profits before people."

How quickly we forget.

TIMELINE OF EVENTS

DECEMBER 21, 1898:
Marie and Pierre Curie discover radium.

1901: Scientists learn that radium can destroy human tissue and tumors and begin using radium as a medicine.

1903: Pierre Curie says that radium has the power to seriously injure and possibly kill people. Meanwhile, the radium craze begins. The *Chicago Daily Tribune* calls the new element the "greatest find of history."

1906: The death of a laboratory worker due to radium burns is reported to the French Academy of Medicine.

1913: Sabin von Sochocky invents his glow-in-the-dark radium paint.

1914: The American Medical Association adds radium to its list of "New and Nonofficial Remedies."

SUMMER 1914: The First World War begins.

ca. 1915: Cosmetics companies launch radium-infused beauty products. The range eventually includes face creams, soaps, and rouge.

JANUARY 1916: The Radium Luminous Materials Corporation opens its dial-painting studio in Newark, New Jersey.

FEBRUARY 1, 1917:
Fourteen-year-old Katherine Schaub starts work at the Radium Luminous Materials Corporation (later called the United States Radium Corporation, or USRC).

APRIL 6, 1917:
The United States joins the First World War. As a result, the New Jersey studio increases its workforce. Nearly four hundred dial-painters are hired.

NOVEMBER 11, 1918:
The First World War ends.

SEPTEMBER 12, 1922: Twenty-four-year-old dial-painter Mollie Maggia dies.

SEPTEMBER 1922: Radium Dial, another radium firm, opens a new dial-painting studio in Ottawa, Illinois.

JANUARY 30, 1923: In New Jersey, Dr. Szamatolski correctly identifies that radium in the glow-in-the-dark paint is hurting the dial-painters.

SEPTEMBER 1924: The first mention is made in medical literature of "radium jaw," by the oral surgeon Dr. Blum.

FEBRUARY 5, 1925: New Jersey dial-painter Marguerite Carlough files suit against USRC, becoming the first dial-painter to do so.

JUNE 16, 1925: Sarah Carlough Maillefer becomes the first dial-painter to be tested for radium.

JUNE 7, 1925: Dr. Leman, the chief chemist of USRC, dies. Dr. Harrison Martland investigates his death, making medical history by measuring radioactivity in a human body for the first time. In so doing, Martland proves that Leman died from radium poisoning.

DECEMBER 5, 1925: Dr. Martland publishes a groundbreaking study that fully solves the mystery of the dial-painters' illnesses.

MAY 18, 1927:
Grace Fryer files suit against USRC, represented by lawyer Raymond H. Berry. Dial-painters Katherine Schaub, Edna Hussman, and Mollie Maggia's sisters Quinta McDonald and Albina Larice soon join the lawsuit too.

SEPTEMBER 4, 1927:
Twenty-four-year-old dial-painter Ella Cruse dies in Ottawa, Illinois.

JUNE 4, 1928: The New Jersey girls' lawsuit is settled out of court.

JUNE 7, 1928: Radium Dial runs a newspaper advertisement to assure the Ottawa dial-painters they are safe.

OCTOBER 29, 1929:
The U.S. stock market collapses and sets America spiraling into the Great Depression of the 1930s.

MARCH 30, 1932:
Radithor consumer Eben Byers dies. In the wake of his death, the U.S. Food and Drug Administration outlaws radium "cures."

JULY 4, 1934: Marie Curie dies of radiation poisoning.

DECEMBER 17, 1935:
A verdict is given in New Jersey in the case of former dial-painter Irene La Porte. The court decides that because there was limited knowledge of radium's dangers in 1917, USRC does not have to pay compensation for Irene's death. This ruling applies to all the lawsuits involving New Jersey dial-painters.

DECEMBER 1936:
Radium Dial closes its studio in Ottawa and leaves Illinois.

JULY 21, 1937: Former Ottawa dial-painter Catherine Wolfe Donohue signs with lawyer Leonard Grossman, who agrees to represent her appeal for compensation before the Illinois Industrial Commission (IIC).

APRIL 5, 1938: The IIC finds Radium Dial guilty in Catherine's case. The company later appeals the verdict multiple times.

JULY 27, 1938: Catherine Wolfe Donohue dies at the age of thirty-five.

SEPTEMBER 1, 1939: The Second World War begins, leading to a massive demand for radium dials.

OCTOBER 23, 1939: The Supreme Court dismisses Radium Dial's final appeal in Catherine Donohue's case. Justice finally prevails for the dial-painters.

MAY 2, 1941: The National Bureau of Standards issues federal safety standards for radium dial-painting.

DECEMBER 8, 1941: The United States declares war on Japan, joining the Second World War.

DECEMBER 28, 1942: U.S. president Roosevelt authorizes the development of the atomic bomb, requiring thousands of workers to handle radioactive materials. Thanks to the dial-painters, safety standards are put in place to protect them.

AUGUST 6, 1945: The United States drops an atomic bomb on Hiroshima, Japan, which ultimately leads to the end of the Second World War.

1956: Postwar studies on the dial-painters begin after the Atomic Energy Commission (AEC) starts examining the long-term risks of radiation exposure.

1969: The AEC approves the establishment of the Center for Human Radiobiology, which aims to study the dial-painters for their full life spans.

1970: The Occupational Safety and Health Administration is created. It aims to ensure safe working conditions in all industries across the United States.

MARCH 1991: The New Jersey Supreme Court finds the corporate successor of USRC "forever" liable for its radioactive contamination of the community.

SEPTEMBER 2, 2011: Radium Girls' Day is declared in Illinois, with the unveiling of the girls' memorial statue.

2019: The radioactive cleanup in Ottawa continues.

GLOSSARY

Aeronautical: Relating to the design and construction of airplanes (*aeronautical instruments* are tools used on planes).

Anemia: A medical condition in which a person doesn't have enough red blood cells.

Arthritis: A medical condition in which a person's joints have become painful.

Assets: The things that a person or company owns, such as property or financial investments.

Atomic bomb: A special kind of bomb that gets its energy from the splitting of an atom.

Autopsy: A medical examination of a person after they have died in order to discover the cause of their death.

Body burden: A scientific term meaning the amount of radium a person has in their body.

Bureau of Labor Statistics: A U.S. government agency responsible for monitoring the labor market, including working conditions.

Compensable: Entitled to compensation.

Compensation: Money that a person may receive if they have been hurt in some way.

Corporate successor: A company that takes control of another firm. The original firm's assets may be bought by their successor and they may change the company's name.

Corset: An item of women's underclothing that fits tightly around the woman's waist and hips in order to shape her figure.

Darkroom: A room that has no windows and no natural light and is deliberately made dark. In the dial-painting studio, it was the room in which the women's work would be checked because in the darkroom, their bosses could see only the luminous paint on the dials and no other light.

Department of Labor: A U.S. government department with responsibility for the welfare of workers and improving working conditions.

Diphtheria: An infectious disease that gives you a fever and makes it difficult to swallow and breathe.

Element: A substance such as radium, carbon, oxygen, or gold that is made up of only one type of atom. (You can discover all the elements that exist by looking at a scientific chart called the periodic table of elements, which lists them all.)

Extract (in relation to radium extraction): Though radium is an element, it is not naturally occurring. This means it needs to be mined or extracted from other sources. To extract—or get—radium was a huge job in the 1910s and 1920s. From a whole ton of ore (a natural substance such as rock or earth), only five to seven milligrams of radium could be obtained, an amount about the size of the head of a pin. The method involved combining sixty tons of water and six tons of chemicals, acids and alkalis with the original ton of ore. This combination would then be put through nine hundred refining processes, including a one-month standing period in a vat. At the end of it all, the resulting radium salts would be put into a dish smaller than a butter pat.

Great Depression: In the 1930s, the U.S. economy was in such a crisis that the terrible economic recession of the era gained this nickname. It lasted for most of the decade.

Half-life: The amount of time that a radioactive substance takes to lose half its radioactivity. Radium-226 has a half-life of sixteen hundred years.

Humanitarian: A person who wants to help people who are suffering or wanting to help people who are suffering.

Industrial: Relating to industry or business.

Insidious: Bad and happening gradually without anyone noticing.

Isotope: A different type or variety of an element. An isotope has the same number of protons in its atomic nucleus as all other isotopes of an element, but each isotope has a different number of neutrons. This gives it different physical properties and means each isotope may behave in a slightly different way.

Jugular vein: A large vein in the neck.

Lay off: When a company decides to stop employing a worker (often many workers at the same time) so they lose their job.

Lesion: An injury or wound on someone's body.

Lip-pointing: The technique used by the dial-painters, which saw them putting their paintbrushes in their mouths. They would suck on the bristles of the brush and then pull it out from between their pursed lips, which forced the bristles into a neat point. This point enabled the women to paint very delicately without going over the edges.

Luminous: Something that glows in the dark or shines brightly.

Lump sum: A one-time payment.

Malignant: Harmful.

Mesothorium: An isotope of radium, numbered radium-228.

Monopoly: When one company has exclusive control of an industry, product or service.

Mortgage: A bank loan taken out specifically to buy a house, or money you can borrow from a bank *because* you own a house. If you fail to pay back the loan, the bank can take ownership of your property.

Necrosis: A medical term meaning the death of a part of the body.

Occupational: Relating to someone's job or occupation.

Phosphorescence: A glow in the dark that endures for a long time.

Phosphorus: Another element. Various isotopes of it are used today to make fireworks, baking powder, and in radiotherapy. Red phosphorus is used to make matches.

Phossy jaw: In the nineteenth and early twentieth century, *white* phosphorus was used to make matches, but it was poisonous. "Phossy jaw" was the nickname given to the terrible condition suffered by the poisoned matchstick-makers—who were known as the Match Girls—in which their jawbones were slowly destroyed.

Physiology: The scientific study of living organisms, including people and their bodies.

Pneumonia: A disease in which the lungs are affected, making it difficult to breathe.

Radiation: The rays and particles emitted or given off by a radioactive element. There are three types of radiation: alpha, beta, and gamma.

Radioactive: Giving off energy in the form of powerful rays and particles.

Radiobiology: The study of how radiation affects living things.

Radium: A highly radioactive, luminous element. On the periodic table, it is part of the alkaline earth group of metals.

Rheumatism: A medical condition that makes your joints and muscles stiff.

Rosary: A string of special beads that Catholics use to count prayers. Rosary can also refer to the prayers themselves.

Sarcoma: A cancerous tumor of the bone.

Syphilis: A disease that is passed on through sexual intercourse.

Sorority: A group of women.

Spontaneously: Happening suddenly or naturally, without warning or being planned and without outside forces affecting it. (When Edna Hussman had a "spontaneous fracture" of her leg, she broke the bone without falling over or banging it; the bone simply broke.)

Statute of limitations: A legal term meaning a deadline is placed on when a lawsuit can be filed. After the deadline has passed, no legal case can be brought against the offender, even if they are guilty.

Timepiece: Another word for a watch or clock.

Tumor: A growth of new tissue or cells somewhere on or in the body that can be benign (safe) or malignant (harmful).

Vertebrae: The little bones that make up the spine in your back.

Wall Street crash: The name for the most dramatic stock market crash in U.S. history, which occurred in October 1929.

Zinc sulfide: A yellow-white powder that can be used to make things glow.

ABBREVIATIONS

CHR   Health Effects of Exposure to Internally
Deposited Radioactivity Projects Case Files.
Center for Human Radiobiology, Argonne
National Laboratory. General Records of the
Department of Energy, Record Group 434.
National Archives at Chicago.

HMP   Harrison Martland Papers, Special
Collections, George F. Smith Library of the
Health Sciences, Rutgers Biomedical and
Health Sciences, Newark

PPC   Pearl Payne Collection, LaSalle County
Historical Society and Museum, Utica,
Illinois

RBP   Raymond H. Berry Papers, Library of
Congress, Washington, DC

AL   Albina Maggia Larice

CD	Catherine Wolfe Donohue
CP	Charlotte Nevins Purcell
EH	Edna Bolz Hussman
GF	Grace Fryer
KS	Katherine Schaub
MR	Marie Becker Rossiter
PP	Pearl Payne
QM	Quinta Maggia McDonald
VS	Sabin von Sochocky
NCL	National Consumers League
USRC	United States Radium Corporation

PHOTO
ACKNOWLEDGMENTS

Page 4   *New York Evening Journal*

Page 6   The Pearl Payne Collection, LaSalle County
                Historical Society and Museum, Utica, Illinois

Page 11   CHR. Image supplied to National Archives by
                Mary Truesdale.

Page 12   CHR

Page 19   CHR

Page 21   CHR

Page 24   Courtesy of Rose Penta and the Maggia family

Page 26   *American Weekly*

Page 29   *Ottawa Daily Times*

Page 30   *Chicago Daily Times*, courtesy of Sun-Times
                Media

Page 31   Advertisement by Westclox. Sourced from
                the Pearl Payne Collection, LaSalle County
                Historical Society and Museum, Utica, Illinois

Page 34 *American Weekly*

Page 40 Courtesy of Darlene Halm and the Looney family

Page 41 Ottawa town directory 1928. Sourced from CHR.

Page 42 Courtesy of Dolores Rossiter and Patty Gray

Page 44 CHR

Page 50 *American Weekly*

Page 53 *American Weekly*

Page 56 CHR

Page 61 Harvard School of Public Health and Dade W. Moeller, sourced via *Deadly Glow* by Dr. Ross Mullner (American Public Health Association, 1999)

Page 64 *Newark Ledger*

Page 73 Portrait of Alice Hamilton, MD, resident and specialist in industrial diseases. JAMC_0000_0258_0399. Hull-House digital image collection, Special Collections and University Archives, University of Illinois at Chicago (left). Courtesy of the Babson College Archives (right).

Page 76 CHR

Page 78 Courtesy of Darlene Halm and the Looney family

Page 145   Raymond H. Berry Papers, reel 2, Library of
            Congress, Washington, DC

Page 147   Raymond H. Berry Papers, reel 2, Library of
            Congress, Washington, DC

Page 148   Raymond H. Berry Papers, reel 1, Library of
            Congress, Washington, DC

Page 149   *Newark Evening News*

Page 156   *The Pittsburgh Press*

Page 159   *Chicago Daily Times*, courtesy of Sun-Times
            Media

Page 166   Unknown newspaper, HMP

Page 169   Unknown newspapers, HMP

Page 171   Unknown newspaper, HMP

Page 185   Reproduced by permission of Argonne
            National Laboratory, sourced from *Deadly
            Glow* by Dr. Ross Mullner (American Public
            Health Association, 1999)

Page 187   Unknown newspaper, HMP

Page 191   Unknown newspaper, HMP

Page 196   CHR

Page 202   *Ottawa Daily Republican-Times*

Page 206   Courtesy of Robert Eyerkuss and his family

Page 210   Atlantic Portrait Galleries, *The World*, sourced
            from Harrison Martland Papers, Special

Collections, George F. Smith Library of the Health Sciences, Rutgers Biomedical and Health Sciences, Newark

Page 216   Used with permission of Darlene Halm and the Looney family, sourced from *Deadly Glow* by Dr. Ross Mullner (American Public Health Association, 1999)

Page 226   Unknown newspaper, Raymond H. Berry Papers, reel 2, Library of Congress, Washington, DC

Page 230   Unknown newspaper, HMP

Page 233   Collection of Ross Mullner

Page 241   Lippincott, Williams, and Wilkins, sourced from *Deadly Glow* by Dr. Ross Mullner (American Public Health Association, 1999)

Page 243   HMP

Page 247   CHR

Page 255   *Chicago Daily Times*, courtesy of Sun-Times Media

Page 259   *Chicago Daily Times*, courtesy of Sun-Times Media

Page 269   *Chicago Daily Times*, courtesy of Sun-Times Media

Page 273   *Chicago Daily Times*, courtesy of Sun-Times Media

PHOTO ACKNOWLEDGMENTS

Page 281   *Chicago Daily Times*, courtesy of Sun-Times Media

Page 285   The Pearl Payne Collection, LaSalle County Historical Society and Museum, Utica, Illinois

Page 286   *Chicago Daily Times*, courtesy of Sun-Times Media

Page 301   *Chicago Herald and Examiner*

Page 305   *Chicago Daily Times*, courtesy of Sun-Times Media

Page 307   *Chicago Daily Times*, courtesy of Sun-Times Media

Page 310   *Chicago Daily Times*, courtesy of Sun-Times Media

Page 311   *Chicago Herald and Examiner*

Page 316   *Chicago Herald and Examiner*

Page 317   *Chicago Daily Times*, courtesy of Sun-Times Media

Page 322   *Chicago Daily Times*, courtesy of Sun-Times Media

Page 325   Unknown newspaper, sourced from the scrapbooks of Leonard Grossman, lgrossman.com

Page 327   *Chicago Daily Times*, courtesy of Sun-Times Media

PHOTO ACKNOWLEDGMENTS

Page 337   Courtesy of the family of Charlotte Purcell

Page 344   Courtesy of the family of Charlotte Purcell

NOTES

PROLOGUE

"my beautiful radium" Quoted in "The Radium Girls," Medical Bag, January 1, 2014, www.medicalbag.com/profile-in-rare-diseases/the-radium-girls/article/472385/.

"These gleamings" Marie Curie, *Pierre Curie*, translated by C. and V. Kellogg (Macmillan, 1923), 104.

"it reminds one" Hugh S. Cumming (U.S. Surgeon General), transcript of the national radium conference, December 20, 1928, RBP, reel 3.

"the unknown god" Quoted in Claudia Clark, *Radium Girls* (Chapel Hill: The University of North Carolina Press, 1997), 49.

"the gods of" George Bernard Shaw, *The Quintessence of Ibsenism* (New York: Courier Corporation, 1994).

CHAPTER 1

"liquid sunshine" Quoted in John Conroy, "On Cancer, Clock Dials, and Ottawa, Illinois, a Town That Failed to See the Light," 1, 14.

"lip, dip, paint" Melanie Marnich, *These Shining Lives* (New York: Dramatists Play Service, Inc., 2010), 16.

"The first thing" Mae Cubberley Canfield, examination before trial, RBP, reel 2.

CHAPTER 2

"The girls" KS, "Radium", *Survey Graphic* (May 1932), 138.

"The place was" Florence E. Wall article, Orange Public Library.

"hands, arms, necks" William B. Castle, Katherine R. Drinker, and Cecil K. Drinker, "Necrosis of the Jaw in Workers Employed in Applying a Luminous Paint Containing Radium," *Journal of Industrial Hygiene* 8, no. 8 (August 1925): 375.

"When I would" EH affidavit, July 15, 1927, RBP, reel 1.

"Without doing so" EH affidavit, July 15.

"one of the" VS, "Can't You Find the Keyhole?" *American* (January 1921), 24.

"Do not do" VS, quoted in GF, court testimony, January 12, 1928.
"She told me" GF, ibid.

CHAPTER 3
"most hygienic" VS, quoted in Clark, *Radium Girls*, 17.
"Locked up in" VS, "Can't You Find the Keyhole?" 24, 108.
"What radium means" VS, "Keyhole?" 24.

CHAPTER 4
"My sister" QM, quoted in "Radium Death is Specter," *Star-Eagle*.
"Painting numbers" Amelia Maggia, quoted by Knef, unknown newspaper, USRC.
"not by an" "Poisoned! As They Chatted Merrily at Their Work," *American Weekly*, February 28, 1926.
"Radium may be" *Newark Evening News*, February 1922.
"slowly ate its" Knef, quoted in "Doctor Bares Deadly Radium Disease Secret," *Star-Eagle*.
"painful and terrible" QM, quoted in "Radium Death is Specter," *Star-Eagle*.

CHAPTER 5
"Girls wanted" Radium Dial advertisement, *Ottawa Daily Republican-Times*, September 16, 1922.
"Several girls" Radium Dial advertisement, *Ottawa Daily Republican-Times*.
"It was fascinating" CD, quoted in John Main, "Doomed Radium Victims Left Defenseless Too," *Chicago Daily Times*, July 9, 1937.
"Miss Lottie Murray" CD, quoted in Helen McKenna, "Victim Faints at Death Query in Radium Suit," *Chicago Daily Times*, February 10, 1938.
"lip, dip" Marnich, *These Shining Lives*, 16.
"18 years or" Radium Dial advertisement, *Ottawa Daily Republican-Times*, September 16, 1922.
"When I was" CP, quoted in "Ottawa Radium Company, Now in NY, to Fight Women," *Chicago Daily Times*, July 8, 1937.
"washing was a" Report on dial-painting studios, edited by Edsall and Collis, *Journal of Industrial Hygiene* 15, no. 5 (1933): CHR.
"The girls were" Bruce Grant, "Ghost Women Await Court's Decision on Radium Poisoning," *Chicago Herald-Examiner*, February 27, 1938.
"humorously termed" Grant, "Ghost Women Await Court's Decision."
"We were extremely" Unknown dial-painter, quoted in Arthur J. Snider, "Ranks of 'Living Dead' Dwindle in 25 Years," *Chicago Daily Times*, 1953.
"We expect you" Westclox Manual for Employees, Westclox Museum.

CHAPTER 6
"some occupational" Dr. Barry, court testimony, January 4, 1928.

"The word radium" KS, court testimony, April 25, 1928.
"dangerous practice" Charles Craster to John Roach, January 3, 1923, RBP, reel 3.
"caused by the" Dr. M. Szamatolski to Roach, January 30, 1923, RBP, reel 3.
"I feel quite" Szamatolski to Roach, April 6, 1923, RBP, reel 3.

CHAPTER 7

"The practice" Bob Bischoff, CHR.
"Her attitude" Interview with Patty Gray.
"Many of the" CD, court testimony, quoted in Grant, "Ghost Women Await Court's Decision."
"We used to" MR to Catherine Quigg, *Learning to Glow: A Deadly Reader*, edited by John Bradley (Tuscon: University of Arizona Press, 2000), 113.
"turn the lights" CP, quoted in interview with Felicia Keeton.
"just for fun" MR to Quigg, *Learning to Glow*, 113.

CHAPTER 8

"not decisive" Irene Rudolph death certificate, RBP, reel 2.
"terrible and" KS, "Radium," 138.
"A foreman there" Memo on KS visit to the Department of Health, July 19, 1923, RBP, reel 3.
"I began" KS, "Radium," 138.
"flinty" Barry, court testimony, January 4, 1928.
"I kept thinking" KS, "Radium," 138.
"My foot was" GF, court testimony, January 12, 1928.
"I said nothing" GF affidavit, June 8, 1927, RBP, reel 1.

CHAPTER 9

"You ought to" Dr. Davidson, quoted in Wiley notes on her interview with the dentist, RBP, reel 3.
"If I could" Dr. Davidson, quoted in Wiley.
"We do not" USRC to its insurance company, quoted in Clark, *Radium Girls*, 38.
"We discussed employment" KS, court testimony, April 25, 1925.
"I have been" GF, quoted in "Girl Radium Victim in Martyr Role," *Graphic*, May 25, 1928.
"pus bags" Katherine Wiley notes, RBP, reel 3.
"there is little" Lenore Young advising what Hazel's family have told her the doctors have said, letter to Roach, February 8, 1924, RBP, reel 3.

CHAPTER 10

"There seemed" Cecil K. Drinker to Andrew McBride, June 30, 1925, RBP, reel 1.

"persisted in the" Castle, Drinker, and Drinker, "Necrosis of the Jaw," *Journal of Industrial Hygiene* (August 1925).
"After seeing one" Wiley to Roeder, January 17, 1925, RBP, reel 3.
"to stick to" Wiley, quoted in Clark, *Radium Girls*, 66.
"As far as" Wiley notes, RBP, reel 3.
"They have none" Wiley to Alice Hamilton, March 4, 1925, RBP, reel 3.
"An investigation" Wiley notes, RBP, reel 3.
"Put it in" Wiley notes, RBP, reel 3.
"practically normal" Table of results from Castle, Drinker, and Drinker, enclosed with letter from Harold Viedt to Roach, June 18, 1924, RBP, reel 1.
"He tells everyone" Dr. Alice Hamilton to Dr. Katherine Drinker, April 4, 1925, RBP, reel 1.
"Rumors quieted" USRC memo.

CHAPTER 11
"nervous case" Wiley notes, RBP, reel 3.
"I could not" KS, "Radium," 138.
"The pain" KS, quoted in "Poisoned—As They Chatted."
"I had stopped" KS, "Radium," 139.
"Why should I" KS, quoted in "Woman Doomed Rests All Hopes in Her Prayers," *Graphic*.
"It seemed to" QM affidavit, August 29, 1927, RBP, reel 1.
"white shadow" Humphries, court testimony, April 25, 1928.
"The whole situation" Roach, quoted in "Occupational Diseases—Radium Necrosis," information secured by Miss E. P. Ward, CHR.
"radium jaw" Blum, address to the American Dental Association, September 1924.
"lingering between" Hoffman to Roeder, December 13, 1924, RBP, reel 2.
"I seriously" Hoffman to Roeder, December 29, 1924, RBP, reel 2.

CHAPTER 12
"I began to" CD, court testimony, quoted in *Ottawa Daily Republican-Times*, February 10, 1938.
"The whole family" Interview with Jean Schott.
"so as not" S. Kjaer, "Occupational Diseases—Radium Necrosis: Observations on Fieldwork," CHR.
Following quotations, Kjaer, "Occupational Diseases."
"Radium paints" Ethelbert Stewart, quoted in "U.S. Labor Expert Calls for Radium Paint Inquiry," *World*, July 17, 1928.
"the expense" Stewart to Hamilton, December 17, 1927, RBP, reel 3.

CHAPTER 13
"the disease in" VS to Hoffman, February 14, 1925, RBP, reel 3.

"My dear Mr." Wiley to Roeder, March 2, 1925, RBP, reel 1.
"We believe that" Drinker to Roeder, June 3, 1924, RBP, reel 1.
"it would seem" Drinker to Viedt, April 29, 1924, quoted in Ross Mullner, *Deadly Glow* (American Public Health Association, 1999), 58.
"In our opinion" Drinker report, June 3, 1924, RBP, reel 1.
Following quotations, Drinker report.
"practically normal" Table of results from the Castle, Drinker, and Drinker report, RBP, reel 1.
"mystified" Roeder to Drinker, June 6, 1924, RBP, reel 1.
"a real villain" Katherine Drinker to Hamilton, April 17, 1925, RBP, reel 1.
"stupid enough" Hamilton to Wiley, February 2, 1925, RBP, reel 3.

CHAPTER 14

"They had impressed" Hoffman, court testimony, January 12, 1928.
"palm off" Roeder, quoted in Kjaer study, RBP, reel 2.
"We are not" Roeder to Drinker, April 9, 1925, RBP, reel 1.
"[He] told me" EH affidavit, July 15, 1927, RBP, reel 1.
"a very depressing" KS, "Radium," 139.
"Since [my] first" KS, *Graphic*.
"To be under" KS, "Radium," 139.
"extremely rotten" Martland, court testimony, April 26, 1928.
"small, rapid" Marguerite Carlough form, Kjaer study, CHR.
"The women were" Hoffman, court testimony, January 12, 1928.
"The cumulative effect" Ibid.
"We are dealing" Hoffman's report, quoted in Mullner, *Deadly Glow*, 66.
"Miss Carlough may" Hamilton to Katherine Drinker, April 4, 1925.
"It has seemed" Hoffman, JAMA, 1925.

CHAPTER 15

"One of the" Martland, "The Danger of Increasing the Normal Radioactivity of the Human Body," HMP.
"The first case" Martland, court testimony, December 6, 1934.
"removed to receive" "Interest Keen in Radium Inquiry," *Newark Evening News* (June 19, 1925).
"I have nothing" Martland, quoted in unknown newspaper, HMP.
"We have nothing" Martland, quoted in "Interest Keen in Radium Inquiry," *Newark Evening News* (June 19, 1925).
"No" "Interest Keen in Radium Inquiry," *Newark Evening News* (June 19, 1925).

CHAPTER 16

"Nothing was found" Viedt, quoted in unknown newspaper, HMP.
"the latter" Ibid.
"a type of" Martland, "The Danger of," HMP.

"I then took" Martland, court testimony, April 26, 1928.
"There is nothing" Martland to McBride, August 28, 1925, HMP.
"There is not" Ibid.
"It must be" KS, "Radium," 139.
"He told me" GF affidavit, July 18, 1927, RBP, reel 1.
"He told me that my trouble" QM affidavit, August 29, 1927, RBP, reel 1.
"The doctors told" KS, "Radium," 139.
"The county medical" Ibid.
"gave me hope" Ibid.

CHAPTER 17

"Do not do" VS, quoted by GF, court testimony, January 12, 1928.
"*all your trouble*" GF affidavit, July 18, 1927, RBP, reel 1.
"Why didn't you" Question derived from Berry's evidence that GF "asked [VS] why it was [he] hadn't informed them" of the danger, court transcript, April 1928.
"aware of these" Court transcript, April 27, 1928.
"warned other members" Berry, citing statement of VS to Martland and Hoffman, legal notes, RBP, reel 1.
"The matter was" Court transcript, April 27, 1928.
"I don't believe" GF quoted in "Girl Radium Victim in Martyr Role," *Graphic*, May 25, 1928.
"Miss Molly" The List of the Doomed, HMP.
"I know I" KS, "The Legion of the Doomed," *Graphic*.
"Her face" "Poisoned—As They Chatted."
"mentally deranged" USRC memo, July 20, 1927.
"When you're sick" KS, quoted in *Sunday Call*.
"She is not" Josephine Schaub, quoted in Dorothy Dayton, "Girls Poisoned with Radium Not Necessarily Doomed to Die," *New York Sun*, May 17, 1928.
"half dead" Hoffman, quoted in *Orange Daily Courier*, June 9, 1928.

CHAPTER 18

"I feel better" GF, quoted in unknown newspaper, RBP, reel 2.
"While other girls" KS, "The Legion of the Doomed," *Graphic*.
"unbias opinion" Flinn to KS, December 7, 1925, RBP, reel 3.
"radium could" Berry, legal notes, RBP, reel 1.
"Suits Are Settled in Radium Deaths," *Newark Evening News*, May 4, 1926.
"Mr. Carlough" "Suits Are Settled."
"I feel we" GF, *Graphic*.
"An industrial" Flinn, "Radioactive Material: An Industrial Hazard?" *JAMA* (December 1926).
"more bias" Hoffman, deposition, August 25, 1927, RBP, reel 1.
"I cannot but" Flinn to Drinker, January 16, 1926, RBP, reel 3.

"Your blood" GF affidavit, July 18, 1927, RBP, reel 1.
"He told me" GF, court testimony, January 12, 1928.

CHAPTER 19

"They were both" Interview with Mary Carroll Cassidy.
"I quit ten" Elizabeth Frenna, CHR.
"I remember when" Mr. Callahan, CHR.
"We were watched" Hazel McClean, CHR.
"Supervisor wasn't" Ida Zusman, CHR.
"We had our" CD, court testimony, legal brief.
"The company left" CD, court testimony, quoted in *Chicago Herald-Examiner*, February 12, 1938.

CHAPTER 20

"in a spirit" Hoffman to Roeder, November 6, 1926, RBP, reel 2.
"Mr. Roeder is" Clarence B. Lee to Hoffman, November 16, 1926, RBP, reel 2.
"You must take" Hoffman to GF, December 9, 1926, RBP, reel 3.
"obliteration" GF medical notes, RBP, reel 2.
"I can hardly" GF, quoted in Florence L. Pflazgraf, "Radium Victim Battles Death with Courage," *Orange Daily Courier*, April 30, 1928.
"We regret" Hood, Lafferty, and Campbell to GF, March 24, 1927, RBP, reel 2.
"[Dr. Martland] agrees" Hoffman to GF, December 9, 1926.
"It's awfully hard" GF, quoted in Pflazgraf, "Radium Victim Battles Death with Courage."
"Her Body Wasting, She Sues Employer: Woman Appears in Court with Steel Frame to Hold Her Erect," *Newark Evening News*, May 20, 1927.

CHAPTER 21

"denie[d] that" USRC legal reply, July 20, 1927, RBP, reel 1.
"So far as" Berry to USRC lawyers Collins & Collins, June 8, 1927, RBP, reel 3.
"I [have] examined" Flinn, "Newer Industrial Hazards," *JAMA* 197, 28.
"In these negotiations" DeVille and Steiner, "New Jersey Radium Dial Workers."
"double-dealing" Martland's opinion, quoted in Berry to Hamilton, January 6, 1928, RBP, reel 3.
"Our records" New Jersey Board of Medical Examiners to Berry, September 29, 1927, RBP, reel 3.
"a fraud" Consumers League to World, March 25, 1929, NCL files, Library of Congress.

CHAPTER 22

"The next day" Nellie Cruse, quoted in Mary Doty, "Kin Reveal Agony of Radium Victims," *Chicago Daily Times*, March 18, 1936.
"That's all bunk" Cruse family doctor, quoted in Doty, "Kin Reveal Agony."

"The next day" Nellie Cruse, quoted in Doty, "Kin Reveal Agony."
"She suffered" Cruse, quoted in Doty, "Kin Reveal Agony."
"Miss Cruse's" Ella Cruse obituary, *Ottawa Daily Republican-Times*, September 6, 1927.
"Life has never" Nellie and James Cruse, quoted in Doty, "Kin Reveal Agony."
"She had been" Ella Cruse obituary, *Ottawa Daily Republican-Times*, September 6, 1927.

CHAPTER 23
"a real villain" Wiley, quoted in Clark, *Radium Girls*, 111.
"No evidence" Initial Amelia Maggia autopsy report, November 3, 1927, RBP, reel 3.
"Each and every" Amelia Maggia form, Kjaer study, CHR.
"This case is" Martland, quoted in "Former Radium Worker Dies," *Newark Evening News*, December 14, 1927.

CHAPTER 24
"Grace is so" Florence L. Pflazgraf, "Radium Victim Battles Death with Courage," *Orange Daily Courier*, April 30, 1928.
"We were instructed" Court transcript, January 12, 1928.
Following quotations in courtroom, Court transcript, January 12, 1928.
"Everything was going" KS, "Radium," 139.
"I was awakened" KS, "Radium," 139.
"I haven't had" KS to Berry, February 1928, RBP, reel 3.
"safe from intrusion" KS to Berry, February 1928, RBP, reel 3.

CHAPTER 25
"The young lady" Court transcript, April 25, 1928.
Following quotations in courtroom, Court transcript, April 25, 1928.
"sadly smiling" "5 Girls Hear Scientists Predict Their Deaths," *Star-Eagle*, April 26, 1928.
"maintained an attitude" Unknown newspaper, RBP, reel 2.
"of which they" "5 Girls Hear Scientists Predict Their Deaths," *Star-Eagle*, April 26, 1928.
"Were you ever" Court transcript, April 25, 1928.
Following quotations in courtroom, Court transcript, April 25–27, 1928.
"We should" USRC memo, July 20, 1927.
"Well, Mr. Berry" Court transcript, April 27, 1928.
Following quotations in courtroom, Court transcript, April 27, 1928..
"heartless and" KS, "Radium," 140.

CHAPTER 26
"Grace" Grace Fryer Sr., quoted in "Radium Case Off Till Fall," *Newark Ledger*, April 29, 1928.

"far from" Berry to Charles Norris, May 5, 1928, RBP, reel 3.
"These girls are" Dr. Gettler, sworn statement, May 9, 1928, RBP, reel 1.
"Everywhere" KS, "Radium," 140.
"Letters came" KS, "Radium," 140.
"Don't think" KS, quoted in "Doomed to Die, Tell How They'd Spend Fortune," *Sunday Call*, May 13, 1928.
"I couldn't say" GF, "The Legion of the Doomed," *Graphic*.
"My body means" GF, "The Legion of the Doomed."

CHAPTER 27
"To Judge" Berry's diary, May 23, 1928, CHR.
"Pains like streaks" KS, *Graphic*.
"Just because I" Judge Clark, quoted in "Radium Men Talk Terms of Settlement," *Newark Evening News*, May 31, 1928.
"There is no" Judge Clark, quoted in unknown newspaper, RBP, reel 2.
"Radium Victims Reject Cash Offers: Will Push Cases; Parleys Now Off," *Orange Daily Courier*, June 2, 1928.
"I will not" GF, quoted in "3 Women to Spurn Radium Offer Unless Firm Pays for Litigation," *Star-Eagle*.
"absolutely refuse" GF, quoted in ibid.
"smiling sorority" Ibid.
"You can say" Judge Clark, quoted in "Radium Suits Settled in Main Details," *Newark Evening News*, June 4, 1928.
"[USRC] hopes" Ibid.
"I have" Berry to Norris, June 6, 1928, RBP, reel 3.
"I want to" Judge Clark to five women, unknown newspaper, RBP, reel 2.
"I think Mr." EH, quoted in "Radium Victims Figuring How to Spend Awards," *Star-Eagle*, June 6, 1928.
"God has heard" KS, quoted in "Cash Welcomed by Radium Victims as Release from Poverty Worry," *Newark Ledger*, June 5, 1928.
"quite pleased" GF, quoted in "'Ray Paint' Victims Praise Settlement," *World*, June 6, 1928.
"I'd like to" GF, quoted in "Cash Welcomed by Radium Victims as Release from Poverty Worry," *Newark Ledger*, June 5, 1928.
"It is not" GF, unknown newspaper, RBP, reel 2.
"You see" GF, *Graphic*.

CHAPTER 28
"More Deaths Raise Radium Paint Toll to 17," *Ottawa Daily Republican-Times*, June 4, 1928.
"The girls became" CD, quoted in Guy Housley, "Radium Dial Deals Death to Ninth of 'Suicide Club,'" *Ottawa Daily Republican-Times*, March 14, 1936.
"they separated" MR, quoted in interview with Dolores Rossiter.

"When I asked" CD, court testimony, quoted in unknown newspaper, www.lgrossman.com/pics/radium/.

"Why, my dear" Reed, quoted in Virginia Gardner, "Former Watch Painter Faints," *Chicago Daily Tribune*, February 11, 1938.

"Neither of us" CD, court testimony, quoted in "Radium Victim Tells 'Living Death'; She Faints as Doctor Charts Doom," *Chicago Herald-Examiner*, February 11, 1938.

"There is no" Reed, quoted in ibid. and legal brief.

"Are the workers" MR, court testimony, quoted in Virginia Gardner, "Radium Test Case Finished; 9 Women Heard," *Chicago Daily Tribune*, February 12, 1938.

"You don't" Reed, quoted in ibid.

"technical experts" Statement by the Radium Dial Company, *Ottawa Daily Republican-Times*, June 7, 1928.

Following quotations, ibid.

"He said that" CD, court testimony, quoted in Bruce Grant, "Radium Bedside Court Sees How Women Dared Death," *Chicago Herald-Examiner*, February 12, 1938.

"Radium will put" Mr. Reed, quoted in MR testimony, *Chicago Herald-Examiner*, February 12, 1938.

"ever-watchful" *Ottawa Daily Republican-Times*, June 11, 1928.

"They went to" Interview with Dolores Rossiter.

CHAPTER 29

"like Cinderella" KS, "Radium," 140.

"I bought the" Ibid.

"Not a cent" GF, quoted in Robert E. Martin, "Doomed to Die—and They Live!" *Popular Science* (July 1929), 136.

"What for?" Ibid.

"For the future!" Ibid.

"survived the early" Clark, *Radium Girls*, 118.

"I am of" Martland to Robley Evans, June 13, 1928, HMP.

"Someone may find" GF, *Graphic*.

"There is no" Stewart, quoted in "U.S. Labor Expert Calls for Radium Paint Inquiry," *World*, July 17, 1928.

"The new methods" Ibid.

"real country life" KS, "Radium," 140.

"splendid" Berry to KS, September 11, 1928, RBP, reel 1.

"I loved to" KS, "Radium," 140.

"I am writing" KS to Martland, June 28, 1928, HMP.

"All five patients" Dr. Failla, test results, November 20, 1928, RBP, reel 2.

"improper diet" Flinn, "Elimination of Radium," *JAMA*.

"tendency" Ibid.

"He died" Martland, quoted in *Star-Eagle*, November 1928.

"a whitewash" Florence Kelley to Wiley, January 2, 1929, NCL files, Library of Congress.

"cold-blooded" Ibid.

"The Radium Corp." Berry to Krumbhaar, December 5, 1928, RBP, reel 3.

"My advice to" Delegate, "Transcript of the National Radium Conference," December 20, 1928.

CHAPTER 30

"Only once" CD, court testimony, quoted in *Ottawa Daily Republican-Times*, February 10, 1938.

"Further steps" Kjaer report, CHR.

"intention" Joseph A. Kelly to Kjaer, March 22, 1929, CHR.

"I feel that" Kjaer to Weeks, March 15, 1929, CHR.

"*One dial-painter*" Kjaer, "Radium Poisoning: Industrial Poisoning from Radioactive Substances," *Monthly Labor Review* (date unknown), CHR.

"a high standard" Statement by the Radium Dial Company, *Ottawa Daily Republican-Times*, June 7, 1928.

"He was" Interview with Darlene Halm, July 20, 2016.

"We'd all be" Interview with Jean Schott.

"She knew she" Ethel Looney, quoted in "'Living Dead' Await That Fateful Day," *Chicago Herald-Examiner*, March 18, 1936.

"Well, Mother" Margaret Looney, quoted in ibid.

"*No*" Jack White, quoted by Darlene Halm in interview, July 20, 2016.

"I think it" Interview with Darlene Halm, July 20, 2016.

"They wanted the" Darlene Halm, quoted in Martha Irvine, "'Radium Girls' Wrote Tragic Chapter in Town's History," *Buffalo News*, October 11, 1998.

"the flat bones" Margaret Looney exhumation autopsy report, 1978, CHR.

"very strongly" Ibid.

"The teeth are" Margaret Looney original autopsy report, August 27, 1929.

"*The young woman's*" Margaret Looney obituary, *Ottawa Daily Republican-Times*, August 16, 1929.

"Miss Looney's" Ibid.

CHAPTER 31

"These women are" Ewing to Krumbhaar, April 30, 1929, RBP, reel 2.

"People are now" GF, quoted in "Radium Victims Figuring How to Spend Awards," *Star-Eagle*, June 6, 1928.

"The doctors don't" KS to Berry, November 8, 1928, RBP, reel 3.

"the jewel" KS to Berry, March 7, 1929, RBP, reel 3.

"hollyhocks" KS, "Radium," 140.

"paper fortunes" *Chicago Daily Tribune*, October 1929, quoted in Ron Grossman, "Recalling a Steeper Stock Market Plunge," *Chicago Tribune*, August 15, 2011.

"For a time" KS, "Radium," 156.
"kept close" "First Woman Radium Victim Will Go to Grave Tomorrow," *Newark Ledger*.
"The bones of" Martland, quoted in "Radium Victim Offered Body to Help Science Save Others," *Newark Ledger*.
"I agree not" Terms of Mae Cubberley Canfield settlement, March 8, 1930, RBP, reel 1.

CHAPTER 32

"They say" KS to Martland, October 5, 1930.
"I work" GF, "The Legion of the Doomed," *Graphic*.
"I found a" Martland, court testimony, December 6, 1934.
"He told me" Vincent La Porte, court testimony, November 26, 1934.
"I am now" Martland, quoted in Mullner, *Deadly Glow*, 72.
"You couldn't take" Martland, court testimony, December 6, 1934.
"I believe" Martland to Sir Humphrey Rolleston, April 2, 1931, HMP.

CHAPTER 33

"I'm sorry" CD, court testimony, legal brief.
All remaining quotations in chapter, Ibid.

CHAPTER 34

"I have been" KS, "Radium," 157.
"exploitation" Krumbhaar to Berry, February 12, 1932, RBP, reel 3.
"highly hysterical" Dr. May to Dr. Craver, November 7, 1931, quoted in Sharpe, "Radium Osteitis with Osteogenic Sarcoma," September 1971.
"the very depressed" Ewing to KS, GF, AL, and EH, February 10, 1932.
"The Radium Water Worked Fine until His Jaw Came Off," *Wall Street Journal*.
"It is my" KS, "Radium," 157.
"adventure" KS, "Radium," 157.

CHAPTER 35

"I feel better" GF, quoted in "Radium Victims Investing Money," *Newark Evening News*.
"Home always" EH, quoted in ibid.
"What good would" EH, quoted in "Radium Poison Survivors Continue to Cheat Death," *Newark Evening News*, March 9, 1938.
"I know they" AL, quoted in "Doomed to Die, Tell How They'd Spend Fortune," *Sunday Call*, May 13, 1928.
"I am not" GF, quoted in "5 Women Smile, Fearing Death, in Radium Case," *Newark Ledger*, January 13, 1928.
"It was not" Grace Fryer Sr., quoted in unknown newspaper, CHR.
"radium sarcoma" GF death certificate.

"The family" Interview with Art Fryer Jr.

"I will never" Art Fryer Sr., interviewed by his grandson, quoted in interview with Art Fryer Jr.

CHAPTER 36

"no visible indication" Margaret Looney obituary, *Ottawa Daily Republican-Times*, August 16, 1929.

"God has sure" CD to PP, 29 April 1938, PPC.

"one of the" "Mid-Winter Bride Will Pledge Vows at St. Columba," *Ottawa Daily Republican-Times*, January 22, 1932.

"They were just" Interview with Don Torpy.

"They were all" Interview with Jean Schott.

"It was confusing" Interview with Mary Carroll Cassidy.

CHAPTER 37

"There was no" Interview with Jan Torpy.

"Tom was" Interview with Mary Carroll Cassidy.

"After that" Tom Donohue, speaking at CD inquest, July 28, 1938.

"I firmly believe" PP to Catherine O'Donnell, June 23, 1938, PPC.

"I told him" Dr. Charles Loffler, court testimony, quoted in Mullner, *Deadly Glow*, 105.

"Nothing even approaching" Statement by the Radium Dial Company, *Ottawa Daily Republican-Times*, June 7, 1928.

"very suspicious" Radium Dial 1928 test results, CHR.

"She never felt" Interview with Jan Torpy.

"I can't do" CP, quoted in Griffin, "Society of the Living Dead," *Toronto Star*, April 23, 1938.

"I have received" CD, court testimony, legal brief.

Following quotations, Ibid.

"I don't think" Reed, quoted in CD testimony, *Chicago Herald-Examiner*, February 12, 1938.

"There is nothing" Reed, quoted in CD testimony, quoted in Mullner, Deadly Glow, 101.

"He refused" CD, court testimony, *Chicago Herald-Examiner*, February 12, 1938.

"Was disease" Mary Robinson death certificate.

CHAPTER 38

"that earlier" Quigg, *Learning to Glow*, 114.

"She was a" CD, quoted in "'Living Dead' Await That Fateful Day," *Chicago Herald-Examiner*, March 18, 1936.

"When Attorney Cook" John Main, "15 Walking Ghosts Jilted by Justice," *Chicago Daily Times*, July 7, 1937.

"an almost" Ibid.

"I hated to" Jay Cook, quoted in *Chicago Daily Times*, July 9, 1937.
"There are medicines" CD, quoted in "Mrs. Donohue Calm at Radium Decision News," *Ottawa Daily Republican-Times*, April 5, 1938.
"not...merely" Irene La Porte v. USRC, December 17, 1935.
Following quotations, Ibid.

CHAPTER 39
"We never talk" Tom Donohue quoted in Mary Doty, "Fears Haunt Victims of Radium in Ottawa," *Chicago Daily Times*, March 19, 1936.
"As long as" CD, quoted in Helen McKenna, "'Fighting Irish' Heart Sustains 'Living Dead,'" *Chicago Daily Times*, February 13, 1938.
"We'll always be" PP, quoted in "Times Thanked by Living Dead," *Chicago Daily Times*, February 11, 1938.
"They shoot to" Mary Doty, "Ottawa's Doomed Women," *Chicago Daily Times*, March 17, 1936.
"Some [girls]" Ibid.
"Her parents" Mary Doty, "Fears Haunt Victims of Radium in Ottawa," *Chicago Daily Times*, March 19, 1936..
"I am in" CD, quoted in "'Living Dead' Await That Fateful Day," *Chicago Herald-Examiner*, March 18, 1936.
"This day" Tom Donohue, court testimony, quoted in Clark, *Radium Girls*, 184.
Following quotations, Ibid.
"Irish temper" Interview with Kathleen Donohue Cofoid.
"I don't think" Ibid.
"I swang at" Tom Donohue, court testimony, quoted in Clark, *Radium Girls*, 184.

CHAPTER 40
"controlling interests" Hobart Payne to Clarence Darrow, May 17, 1937, PPC.
"typical of" Interview with Mary Carroll Cassidy.
"They know that" Ibid.
"You took whatever" Ibid.
"We used to" Interview with Donald Purcell.
"Tom was nearly" Brother-in-law, quoted in Mullner, *Deadly Glow*, 106.
"They were on" Interview with Mary Carroll Cassidy.
"Part of her" Hobart Payne to Darrow, May 17, 1937, PPC.
"It was so" Interview with Mary Carroll Cassidy.
"She was an" Interview with Dolores Rossiter, July 26, 2016.
"their last stand" John Main, "Radium Death on Rampage," *Chicago Daily Times*, July 7, 1937.
"Without a lawyer" Main, "Doomed Radium Victims Left Defenseless, Too," *Chicago Daily Times*, July 9, 1937.

"That's what" CD, quoted in ibid.
"The Radium Dial" *Chicago Daily Times*, July 7, 1937.
"I can't recall" William Ganley, quoted in "Ottawa Radium Company Now in New York," *Chicago Daily Times*, July 8, 1937.

CHAPTER 41

"We were at" CD, quoted in Griffin, "Society of the Living Dead," *Toronto Star*, April 23, 1938.
"My heart is" Grossman to PP, October 15, 1938, PPC.
"the paint was" "Doomed Ottawa Women Seek Compensation for Death," *Daily Pantagraph*, July 24, 1937.
"We should have" Grossman, courtroom proclamation, quoted in ibid.
"We do not" Ibid.

CHAPTER 42

"She hasn't long" PP, quoted in Bruce Grant, "Ghost Women Await Court's Decision on Radium Poisoning," *Chicago Herald-Examiner*, February 27, 1938.
"It had good" Interview with Mary Carroll Cassidy.
"My body" CD, court testimony, quoted in "Firm Discounted Radium Fears," *Newark Evening News*, February 11, 1938.
"You could see" Interview with James Donohue.
"People are afraid" CD, quoted in Helen McKenna, "Fighting Irish Heart Sustains Living Dead," *Chicago Daily Times*, February 13, 1938.
"He used to" Interview with James Donohue.
"I suffer so" CD to PP, December 7, 1937, PPC.
"This is the" Grossman quoted in Win Green, "April Decision in Radium Test," *Ottawa Daily Republican-Times*, February 12, 1938.
"with every" Grossman to PP, Season's Greetings card, December 1937, PPC.
"right through" Dalitsch, court testimony, legal brief.
"near death" Loffler, court testimony, quoted in *Ottawa Daily Republican-Times*, February 11, 1938.

CHAPTER 43

"Mrs. Donohue" *Chicago Herald-Examiner*, February 11, 1938.
"toothpick woman" Helen McKenna, "Living Dead Ask Radium Co. Pay," *Chicago Daily Times*, February 10, 1938.
"Human lives" Grossman, legal brief.
"weak and" Unknown newspaper, collection of Ross Mullner.
"faltering" Helen McKenna, "Victim Faints at Death Query in Radium Suit," *Chicago Daily Times*, February 10, 1938.
"That's the way" CD, court testimony, quoted in McKenna, "Living Dead Ask Radium Co. Pay," *Chicago Daily Times*, February 10, 1938.

"After those" CD, court testimony, quoted in Bruce Grant, "Radium Bedside Court Sees How Women Dared Death," *Chicago Herald-Examiner*, February 12, 1938.

"After Miss Marie" CD, court testimony, quoted in "'Living Death' Told by Woman Victim of Radium Poison," *Chicago Herald-Examiner*, February 11, 1938.

"Oh!" MR, quoted in ibid.

"That is the" CD, court testimony, quoted in Virginia Gardner, "Woman Tells 'Living Death' at Radium Quiz," *Chicago Daily Tribune*, February 11, 1938.

"assumed responsibility" Frances Salawa, CHR.

"Mr. Reed said" CD, court testimony, quoted in Grant, "Radium Bedside Court Sees How Women Dared Death."

"He refused" Ibid.

"After two years" CD, court testimony, quoted in *Ottawa Daily Republican-Times*, February 10, 1938.

"These are" CD, court testimony, quoted in *Chicago Tribune, Chicago Daily Times, Chicago Herald-Examiner*, February 11, 1938.

CHAPTER 44

"The condition" Dalitsch, court transcript, legal brief.

Following quotations, Ibid.

"permanent, incurable" Legal brief.

"In her" Dalitsch, court testimony, legal brief.

"The woman's sobs" Bruce Grant, "Woman Tells How Radium Dooms Her," *Chicago Herald-Examiner*, February 11, 1938.

"She is in" Attending physician, quoted in *Chicago Daily Times*, February 10, 1938.

"Death Is the Third Person Here," *Detroit Michigan Times*, February 14, 1938.

"Is her condition" Court transcript, legal brief.

Following quotations, ibid.

"She is beyond" Weiner, court testimony, quoted in *Ottawa Daily Republican-Times*, February 11, 1938.

"She has but" Loffler, court testimony, quoted in Gardner, "Woman Tells 'Living Death' at Radium Quiz."

"That is" Grossman, quoted in Grant, "Woman Tells How Radium Dooms Her."

CHAPTER 45

"It's too" CD, "'Living Dead' Hear New Radium Plea," *Chicago Illinois American*, June 6, 1938.

"Show us" Grossman, court transcript, quoted in Virginia Gardner, "Radium Test Case Finished: 9 Women Heard," *Chicago Daily Tribune*, February 12, 1938.

"Here's how" CD, court testimony, quoted in "'Living Death' Case Hearing Ends," *Dubuque Iowa Herald*, February 13, 1938.

"We dipped" CD, court testimony, quoted in Gardner, "Radium Test Case Finished."

"Then shaped" Ibid.

"a shudder ran" "'Living Death' Case Hearing Ends."

"I did this" CD, court testimony, quoted in Grant, "Ghost Women Await Court's Decision on Radium Poisoning."

"That was" CD, court testimony, quoted in "Court Convenes at Bedside in Dying Woman's Damage Suit," *Denver Colorado Post*, February 11, 1938.

"Did any" Grossman, court transcript, quoted in *Ottawa Daily Republican-Times*, February 11, 1938.

Following quotations, Ibid.

"We even ate" CD, court testimony, compiled from quotes in *Ottawa Daily Republican-Times, Chicago Daily Times, Chicago Herald-Examiner*.

"This is a" Court transcript, quoted in Gardner, "Radium Test Case Finished."

Following quotations, Ibid.

CHAPTER 46

"criminally careless" "The Radium Poison Tragedies," *Springfield Illinois State Register*, February 22, 1938.

"Once that" Interview with Mary Carroll Cassidy.

"I just remember" Ibid.

"You have my" Letter to CD, quoted in in Win Green, "Nation-Wide Interest Shown in Radium Case," *Ottawa Daily Republican-Times*, March 1938.

"I cannot imagine" Grossman, legal brief.

"The Industrial" Marvel's judgment, quoted in "'Living Death' Victim Wins Life Pension," *Chicago American*, April 5, 1938; William Mueller, "'Living Dead' Win Radium Test Case," *Chicago Daily Times*, April 5, 1938.

"Justice has" Grossman, quoted in unknown newspaper, lgrossman.com.

"cries but" Tom Donohue, quoted in "Mrs. Donohue Calm at Radium Decision News," *Ottawa Daily Republican-Times*, April 5, 1938.

"I am glad" CD, quoted in "'Radium' Victim Granted Pension of $277 a Year," *American*, April 6, 1938.

"The judge is" CD, quoted in "Mrs. Donohue Calm at Radium Decision News."

"It should have" Ibid.

"I wonder if" CD, quoted in "Radium Victim Asserts Death Races Pension," *American*, April 6, 1938.

"Now maybe" CD, quoted in unknown newspaper, collection of Ross Mullner.

"I hope the" Ibid.

CHAPTER 47

"I only wish" CD to PP, April 29, 1938.

"In my opinion" Dr. Dunn, quoted in "Hold Hearing in LaSalle on Radium Poison Appeal," *Daily News-Herald*, June 6, 1938.

"If Mrs." Grossman, quoted in "Hold Hearing in LaSalle on Radium Poison Appeal."

"The doctors" CD to Father Keane, June 22, 1938, quoted in *Chicago Daily Times*, June 24, 1938.

"It was" CD to PP, PPC.

"lovely time" Olive Witt to PP, July 18, 1938, PPC.

"I live" PP, quoted in Griffin, "Society of the Living Dead."

"She had held" Grossman, quoted in "Death Halts Collection of Award," *Chicago Daily Times*, July 27, 1938.

"a cool, calculating" Grossman, quoted in *Chicago Daily Times*, July 28, 1938.

"We, the jury" Unknown newspaper, possibly *Ottawa Daily Republican-Times*, Catherine Wolfe Donohue Collection, Northwestern University.

"one of the" Walsh, "Jury Blames Dial. Co. for Radium Death."

EPILOGUE

"If it hadn't" AEC official, quoted in Mullner, *Deadly Glow*, 127.

"invaluable" Ibid.

"Every one of" NCL memo, November 1959, NCL files, Library of Congress.

"the terrible future" AEC official, quoted in Mullner, *Deadly Glow*, 134.

"incalculable value" Ibid.

"vital insight" Ibid.

"essential to the" Argonne National Laboratory press release.

"If we can" Lester Barrer, quoted in Malcolm M. Manber, "Radium Workers Well," *Newark Evening News*, July 15, 1962.

"give the world" Plainfield Courier, March 21, 1959.

"Wanted" Theodore Berland, "Wanted: Radium Workers of the Roaring Twenties," *Today's Health*, November 1959.

"Each of these" John Rose, quoted in Roy Gibbons, "Vast Search Is on for Radium Fad Victims," *Chicago Sunday Tribune*, March 18, 1959.

"a reservoir" Roscoe Kandle, CHR.

"The source of" Kjaer notes, 1925, quoted in "Historic American Buildings Survey."

"moral obligation" Mullner, *Deadly Glow*, 136.

"huge and spotty" Interview with Jan Torpy.

"I witnessed" MR, November 13, 2010, accessed 2015, http://www.mywebtimes.com/news/local/video-she-was-a-fighter/article_f7f6b1e8-1412-5e0a-8574-763be17400ee.html.

"forever" New Jersey Supreme Court judgment, quoted in Clark, *Radium Girls*, 201.

"the normal" Martland, quoted in Mullner, *Deadly Glow*, 72.

"She was probably" Interview with Jan Torpy.

"It was nothing" Interview with Don Torpy.

"far from won" Frances Perkins, quoted in "Sec. Perkins Says

Compensation for Workmen Inadequate," *Ottawa Daily Republican-Times*, October 17, 1939.

"I'm *angry*" Unnamed Looney sister, quoted in Irvine, "Suffering Endures."

"Every family" Jean Schott, quoted in Denise Grady, "A Glow in the Dark, and a Lesson in Scientific Peril," *New York Times*, October 6, 1998.

"No monuments" Mullner, *Deadly Glow*, 143.

"The radium girls" Official proclamation from the State of Illinois Executive Department, September 2011, now on display at the Ottawa Historical and Scouting Heritage Museum.

"dial-painters who" Radium Girls statue sign, Ottawa, Illinois.

"The studies of" Mullner, *Deadly Glow*, 6.

"The suffering" Mullner, *Deadly Glow*, 143.

"I always admired" Interview with Kathleen Donohue Cofoid.

POSTSCRIPT

"We girls" Eleanor Eichelkraut, quoted in Bill Richards, "The Dial Painters," *Wall Street Journal*, September 19, 1983.

"I felt lucky" Beverley Murphy, quoted in *Ottawa Daily Times*.

"We slapped" Lee Hougas, quoted in Conroy, "On Cancer, Clock Dials."

"for kicks" Pearl Schott, quoted in Richards, "The Dial Painters."

"I'd come" Martha Hartshorn, quoted in JoAnn Hustis, "Radium Dial Deaths of Women Topic of TV News Show Tonight," *Ottawa Daily Times*, September 20, 1983.

"The company" Martha Hartshorn, quoted in Richards, "The Dial Painters."

"I had to" Pearl, quoted in Anna Mayo, "We Are All Guinea Pigs," *Village Voice*, December 25, 1978.

"A man from" Carol Thomas, quoted in Hustis, "Radium Dial Deaths of Women Topic of TV News Show Tonight."

"Employees are" Holm, quoted in Jim Ridings, *Ottawa Daily Times*, May 1978.

"A lot of" Unnamed dial-painter, quoted in Mayo, "We Are All Guinea Pigs."

"They didn't have" Carol Thomas, quoted in *Ottawa Daily Times*, September 23, 1983.

"Luminous Processes" *Ottawa Daily Times*, May 1, 1978

SELECT
BIBLIOGRAPHY

BOOKS

Bradley, John, ed. *Learning to Glow: A Nuclear Reader*. Tucson: University of Arizona Press, 2000.

Clark, Claudia. *Radium Girls: Women and Industrial Health Reform, 1910–1935*. Chapel Hill: University of North Carolina Press, 1997.

Mullner, Ross. *Deadly Glow: The Radium Dial Worker Tragedy*. Washington, DC: American Public Health Association, 1999.

Neuzil, Mark and William Kovarik. *Mass Media and Environmental Conflict: America's Green Crusades*. New York: Sage Publications, 1996.

FILM

Radium City. Directed by Carole Langer. Ottawa, Illinois: Carole Langer Productions, 1987.

INTERVIEWS

Original interviews conducted by the author in the United States in October 2015 with the following, with her sincere thanks:

Michelle Brasser

Mary Carroll Cassidy

Mary Carroll Walsh

Kathleen Donohue Cofoid

James Donohue

Eleanor Flower

Art Fryer (interview conducted in December 2015 via Skype)

Patty Gray

Len Grossman

Darlene Halm

Felicia Keeton

Ross Mullner

Randy Pozzi

Donald Purcell

Dolores Rossiter

Jean Schott

Don Torpy and Jan Torpy

MISCELLANEOUS ARTICLES AND PUBLICATIONS

In addition to the below sources, various other newspapers, magazines and periodicals were used. See Notes.

Conroy, John. "On Cancer, Clock Dials, and Ottawa, Illinois, a Town That Failed to See the Light," National Archives.

DeVille, Kenneth A. and Mark E. Steiner. "The New Jersey Radium Dial Workers and the Dynamics of Occupational Disease Litigation in the Early Twentieth Century." *Missouri Law Review* 62, no. 2 (1997): 281–314.

Irvine, Martha. "Suffering Endures for Radium Girls." *Associated Press*, October 4, 1998.

National Park Service. "Historic American Buildings Survey: U.S. Radium Corporation."

Schaub, Katherine. "Radium." *Survey Graphic* (May 1932): 138.

Sharpe, William D. "Radium Osteitis with Osteogenic Sarcoma: The Chronology and Natural History of a Fatal Case." *Bulletin of the New York Academy of Medicine* 47, no. 9 (September 1971): 1059–1082.

SPECIAL COLLECTIONS

Catherine Wolfe Donohue Collection. Northwestern University, Chicago, Illinois.

Harrison Martland Papers. Special Collections. George F. Smith Library of the Health Sciences, Rutgers Biomedical and Health Sciences, Newark, New Jersey.

Health Effects of Exposure to Internally Deposited Radioactivity Projects Case Files. Center for Human Radiobiology, Argonne National Laboratory, General Records of the Department of Energy. Record Group 434. National Archives at Chicago, Illinois.

Pearl Payne Collection. LaSalle County Historical Society and Museum, Utica, Illinois.

Raymond H. Berry Papers. Library of Congress, Washington, DC.

WEBSITES

ancestry.com (with access to the records of the U.S. Census, town directories, Social Security records, First World War and Second World War draft registration cards, and the Index of Births, Marriages, and Deaths)

history.com

lgrossman.com

mywebtimes.com

thehistoryvault.co.uk

usinflationcalculator.com

———— ≋ ————

For further reading, D. W. Gregory's *Radium Girls* (Dramatic Publishing, 2003) is a play about the Orange women, while *These Shining Lives* by Melanie Marnich (Dramatists Play Service, Inc., 2010) depicts the Ottawa dial-painters.

INDEX

Note: Page numbers in *italic* refer to photographs.

hired as dial-painter, 11
illnesses from radium poisoning, 149–150
photographs of, *196, 206*
receives settlement, 196, *196*, 205, *206*
USRC restricts medical care payments for, 241–242
Bureau of Labor Statistics, 78–81, *210*, 212–215
Byers, Eben, 242–244

C

cancerous tumors. *See* sarcomas
Carlough, Marguerite, 19, 65, 91–92, 102–105, 107–108
   death of, 128–129, *129*
   diagnosed with radium poisoning, 115
   Dr. Hoffman's appeal on behalf of, 72–73
   Drinkers' examination of, 61–62
   hired as dial-painter, 11
   illnesses from radium poisoning, 48, 49–51, 94–95
   lawsuit against radium company, 73–74, 82–83, 97, 115–116
   medical bills, 94, *94*
   photograph of, *50*
   settlement from USRC, 132, *132*
Carlough, Sarah (Maillefer), 83
   diagnosed with radium poisoning, 103–107
   Drinkers' examination of, 61–63
   Dr. Martland performs autopsy on, 110–114
   hired as dial-painter, 11
   lawsuit against radium company, 115, 132
   photograph of, *19*
Center for Human Radiobiology (CHR), 333–344
Charleston dance craze, 42
Chicago Daily Times, 272–274, *281*
Clark, William, 192–198
Consumers League. *See* Wiley, Katherine
Cook, Jay, 261–262, 266–268
Corby, Irene. *See* La Porte, Irene
Corcoran, Inez (Vallat), 138, 141–142, *141*, 236

ACKNOWLEDGMENTS

I t has been an incredible privilege to create this young readers' edition of *The Radium Girls*, bringing the women's important story to a whole new generation. It would not have happened without the support of my brilliant publisher, Sourcebooks. Thank you to Kelly Barrales-Saylor for her vision and guidance, Bunmi Ishola, Emma Hintzen, and Cassie Gutman for all their hard work, Grace, Liz, Lizzie, Margaret, Valerie, Dominique, and everyone involved in making the adult book such a bestselling success, and of course the entire Sourcebooks team for championing these women to readers, no matter their age. Thanks also to my agent, Simon Lipskar of Writers House, for making it happen.

I will be eternally grateful to the dial-painters' families for generously contributing to *The Radium Girls*—you enriched it beyond measure—and for supporting it so much upon publication. Sincere thanks to Michelle Brasser,

Mary Carroll Cassidy, Mary Carroll Walsh, James Donohue, Kathleen Donohue Cofoid, Art Fryer, Patty Gray, Darlene Halm, Felicia Keeton, Randy Pozzi, Donald Purcell, Dolores Rossiter, Jean Schott, Don Torpy, and Jan Torpy. You all had gems of insight and information to share, and I am extremely thankful for every last one. Special thanks to Darlene and Kathleen for their friendship and for all the additional support they kindly gave.

Len Grossman—what a generous man you are. Thank you for everything you have done to champion, enhance, and share this story. I am thankful, too, to Alex, HanaLyn, and Dena Colvin for their insights into Raymond Berry, to Christopher and William Martland for allowing me to reproduce quotations from Harrison Martland, and to all those family members of the girls who have contacted me over the years.

A very special thank you to dial-painter Pearl Payne, who carefully saved her own collection of documents about this case, creating an extraordinary archival legacy. The edits made to the original manuscript of *The Radium Girls* for this new edition have sadly seen Pearl cut by name from the narrative, but her enormous contribution to helping me tell her and her friends' stories is second to none. Thank you, dearest Pearl.

I am also indebted to those authors who came before me

on this journey, Claudia Clark and Ross Mullner, whose books were an invaluable resource. Librarians and archivists across America were brilliantly helpful, in particular Bob Vietrogoski of Rutgers, who literally went the extra mile to help. Thanks, too, to all those who gave permission for me to reproduce documents and photographs, including Rose Penta, Irma Fahrer, Robert Eyerkuss and Nancy Sutherland, and to Muriel J. Smith for her help in connecting me to Rose and Irma.

My book *The Radium Girls* was born after I directed the play *These Shining Lives*, which dramatizes the experiences of the Ottawa dial-painters. So I want to say a huge thank you to playwright Melanie Marnich, for first introducing me to their story, and to my incredible cast for bringing it to life. I'm grateful to all my friends and family, with a special shout-out to my amazing niece and nephews—Amelia, Zack, Toby, and Elliot—who I had in my mind's eye as I was adapting the text.

To Duncan Moore, my husband, "thank you" is simply not sufficient for all you have done for this book. I am indebted to you for your love and support but most of all for your perceptive direction and your innate creative wisdom.

I'd also like to say a huge thank you to my passionate readers, who have championed the women's story to such a degree that this young readers' edition became possible.

Last but in no way least, very special thanks to senior

commissioning editor Abigail Bergstrom at S&S UK. Not only for what she has done for me but for what she has done for the dial-painters. Their story has now been told, and it would not have happened without her. Thank you, Abbie, from the bottom of my heart, for giving them a voice.

Kate Moore, 2019

ABOUT
THE AUTHOR

When she was a little girl growing up in England, Kate Moore dreamed of writing books. She now lives in London, where she writes books in between putting on plays and eating scones with cream and jam. Kate's never glowed at night herself, but when she first "met" the radium girls (which happened when she put on a play about them), she was dazzled by these very special women and their extraordinary story.

kate-moore.com

@katebooks

To discover more about the radium girls, please visit theradiumgirls.com.